W9-AGX-975

OSMIN'S RAGE

OSMIN'S RAGE

Philosophical Reflections on Opera, Drama, and Text

BY PETER KIVY

PRINCETON UNIVERSITY PRESS

Copyright © 1988 by Princeton University Press
Published by Princeton University Press, 41 William Street,
Princeton, New Jersey 08540
In the United Kingdom: Princeton University Press,
Guildford, Surrey

LIBRARY OF CONGRESS CATALOGING-IN-PUBLICATION DATA

Kivy, Peter.
   Osmin's rage: philosophical reflections on opera, drama,
   and text / by Peter Kivy.   p. cm.
   Bibliography: p.
   Includes index.
   ISBN 0-691-07324-4 (alk. paper)
   1. Opera. 2. Music—Philosophy and aesthetics. I. Title.
ML3858.K53 1988
782'.01—dc19   87-26339

This book has been composed in Linotron Baskerville

Printed in the United States of America by
Princeton University Press,
Princeton, New Jersey

To Joan Pearlman
and her three ladies

"The passage 'Drum beim Barte des Propheten' is indeed in the same tempo, but with quick notes; but as Osmin's rage gradually increases, there comes (just when the aria seems to be at an end) the allegro assai, which is in a totally different measure and in a different key; this is bound to be very effective. For just as a man in such a towering rage oversteps all the bounds of order, moderation and propriety and completely forgets himself, so must the music too forget itself. But as passions, whether violent or not, must never be expressed in such a way as to excite disgust, and as music, even in the most terrible situations, must never offend the ear, but must please the hearer, or in other words must never cease to be *music*, I have gone from F (the key in which the aria is written), not into a remote key, but into a related one, not, however, into its nearest relative D minor, but into the more remote A minor."

Mozart (to his father, 26 September 1781)

CONTENTS

This book is about the opera. It is by someone who is trained primarily as a philosopher, secondarily as a musician and musicologist. If there can be such a thing as "the philosophy of the opera," the following pages are meant to be a contribution to that ill-defined and perhaps nonexistent enterprise.

But the philosophical argument of this book is not spun out of the airy speculations of *a priori* aesthetics. (I am not giving the rule to art.) It is firmly based, I hope, in musical and music-historical fact. It is of necessity, therefore, an interdisciplinary study, with all of the dangers such studies entail, the principal one being the danger of not knowing what you are talking about at some point or other. Needless to say, no one, these days, can be at the cutting edge of research in more than one discipline, and seldom even at the cutting edge in more than a part of the discipline one practices. The subject I have undertaken, and the method employed, require that I talk about music and musical documents *in concreto*; and although I have tried as hard as I could not to make any obvious blunders in those particulars, I am sure I have failed at times. I do hope, however, that the reader will try to distinguish between those possible errors of musicological fact that do *not* affect the philosophical argument being put forward and those (few, I trust) that might. As many musicologists have come to realize (and verbalize), musicology cries out, at this stage of its development, for enrichment from other disciplines; in this it is far behind art history, literary studies, and the rest of the humanities and social sciences, perhaps because of the peculiarly self-contained nature of musical syntax and structure, so seemingly recalcitrant to general humanistic understanding. Music, however, is of this world, not of the musician's world alone. It *must* be talked about from the outside as well as from within, if it is to maintain itself as a humanistic study and not collapse into itself entirely to become a self-contained "windowless monad."

Because I am well aware of the possibility of dilettantism, I have stayed as close as I could to the well-trodden paths of music history. Nothing, therefore, that I say about the history of opera is new, and some of it may be outmoded. What has been replaced by the most recent scholarship of which I may not be aware will not, I hope, greatly alter the most general facts; and those, intact, are all that my argument requires.

But if I have said nothing new about the history of the opera, and if such musical analysis as I must sometimes offer is unoriginal and pretty well beyond dispute, what do I have to offer that has not been offered before? Three things, I think, which add up to an argument about the aesthetics of the opera that sheds new light on some old truths and puts some new truths in an old setting.

First, I have given some familiar theoretical writings on, and relevant to, the foundations of the opera a close philosophical reading. I do not mean to suggest by that that musicologists do not read texts closely, or that they need philosophers to correct them. But historians of music look at texts from one point of view, philosophers from another; and it is the—or a—philosophical point of view that I offer here.

Second, I have drawn connections between opera in the eighteenth century and some seventeenth- and eighteenth-century texts in psychology and philosophy that, so far as I know, have not been drawn before, and provide a new understanding of the formal, representational, and psychological underpinnings of such operatic masterpieces as the operas of Handel and Mozart.

Third, I have drawn from my new reading of the familiar texts, and my familiar reading of the new texts that I have brought to bear on the concept of opera, some conclusions about opera aesthetics that are new: not, perhaps, new in the sense that they tell us something about the opera that we did not believe before, but new in the sense that they give us some new reasons to think those beliefs are true. It is sometimes said that philosophy consists in finding bad reasons for what you already believe. I do think I have found some new reasons for what many people already believe about opera. I also am tempted to think that my reasons are good. That, however, remains to be determined by all of the usual critical tests.

The testing, of necessity, has already begun. *Osmin's Rage* was carefully read, prior to publication, by three scholars of diverse disciplines and viewpoints. I am deeply indebted to all of them, both for their supportive praise and for their constructive criticism.

Carolyn Abbate has given me the musicologist's viewpoint, which is, as one might expect, basically historical. She has tried to keep me music-historically honest, to the extent possible for a philosopher who, as it was once said of Herbert Spencer, thinks a tragedy is a theory killed by a fact. I am in her debt for saving me from a number of historical bloopers and for forcing me to make my meaning clearer.

Jerrold Levinson, from my own discipline, has provided me with the devil's advocacy that any philosopher requires to hone distinctions and fine-tune arguments. I am grateful to him now, as in the past, for his criticism and appreciation of my work on the philosophy of music.

I owe a really special debt of gratitude to my third and most sympathetic reader, Paul Robinson, a distinguished intellectual historian who, like myself, has poached on the musical preserve. His splendid book *Opera and Ideas from Mozart to Strauss* appeared after my manuscript was completed. Had I read his book before I wrote mine, I would have known by direct acquaintance what the standard of excellence was that I was aspiring to.

No one has been more fortunate, I am sure, in their editors than I have been in mine at Princeton University Press. This is the third of my books on music and philosophy that Sanford ("Sandy") G. Thatcher, now Editor-in-Chief at Princeton, has shepherded into print. And, as always, I owe him more than I can really explain in a preface. But I am now doubly blessed by the presence at the Press of its Fine Arts Editor, Eric Van Tassel, who is a professional musicologist and writer on music. His musical as well as editorial expertise has helped make *Osmin's Rage* a better book.

Like tipping the headsman, and serving something of the same purpose, it is customary to let one's readers and editors off the hook. That I now cheerfully do. None of the above named is at all responsible for any of the mistakes in this book. What I have written *I* have written. But I couldn't have done it alone.

Cape Cod
August 1986

ACKNOWLEDGMENTS

Work on the major portion of this book was made possible by a Senior Research Fellowship from the National Endowment for the Humanities. I am profoundly grateful to the people at the Endowment who had enough faith in my project to give me the financial backing it required. In some respects this is a different book from the one I proposed to them, in some respects remarkably the same, considering all of the ground I have covered between then and now. The same or different, I hope that they recognize it, and that it does not displease them.

Figure 1 is reproduced by permission of the Metropolitan Museum of Art, New York. Figure 2 is reproduced from an original in the Uffizi, Florence, by permission of Art Resource/Alinari. Figure 4 is reproduced from Ralph M. Evans, *An Introduction to Color* (copyright © 1948) by permission of John Wiley & Sons, Inc.

PART I

Posing the problem

CHAPTER I

Ecstasy and prophecy

o 1 o   When Dr. Johnson characterized the opera as an "irrational entertainment," he unknowingly tapped a vein of musical thought that ran through the entire history of the art-form to that date, and continued beyond. Indeed, seen as the expression of a general difficulty felt in the setting of words to music, it can be discerned well before the Florentine Camerata came into being and, along with it, the first operatic works.

What Johnson may have meant by "irrational" we shall have occasion to discuss more fully later on. But one thing the word conveys is the sense of "unnaturalness." That the singing (rather than speaking) of words is "unnatural" is something that breaks the surface of musical consciousness with great frequency. Yet it is truly surprising that it should. For what, after all, could be more natural than song? Is there any culture that does not sing? Was there ever a time, when human beings had music at all, that they did not have vocal music? If by "natural" we mean anything like universal to the race, coeval with its very beginnings, existing in "low" as well as in "high" culture, there cannot be anything more natural to human beings than the singing of songs.

Whence comes, then, this charge of unnaturalness? Surely it must arise from the confrontation of theory with practice: at a point where theory is abstract enough to lay a claim to being philosophical, and practice advanced enough to attract the philosopher's eye. One such point, but by no means the earliest in the history of Western music, is the reform of polyphonic church music during the Counter-Reformation, given official impetus by the Council of Trent (1545–1563). It is here that the argument of this book begins.

o 2 o   A generation before the real onset of the Counter-Reformation, Erasmus of Rotterdam had already launched an attack on the abuses he believed had found their way into the music of the Catholic Church, an attack of a kind that was to become all too familiar as the century wore on. The renowned humanist wrote:

> We have introduced an artificial and theatrical music into the church, a bawling and an agitation of various voices, such as I believe had never

been heard in the theatres of the Greeks and Romans. Horns, trumpets, pipes vie and sound along constantly with the voices. Amorous and lascivious melodies are heard such as elsewhere accompany courtesans and clowns. The people run into the churches as if they were theatres, for the sake of the sensuous charm of the ear.[1]

This passage, as Gustave Reese points out, is part of a commentary on I Corinthians 14. It will be instructive to see what echoes of Paul are reverberating here. Paul contrasts "the language of ecstasy," or "speaking in tongues," with prophetic speech, or, in other words, plain speaking. One obvious point that he wishes to make concerns intelligibility.

When a man is using the language of ecstasy he is talking with God, not with men, for no man understands him; he is no doubt inspired, but he speaks mysteries. On the other hand, when a man prophesies, he is talking to men, and his words have power to build; they stimulate and they encourage.[2]

The polyphonic music of which Erasmus speaks, then, is like the language of ecstasy, musically inspired, perhaps, but unintelligible as to text: speaking in tongues. But music that is unintelligible in this sense does not "have the power to build"; it can neither "stimulate" nor "encourage," because the text cannot be understood.

Let us suppose, then, that Paul contrasts "speaking naturally" with some other way of speaking. What could the analogue be in music?

Clearly, singing is not speech. The contrast must be between singing a text—that is, singing words—naturally and unnaturally. How can this contrast be made out? Is there a "natural" as opposed to an "unnatural" way of singing words? In a sense all singing is "unnatural" since the "natural" way of enunciating a text, for the purpose of communication, is to speak and not to sing it.

Returning to the passage from Erasmus with this question in mind, we are struck by a number of suggestive phrases. The music of the Church has become "artificial," a fairly close synonym of "unnatural." It is "theatrical," and consists in "an agitation of various voices." Well, that, of course, is what polyphony must be: many-voiced, that is to say, "an agitation of various voices." Erasmus adds, significantly I think, that it is something "never . . . heard in the theatres of the Greeks and Romans."

Were there one word added here, the word "even," we might understand this as a bit of rhetoric. The theatre of Greece and Rome, then, would be being held up as the paradigm of "a bawling and an agitation of various voices," which the church music of Erasmus' time manages actually to surpass in unintelligibility: it is "a bawling and an agitation of voices" so gross that it "had never been heard [even] in the theatres of the Greeks and Romans," which, the implication would be, were also a pretty gross "bawling and . . . agitation of various voices."

But it is, in fact, much more plausible to read this passage straight, in which case it becomes, I think, illuminating of a deeper philosophical core than first meets the eye. Let us suppose that the theatre of Greece and Rome was being held up—as it would be by the "inventors" of the opera—as a paradigm not of the "unnatural" but rather of the "natural." In that case the "bawling and . . . agitation of various voices" surely "had never been heard in the theatres of the Greeks and Romans" just because they were a paradigm of the opposite: the artificial and unnatural. What then is the "natural," and how might the setting and singing of a text achieve it?

In a painting, a figure is said to exhibit a "natural" pose when the pose is "lifelike": when the posture of a real person is realistically represented. In the spoken theatre, a speech is said to have been delivered "naturally" if it was spoken the way it would have been in the same situation by a real person, in a real conversation. Surely, then, it would not be surprising to have the theatre of Greece and Rome held up, by a Renaissance humanist, as a paradigm of the "natural," as opposed to "a bawling and an agitation of various voices." For ancient tragedy, which Erasmus, like the Florentine Camerata, may have assumed to have been "sung" in some sense or other, had behind it the most powerful and elaborately worked out philosophy of art to appear in the West until well into the eighteenth century. That, of course, was the Aristotelian theory of *mimesis*: just the theory that identified the successful in art with the well represented. To quote Aristotle's familiar definition: "Epic poetry, then, and the poetry of tragic drama, and, moreover, comedy and dithyrambic poetry, and most flute-playing and harp-playing, these, speaking generally, may all be said to be 'representations of life.' "[3]

Now of course the cat is out of the bag; and not a very surprising cat after all. For if any art-theoretical considerations lay behind Erasmus' criticism of Catholic church music, what but Aristotelian ones could they be? Aristotle's were the only ones in the running, and would continue to be for a long time to come. But now that we have started our hare, or, rather, liberated our cat, we are still left with a question. We know that according to Aristotle, all of the arts are "representations of life." We know, further, what it is that tragedy represents. To quote again from Aristotle, this time an even more familiar passage: "Tragedy is, then, a representation of an action. . . . it represents men in action. . . ."[4] But what could church music "represent"? If the charge that it is "unnatural" is linked to the Aristotelian theory of tragedy, then it must be synonymous with unsuccessful or distorted "representation," and, contrariwise, "natural" must be synonymous with successful "representation." Representation of what? Once we know what church music is meant to represent, then we will be able to form some opinion of what makes for good representation; but not before.

o 3 o   We know what instructions were given composers at the Council of Trent, and what practical considerations lay behind them. The canon dealing with music to be used at Mass says, in part:

> The whole plan of singing in musical modes should be constructed not to give empty pleasure to the ear, but in such a way *that the words may be clearly understood by all*, and thus the hearts of the listeners be drawn to the desire of heavenly harmonies, in the contemplation of the joys of the blessed.[5]

The concern is the same as that of Saint Paul, in I Corinthians 14, when he recommends "prophecy" over "speaking in tongues": that the content of the text be understood. And that, we have every right to assume, was one of Erasmus' concerns as well.

In recommending natural speech over "speaking in tongues," or "ecstatic speech," Paul was, of course, saying that if you want to be understood by "normal" people you should speak the way "normal" people do: natural speech is normal speech. What, then, if you want to be understood by normal people when you sing? Clearly, the answer cannot be: Sing the way normal people sing (whatever that way may be). Normal people don't sing very well; normal people sing out of tune; indeed, normal people don't sing much at all. And if a normal person wanted to be as sure as he could be that the message "There is a scorpion on your arm" was understood, he would scarcely sing it. Clearly, then, the answer must be: Sing the way normal people *speak*. How would one do that? Well, if the hypothesis under which Erasmus and the Council of Trent were working is that music is representation, the answer is obvious. If you want to be understood when you sing, *represent in your singing normal human speech*. I do not suggest that that is the answer explicitly given; it clearly is not. For the answer was given in terms of musical practice, not in terms of philosophical theory. What I do suggest is that that theory lay behind that practice.

Perhaps it will be objected that I am reading more into these observations on musical practice than could possibly be there. That is always a possibility, when a philosopher is confronted with a fragmentary text; but I think not, in this case. For if Erasmus and the Cardinals of the

Church did not make their assumptions explicit, others did; nor could it be thought a very audacious claim, after all, that one of the greatest humanists of the sixteenth century, and the participants of the Council of Trent, had at least a passing acquaintance with the Aristotelian corpus. As for a more explicit reference to music representing human speech, we have not far to look. Consider, for example, the following passage from Heinrich Glarean's *Dodecachordon* (1547), written about ten years before the beginning of the Council of Trent and ten years after the death of Erasmus. In praise of the motet of Josquin Desprez *Planxit autem David* (*And David wept*), Glarean writes:

> throughout the motet, there is preserved what befits the mourner, who is wont at first to cry out frequently, then to mourn to himself, turning little by little to sorrowful complaints, thereupon to subside or sometimes, when passion breaks out anew, to raise his voice again, shouting out a cry. All these things we see most beautifully observed in this composition, as will be evident to the attentive reader.[6]

Surely it is not reading anything into this splendid analysis of Josquin—untarnished by four hundred years—to interpret it as ascribing to *Planxit autem David* the musical representation of human utterance, as it would manifest itself in mourning and lamentation. Thus, the concept of music as a representation of human speech was abroad in the world. Ascribing it, therefore, to Erasmus and the Counter-Reformation is not reading the General Theory of Relativity into the *Gilgamesh*. It and its Aristotelian foundations were common coin. What would be surprising would be not their presence in the reform of Catholic church music, but their absence.

Both Erasmus and the Council had two kinds of things on their minds: matters of morals and what might loosely be called matters of "practical aesthetics." Morally, they were concerned with the possible intrusion into the service of music that might be, as the committee of deputies put it, "lascivious or impure,"[7] or, in Erasmus' words, "Amorous and lascivious melodies . . . such as elsewhere accompany courtesans and clowns." Such moral scruples are not our concern here. Relevant are the matters of musical "aesthetics." The Council, as we have seen, was anxious that "the words may be clearly understood by all"; and Erasmus gives us a hint as to what might tend to obscure the text, namely, "a bawling and an agitation of various voices," as well as the fact that "Horns, trumpets, pipes vie and sound along constantly with the voices." In other words, without the rhetoric, we are talking about highly complex, instrumentally doubled polyphony.

People do not ordinarily speak all at once, nor are they accompanied in ordinary speech by woodwinds and brasses. If they did, and if they were, their speech would be as unintelligible as the text of a Mass by Ockeghem. So if you want to sing a text and make it clearly understood, you had better imitate ordinary speech as closely as musically possible: and it would seem that two steps in that direction must be singing without instrumental accompaniment and, *horribile dictu*, the rejection of polyphony.

Now as a matter of fact, polyphony was indeed fighting for its very life: "polyphonic church music at the Council of Trent . . . was in grave danger of being banished from the church altogether."[8] It was saved by, among other things, the labors of Jacobus de Kerle, Palestrina, and others, who were able to produce a new style of polyphony more conformable to the stated goals of the Church: a polyphony that could, *inter alia*, make the text of the Mass at least somewhat more intelligible to the listener.

o 4 o   A detailed account of how the late-sixteenth-century polyphonists—Palestrina at their head—did (and did not) realize the ideals of the Council of Trent and the Counter-Reformation is work for a musicologist, not a philosopher. What I am interested in here, and what I am trying to convince the reader of, is the philosophical idea behind it, namely, the Aristotelian *mimesis* in the form of the musical representation of human speech. Of that something further might be said, with direct reference to the music, without, I think, poaching too blatantly on the historian of music's preserve.

Consider two musical quotations (Example 1), one from Ockeghem, writing in the heyday of pre-Tridentine Netherlandish polyphony, the other from Palestrina, who has come to be seen as the ideal musical embodiment of the Counter-Reformation.

There can be little doubt, I think, that if one were to try to speak the words "Agnus Dei" first in the rhythm of Ockeghem's setting and then in the rhythm of Palestrina's, the latter's would come far closer to the cadence of ordinary speech than would those of the former. Or, to put it in art-theoretical terms, Palestrina's musical lines are more accurate, more lifelike representations of human speech than are Ockeghem's. In a sense, it is simply of no concern to Ockeghem how close to ordinary speech he stays, or how far he strays.

I do not want to suggest by this, by the way, anything so crass as that Ockeghem didn't care about the words he was setting or how he set them, and that Palestrina did. That a musician of Ockeghem's genius (and, it is to be assumed, religious convictions) should have been indifferent to the

EXAMPLE 1

(a) Johannes Ockeghem, *Missa Prolationum*, Agnus Dei

(b) Giovanni Pierluigi da Palestrina, *Missa Papae Marcelli*, Agnus Dei

"correct" setting of the text of the Mass is beyond credence. What I will suggest is that composers like Ockeghem—not just in his own historical period but in other periods as well—were pursuing a different but no less valid aesthetic of text-setting from that of Palestrina, and, so I shall argue, from that of most composers of the modern era. Apropos of this, let me contrast what I want to call the *principle of textual realism* with another approach to the setting of texts that I will call the *principle of opulent adornment*. This requires a digression.

The text of the opening chorus of Heinrich Schütz's *Seven Words from the Cross* reads, in part, "keep in your heart the words he spake, each like a precious jewel!" Now, not all of the words Jesus spoke on the cross were of equal religious or philosophical significance. He said "Father, forgive them . . . ," which is the very epitome of Christian morality. But he also said: "I'm thirsty," which, apart from its human significance, can have little other unless interpreted with plenty of imagination. Yet in so far as each word was spoken *by Jesus*, it takes on, *as an object*, a being of its own, in addition to and even apart from its meaning. Each word is indeed, as Schütz's text says, "a precious jewel"; and a precious jewel deserves an equally precious setting or container. Words are, in religion and elsewhere, not just bearers of meaning, but "sacred objects." They have power. At least in the King James version, the Word was not only with God but *was* God.

What I would like to suggest, then, is that viewing religious words as sacred objects—as, in Schütz's text, "precious jewels"—rather than bearers of meaning, human or divine utterances, gives rise to an entirely different aesthetic of text-setting from the one sanctioned by the Council of Trent, espoused by Palestrina, and shared by most composers since, at least most of the time: an aesthetic that can ignore meaning, declamation, and even expressive character. Palestrina is the interpreter of the text in music: he sets meanings, not words. Ockeghem is, for want of a better description, the adorner, the decorator, of texts in music: he sets *words*, not meanings. Ockeghem, in other words, is governed by the principle of opulent adornment, Palestrina by the principle of textual realism.

It is all rather like the difference between two Madonnas, one by Bernardo Daddi, and the other Filippino Lippi. For Lippi, whatever else the Virgin is, she is a human being; and human beings stand in rooms, rooms stand in the world, with windows that reveal it (Figure 1). For Daddi, whatever else the Virgin is, she is a sacred object of veneration, a precious sacred jewel; and precious jewels are kept in precious, gorgeous settings—golden ones, if you can afford them (Figure 2). Palestrina puts texts in their natural surroundings, which are human utterances. These he represents in music, as Lippi represents the natural background of his

Madonna. Ockeghem sees texts as sacred objects of veneration, as "precious jewels," and puts them in their appropriate place: not in the mouths of men but in sumptuous golden frames and ivory boxes, as Daddi puts his Madonna not in a room, in the world, but in a cabinet of precious metal, closed off from the world. Because he is, in the jeweler's sense, "setting" precious objects, not representing utterances, he can, unlike Palestrina, let his musical imagination take unfettered flight, hindered neither by the meaning nor by the intelligibility of what he "sets." Such a setter of texts is hindered only by his musical powers; and the objects he mounts, some of the most precious in the world or out of it, deserve no less than the most elaborate musical structures the mind of the composer can conjure up. Palestrina prophesies; Ockeghem speaks in tongues.

Who, then, "cares" more for his text, the "setter" of precious jewels or the "interpreter" of meanings? Would it be too much to suggest, if the question must be raised and answered at all, that the answer might be just as well in favor of the former as the latter? For the latter the Word is with God; but for the former the Word is God. Perhaps, then, there is more genuine religious as well as musical fervor in the former than in the latter. That Erasmus and the Council of Trent did not quite see it that way is, of course, another matter, and reflects a profound change in art, thought, religion, society, and the world.

I leave this subject now with no further comment. It was entered on merely to forestall the objection that in the remarks that follow I am doing Ockeghem and his artistic confreres an injustice, as setters of texts.

For present purposes, the following can be observed. The long, supple, complex, almost "instrumental" lines (whatever that would mean in the present context) of Ockeghem follow a musical logic of syntax and structure all of their own. It seems clear that their aesthetic character has not been influenced, except in a minimal way, by textual considerations of the kind that were clearly motivating Palestrina. If Palestrina, in following the spirit of the law of the Council of Trent (he could not have been following the letter, as his Mass was composed before the Council), was influenced in his setting by how he might represent ordinary speech, Ockeghem clearly was following a different law altogether: the law solely of musical development (as the composers of his time understood it). As Reese observes, "The clarity in the treating of the text" in the *Missa Papae Marcelli* "results from the high percentage of note-against-note writing . . . ,"[9] whereas the writing of Ockeghem abounds in melismas of such length that if one really did not know what words were being sung, one would forget what the first syllable was before the musical line arrived at the second.

This, of course, is hardly the whole story of how Palestrina's music ful-

Figure 1. Filippino Lippi, *Madonna and Child* (Jules Bache Collection, The Metropolitan Museum of Art, New York)

Figure 2. Bernardo Daddi, *Madonna and Child* (Vatican Museums)

fills the musico-religious ideals of the Counter-Reformation whereas Ockeghem's does not. Furthermore, I have, needless to say, carefully chosen my examples to illustrate a point. Many a line of Ockeghem's follows the text note-for-syllable; and many a line of Palestrina's displays long-drawn-out melismas of almost Netherlandish duration and complexity. But style, after all, is a matter of what predominates, not what contradicts; and it is the contrast of linear styles that is at issue here. The conclusion I want to put forward is that the linear style of Palestrina—as representative of Tridentine church music—can be plausibly seen as resulting in large measure (I do not say wholly) from the attempt to represent, as closely as musical exigencies will allow, the cadence of normal speech. Musical exigencies include, fortunately, the preservation of polyphony. (We do not speak all at once, in six real parts.) But that is the eternal tension that must exist when music confronts a text, under the governance of the principle of textual realism, or when *any* medium approaches an object of representation; for it is as much a failure for music to become speech (and cease to be "music"), if speech is what it is meant to represent, as it would be for it to wander too far from its object.

o 5 o Let me try, now, to bring together the threads of this rather diffuse argument; although it is yet in an early and unfocused form, its general outline is already discernible, and that outline will be apparent throughout the course of this book, whenever music, drama, and text are confronted by one another, and by the pale cast of philosophical thought.

Music in the West, at least as far back as the sixteenth century (to choose a somewhat arbitrary point), possessed what I think can fairly uncontroversially be described as "inner laws" of its own in respect to its vertical and linear structure, its rhythm, its "form"—in short, its musical "syntax" as a pattern of aesthetically perceived sound. It possessed also, at least from the same period onwards, a surrounding theoretical and practical literature. What the purely musical parameters did *not* possess, I think, until the eighteenth century, and even then often only by implication, was grounding in what might be called broad philosophical (as opposed to theological or grammatical) principles: principles of the kind that came to be called, in the Enlightenment, "aesthetic," and which we think of as part of the "philosophy of art."

In the period which I have taken as the beginning of my argument, the Counter-Reformation (which, no doubt, is beginning *in medias res*), philosophy does indeed enter the musical picture: but only where the questions are not of a purely musical kind; where, that is, they are questions relating to the musical setting of texts. The reason for this, as I have suggested, is that the reigning philosophy of art—indeed, the only well-worked-out one around—was the Platonic and Aristotelian theory of art as imitation. And it was only when music presented a possible object of "representation"—in this case, human utterance—that that theory could gain a foothold on the musical turf. It was the obsession with the intelligibility of texts that drove music into the grasp of philosophy by suggesting a means to intelligibility, namely, the accurate representation of human speech: what I have called the principle of textual realism. Had the aesthetics of text-setting continued to be governed by the principle of opulent adornment, no such confrontation would have occurred.

But when the demands of Aristotelian "imitation" begin to exert a force on the purely musical, music must be diverted from its purely "musical" course. The exquisite balance of music and text in Palestrina was bought, of necessity, at a certain musical cost. The completely unfettered musical intellect cannot find the same satisfaction in Tridentine church music as in the Netherlandish School. Where the demands of representation are heard, the demands of pure music are blunted, unless the philosopher can construe the "purely" musical as in some sense representational (as, for a rare example, Schopenhauer tried unsuccessfully to do). This inevitable conflict between the purely musical and music in the service of textual "representation" shapes, for all time, the aesthetics of opera, and, indeed, of all vocal music, whether the conflict is only between incompatible musical practices, or is egged on by philosophical theorizing, on one side or the other or both. That, essentially, is the argument of this book.

I have said little yet, in detail, about the concept of representation, or anything at all about the related concept of musical "expression." That is to come. But we have here, in my view, already fully formed, the basic philosophical tension that motivates later analyses and disputes over the "strange" aesthetics of the opera. It is the tension between the demands of a pure musical syntax and those of Aristotelian *mimesis*. All that is lacking is a philosophical counterpart to the Aristotelian theory for the purely musical parameters. And that, as I have suggested, did not begin to be forthcoming until the Enlightenment. When it came, it made the issue all the clearer. Could it merely be a matter of chance that the rise of a philosophy of art capable, at least by implication, of justifying a purely musical syntax coincided with the rise of an independent instrumental music which was not just an appendage to but a rival of the vocal idioms that had theretofore dominated the attention of composers? Or perhaps that is paying philosophy too great a compliment.

In any case, the Aristotelian theory of representation, as applied to music, soon had a broader field to occupy than just the church music of Rome. For we are, in the middle of the sixteenth century, on the threshold of the invention of opera. That threshold we now shall cross.

CHAPTER II

The art of invention: opera as invented art

○ 1 ○   I spoke at the close of the preceding chapter of the "invention" of opera; and others have spoken of it in such terms before. Indeed, one would think, if ever there was an "invention" in the arts, it was this. But such claims are never without their detractors; and a claim that has been made for so long, and for so long been taken pretty much for granted, is bound to have gotten creaky with age and, perhaps, now deserves to be set aside as one of the myths of music history. It may even be the case that the notion of an "invented art" itself is logically untenable.

My own view is that there's life in the old myth yet. But an unexamined claim is not worth making. Before, I think we can confidently turn to the "invention" of opera, we must turn to the claim itself that opera can reasonably be thought of as an invented art, or, for that matter, that anything at all can be so thought of. It is a claim not without interest; and, like all interesting claims, not without problems.

○ 2 ○   In his well-known and frequently reprinted essay "Style and Medium in the Motion Pictures," Erwin Panofsky wrote, in 1934: "Film art is the only art the development of which men now living have witnessed from the very beginnings. . . ."[1] This seems to imply two things, almost too obvious to bear mentioning: first, that those beginnings were the beginnings of an *art*; and, second, that those beginnings were discernible as somehow discrete and disconnected from what had gone before— that, in other words, film art was brought into being suddenly, and completely, rather than having developed and evolved slowly and imperceptibly, in some sort of gradual transformation of previously existing forms of art. These two implications might plausibly be conflated into the statement that film art, as opposed to some other arts, was *invented*, was *invented art*.

I say these implications seem almost too obvious to mention. But, in fact, both are problematical. And in order to speak responsibly about any art as an invented one, we must see why.

In discussing whether film is an art, I do not mean to raise the old and, it seems to me, completely discredited question as to whether films, because their production relies heavily on the use of a mechanical contrivance—the motion picture camera—can really be art works at all. Rather, I want to point out that there might be some difficulty in distinguishing between invented "arts" and, to take an equally problematical term, invented "genres." An earlier Panofsky might have begun an earlier essay with the words: "The novel is the only art the development of which men now living have witnessed from the very beginnings." There was a time, I think, when something like that might truthfully have been said. But I don't think the invention of the novel, if it were an invention, would have been the invention of an "art," very strictly construed, because, I imagine, we would insist that it is a genre of the art of literature rather than an art in its own right.

I hope, however, that saying this will put me under no necessity of spelling out, with necessary and sufficient conditions or anything like that, what makes one thing a "genre" and another an "art." I certainly wouldn't be able to do it. All I can say, perhaps, is that there does seem to me to be a certain self-contained character belonging to the film art that does not belong to the novel: its practice is more separated from those other arts which undoubtedly contributed to its development than is the novel from those other literary genres out of which it was made. I am going to assume that film is a paradigm—perhaps *the* paradigm—of invented art; but I should have been intellectually dishonest, I think, not to have pointed out that the distinction between an art and (say) a genre is hardly crystal-clear, hard-edged, or uncontroversial.

What about the second problematic: the notion that the "beginnings" of the film art were discrete, disconnected from, discontinuous to a certain extent with what had gone before; that its origins were sudden; that, in a word, it was invented rather than evolved? The problematical nature of this kind of view stands revealed here, as elsewhere, by that enemy of all discontinuities, the modern historian of art, literature, or music. Pick anything you like for the beginning of an art-form or genre, style or technique—an historian will find you a beginning before that, and fill in the gaps, and so *ad infinitum*. Was the novel invented in the eighteenth century? What about Thomas Nashe? What about *Don Quixote*? Or, for that matter, what about *The Golden Ass* of Apuleius? And it used to be fashionable, I remember, to call the Book of Job the first novel.

Film art, it might be thought, would be immune from the historian's disease of "nothing new under the sun." For, after all, there could be no cinema without cinematography; no moving pictures without a machine to make them move. But even here the searchers after roots will not be put off. What about the *idea* of cinema? And, after all, the cinema, as many writers have liked to look at it, is just another step in the evolution of the representational arts, which goes back to the cave paintings, and then some. The conclusion might very well be reached, on this slippery slope, that *no* art could possibly have been invented; art, after all, is not technology. Machines are invented; arts evolve.

Unfortunately, like all slippery slopes, this one proves too much. For mechanical inventions also have their histories. The steam engine was invented by James Watt, but only if you ignore Newcomen's pumping engine. Newcomen's engine couldn't turn the wheels that started the industrial revolution. But it could pump water out of the mines; and there is, I believe, still an extant example of the machine doing a good day's work somewhere in England. So I guess we will have to settle on Thomas Newcomen as the inventor of the steam engine—but only, of course, if we ignore Hero (or Heron) of Alexandria, who constructed what is known in the trade as a "reaction turbine" about A.D. 100. His engine worked. The trouble is, it couldn't *do* anything. What, after all, did the Alexandrians need a steam engine for in A.D. 100? A can opener needs a can. Hero's engine just spun around, to amuse people. But surely our concept of what a steam engine is does not include what practical tasks (if any) a steam engine can or cannot perform. A steam engine is a device for transforming steam into mechanical motion. A railway steam engine is one for pulling trains, a marine steam engine is one for pushing boats. And Hero's engine, which succeeded in getting considerable mechanical motion out of steam, is a steam engine for doing absolutely nothing. Reason, then, seems to drive us to the conclusion that the real inventor of the steam engine was Hero of Alexandria. However, that will not quite do either; for if our definition of a steam engine is a device that transforms steam into mechanical motion, then any teakettle or pot is a steam engine too, as the lid is made to move up and down, much like a piston, when the pressure gets great enough. The first pot with a lid, used for boiling water, was the first steam engine. The inventor of the pot with a lid for boiling water was, then, *ipso facto*, the inventor of the steam engine; which is tantamount, I take it, to concluding that it was not an invention at all, but something gradually evolved, like the clock, or the sonata. And as the same trick can be turned for any mechanical device and, *a fortiori*, for any work of art, institution, or human practice, we will have to conclude that there are no inventions at all: the concept of invention is an empty one, devoid of instances.

However welcome this conclusion may be to the philosophical skeptic who thinks there are no heaps since we can't tell which grain of sand marks the event, no one else will be much impressed with it. But we will perhaps have to settle for, at least for present purposes, a vague notion of invention, susceptible of degrees. There is no period in history, I suppose, where it would have been true to say that people then living had witnessed the beginning of science, or religion, or the clock (understood as a device for keeping time). Whereas the sudden and rapid development of the rotative steam engine, its association with one man or a small group of men, and its rather extreme discontinuity with anything that had gone before license us, I think to distinguish it from the clock or the wheel by calling it one of the world's great *inventions*. Such a thing, too, by parity of reasoning, is the art of film.

It seems to me, then, that although there are problems and vagaries here, we are justified in taking film art, as I think many people do, to be the paradigm of invented art. Having established that, however, I am not, except tangentially, going to talk about the art of film at all, because, of course, my topic is another invention: the problematical art of the opera. However, I think it has been useful to begin by talking about film, not only to, as it were, lay down some ground rules for and problems with the concept of invented art, but also as a reminder, to those who do see film as a very special historical case of invented art, that we have been through something like this before. For if cinema seems to be the paradigm of the sudden invention and rapid development of an art-form, it would be well to remember, as an antidote to this twentieth-century obsession, that in every bit as self-conscious a way the opera was invented in the closing years of the sixteenth century, having its first recorded instance in 1597 and its first masterpiece, Monteverdi's *Orfeo*, in 1607: a rate of progress that even the precocious art of cinema cannot match.

In what follows I want to talk about how the opera came into being. But I am not interested so much in the invention process itself as in trying to show what the peculiar nature of the opera aesthetic is, by showing what its inventor intended it to be, and how they carried those intentions out. It is an art surrounded by controversy. And although I would not go so far as to say that it is problematical because it is invented (as opposed to evolved), I do maintain that it is problematical because of what its inventors were inventing. To that I will shortly turn my attention. But I suppose my first task is to establish that opera is an art-form, and that it is an invented one. Having tried to do this for film, which is not my topic, I can scarcely do less for opera, which is.

○ 3 ○   It is customary to refer to the sonata, symphony, cantata, and the like as musical forms or genres, not separate art-forms in their own right. What justification, then, could there be for treating opera any differently? Music is the genus, opera simply one among many species of the thing. Whereas cinema, after all, cannot reasonably be thought of as a species of any of the other representational arts. It may have affinities with them all, but stands quite apart, *sui generis*, as a more or less unique artistic practice.

Let me say straightaway that I think this argument is a good one. In the sense in which film art is one of the arts and not an art-part, opera is not one of the arts, although it has a degree of independence that, for example, the fugue or sonata does not have. (How great the degree of independence is is perhaps underscored by the extreme unlikelihood of a great composer of opera being a great composer of anything else, and vice versa.) But opera *is* a part of the art of music, broadly conceived, as the novel is a part of the art of literature. Opera is a musical form or a genre of music. That, indeed, as we shall see, is what helps make it so problematical and controversial, and what constitutes its peculiar aesthetic character.

In any event, the invention of "opera" was really the invention of two things: opera and (what I would like to sharply distinguish it from) "music drama," or, as the seventeenth and eighteenth centuries liked to call it, *dramma per musica*. And although opera, I think it important to insist, is a musical form or genre, part of the art of music, music drama is a separate art altogether, very much in the sense in which cinema is: a thing unto itself, deserving another muse, if there were one available.

That opera and music drama were invented I think will become abundantly clear in my following discussion. But it would not be inappropriate here, nevertheless, to be reminded that the invention of opera, like the invention of anything else, is open to the historian's demand for continuity, development, and roots. A recent work, Nino Pirrotta's *Music and Theatre from Poliziano to Monteverdi*, traces theatre music considerably further back than the performance of the first opera in 1597. And it might be well for us to pause, just briefly, to consider what effect such historical evidence as Pirrotta painstakingly gathers might have on the traditional notion of opera as an invention rather than an evolution. For the light of history tends to blur discontinuities; and the discovery that music, to a degree not perhaps appreciated heretofore, permeated the Italian theatre of the Renaissance for one hundred years before the Camerata might suggest to some (and has, I think, already) that we can no longer talk responsibly about the sudden appearance of the opera. But, I shall argue, we no more have to give up such talk than we have, in the light of history, to declare either that the steam engine was not invented at all, or that it was invented by Mrs. Neanderthal. I hope I have made it seem at least plausible to assert that because inventions have histories it does not follow that they are not inventions. The lady has ancestors—but also a birthday.

I cannot do justice here to the richness of Pirrotta's book or the intricacies of its scholarship. Nor is it my aim. Rather, what I think it relevant to do is to cite some samples of the historical discoveries of his that I take to be suggestive at least of the conclusion that opera, like so much else in the history of art, is evolution rather than invention; that the so-called "invention" of the opera is more a myth than a reality. I hope to show that such is not the case: that Pirrotta's discoveries—which I would not think of questioning—are quite consistent with opera as the art of invention, at least if one is willing to grant that invention is a non-empty set.

o 4 o In 1908, Romain Rolland called attention to Angelo Poliziano's drama *Orfeo*, which there is some evidence to show was performed with a few musical numbers. "It is now almost unanimously accepted," Pirrotta tells us, "that the most probable date for its composition is 1480."[2] None of the music, if indeed there was any, survives; and the date of the first performance, or even whether it was performed at all, is controversial. Nevertheless, Poliziano's *Orfeo* was not an isolated phenomenon, as Pirrotta convincingly shows. And we can form at least some idea of what some of the musical interpolations may have been like from surviving examples. What is most striking is that although the writing was, of course, contrapuntal, many of the musical pieces seem to have been sung by a solo voice with polyphonic instrumental accompaniment.

Of even more interest for present purposes is the fact that some sort of self-conscious aesthetic—"philosophy," if one wants to stretch the term a little—must have surrounded these performances, or, if that is too much of an exaggeration, at least made an occasional appearance in their company. Two statements which Pirrotta quotes in his book are worth quoting again here in this regard. Vincenzo Calmeta, for example, writes of the solo singing of his time, "we must praise the good judgment of those, who in singing put all their effort into expressing the words well . . . *and have them accompanied by the music in the manner of masters accompanied by their servants* . . . not making the thoughts and emotions subservient to the music, but the music to the emotions and thoughts."[3] And Poliziano himself writes, in a similar vein but also in an even more marked anticipation of the aesthetics of the Camerata:

His voice was not entirely that of someone reading, nor entirely that of someone singing; both could be heard, and yet neither separated one from the other; it was, in any case, even or modulated, and changed as required by the passage. Now it was varied, now sustained, now calm and now vehement, now slowing down and now quickening its pace, but always it was precise, always clear and always pleasant. . . .[4]

The conclusion that Pirrotta reads from these passages is also worth quoting:

> Calmeta was not alone in insisting that the music should be "subservient to the emotions and thoughts" expressed by the words. We find the same idea reasserted by Poliziano and developed to form the basis of a style midway between spoken language and song and which relied for its shades of expression on the performer's flexibility. The basic concepts of monodic reform . . . had not only been formulated but had even been put into practice more than a century before the birth of opera.[5]

Should this conclusion be damaging to the notion that opera was an "invention" that rather suddenly came upon the scene as a result, to a large degree, of theory preceding practice? I do not think so, even if it were wholly true. But, to begin with, there is some exaggeration here, as regards both theory and practice, although Pirrotta is certainly correct in seeing these statements, and the practice they both describe and sanction, as a clear anticipation of operatic theory and practice at the end of the sixteenth century. It is an exaggeration of the theoretical moment of these statements of Calmeta and Poliziano to claim that they formulate "The basic concepts of monodic reform" because the basic concepts are not practical precepts at all but philosophical ones, deeply imbued, as we shall soon see, with the Platonic and Aristotelian theory of artistic *mimesis* which I see no real evidence of here. The invention of opera was not, in my view, an event in which philosophical theory played a trivial, *ad hoc* role, being called in at the last minute to give bad reasons for an already existent practice. It was, on the contrary, a major catalyst for practice.

But further, it surely is an exaggeration too to say that monodic practice, as we understand it in the first operas, is already in place here. That the monodic practice of Peri and Caccini must have had predecessors and ancestors any sensible person must allow, and Pirrotta has succeeded brilliantly in showing us what some of them must have been. However, to go from here to the conclusion that the monodic techniques of Peri and Caccini were not therefore an "invention" would, I think, be to confuse Hero of Alexandria's steam engine with James Watt's.

In any case, even the existence of a complete theory one hundred years before the event would not be surprising. One need only think, for example, of the theory of powered heavier-than-air flight, which was fully worked out by Leonardo da Vinci, some hundreds of years before Kitty Hawk, to the extent that a drawing of his for a "helicopter" has recently been declared airworthy by an aeronautical engineer. Even when theory precedes invention, the time must be ripe for theory and practice to couple and give birth.

o 5 o   The major portion of Pirrotta's study is taken up with the "theory" and practice of the sixteenth-century *intermedi*: the predominantly musical interpolations between the acts of Italian Renaissance dramas, which sometimes actually become unified enough in plot and character to achieve the status of "play within a play." These musical performances were truly musical theatre, both elaborate and sophisticated; and if one were to look for an opera before the opera, it would surely be here.

That the *intermedi* were not proto-operas seems abundantly clear from Pirrotta's descriptions, nor does he make any such claim for them. Indeed, he seems more prone to emphasize what distinguishes them from opera and to point out that, far from developing into opera, they continued to flourish alongside the new musical form and were, indeed, influenced by it. In the pre-operatic *intermedi*, "Music did not dominate the stage; it was not as active and dynamic a presence as it was later to become in opera." And after the event, *intermedi* "were no longer immune to the influence of opera, and so came to be performed with more music and more solo singing than their original nature required."[6] The *intermedi*, then, are no more forerunners or proto-operas than the dirigible is a forerunner or proto-airplane. Rather, they were a separate and different realization of the same dream of a musical theatre with, indeed, enough vitality of their own to enable them to co-exist at least for a while with the newer and more viable form, just as the dirigible and airplane, both realizations of the dream of powered flight, shared the same skies during the early years of aviation.

This being the case, it should not be surprising to find here, too, statements of aesthetic principle not unlike those of the theorists and composers of the first true operas. "The description of the singing of choruses included in a report on Gabriele Bombasi's *Alidoro*, a tragedy performed on 2 November 1568 . . . ," Pirrotta points out, "is such that it might seem to be by a member of the Florentine *camerata* . . . , and yet we know that it was written and published well in advance of any musical, or non-musical gathering in the *camerata* of the Bardi family."[7] Of this description, the following excerpt seems most to justify Pirrotta's assertion:

Much thought has been given to these [choruses] by most excellent musicians, who, having looked deeply into their meaning, wrote the songs for them, imitating the words so felicitously, that *one would sooner call them speeches than songs.* For ... *they moved at the pace of ordinary speech,* always avoiding any repetition.[8]

Such obiter dicta should not, I think, be made too much of. That they show a sustained interest, in the Renaissance, in analogies of music to speech cannot be denied. But, as we have seen, the music of Josquin was also described in terms of spoken utterance; and one would hardly look for a precursor of operatic monody there. What gives the theoretical underpinnings of the Camerata their power and originality is not simply such passing observations; it is the sustained effort to portray a music of human speech as a consequence of philosophical presuppositions. Like all inspired theory, it was not the production of novel observations as much as the bringing together of what had often been said before into a coherent whole: an interconnected body of hierarchical premises and conclusions, rather than a collection of fragmented aphorisms. This is the difference that makes what Leonardo said about flight at least a proto-theory, and what Roger Bacon said merely a curiosity. A balanced account of the invention of opera must keep this distinction prominent if it is to make its claim against the ever-growing body of factual knowledge concerning the theory and practice of pre-operatic musical theatre.

○ 6 ○ Needless to say, the discussion so far of Pirrotta's book gives only the smallest sampling of the historical facts adduced. But it is nevertheless representative of those facts that might be thought most damaging to the notion that opera is an "invention" of rather sudden appearance and not something of more gradual, evolutionary origin. And nothing in those facts, or in any others in Pirrotta's study, so far as I can see, necessitates the giving up of that notion. They show an invention with a history. But only The Boy's Book of Great Inventions would lead one to expect anything different. Only God creates *ex nihilo.* Indeed, it seems that Pirrotta himself, in spite of his suspicions about the traditional story of the invention of opera—suspicions born of a more detailed knowledge than heretofore possessed of the prevalence of musical theatre, in both theory and practice, in the century before the opera's appearance—shares the common belief that opera appeared almost fully armed, more like the electric light than the anthropoid ape: in a word, more like an invention than an evolution. "Few other genres," he admits, "have their beginnings as precisely determined as opera."[9]

Nonetheless, some statements of Pirrotta's, which seem to be conclusions drawn from his historical research into Renaissance theatre, are somewhat disturbing, at least on first reflection, to the settled belief that opera is an invented art, at least if the story of that invention is anything like the one I am on the threshold of giving. We had better have a look at these.

To begin with, Pirrotta expresses in his Preface "some qualms about assigning the *Camerata* a leading role in the creation of opera. . . ."[10] But surely the traditional account of the invention of opera does indeed, without any qualms whatever, assign to the Camerata such a role. Had Pirrotta expressed qualms about assigning *the* leading role to those noble gentlemen, one could only share them. For, certainly, the mix of philosophical theory and musical practice that gave birth to opera was far older and more diverse than that. Yet when that is said, there does seem to have been something in the discussions of Bardi *et al.* that was of importance to the development of the new art, even though nothing new originated there.

We can connect Pirrotta's qualms about the role of the Camerata in the invention of opera with a statement much later on which gives them more substance. He says: "I hold Caccini chiefly responsible for the creation of the myth that monody and opera originated in the Florentine *camerata*, for he was the first to propound it."[11] And Pirrotta supports this claim—that is, that it is a "myth that monody and opera originated in the Florentine camerata"—by insisting: "The truth is . . . the ideas and procedures of [the Camerata] . . . have more distant origins in the musical practice of the fifteenth century."

Putting these statements together, we can, I think see precisely what Pirrotta is trying to correct in those accounts of the origin of the opera that might give the Camerata top billing. Certainly, in the light of his research into fifteenth- and sixteenth-century Italian theatre music, Pirrotta must reject the claim that the Camerata produced, *de novo*, either the theory or the practice of solo singing; and we must reject it along with him. But certainly the first chapter of this book, as well as what is still to come, will amply demonstrate that while I do reject it, I still maintain—consistently, I believe—both that opera is an invention and that the composers and theoreticians associated with the Florentine Camerata played *a* major role in the accomplishment. In support of this claim, perhaps it would be useful to say a little about the nature of (at least some) inventions: in particular, what in an "invention" is "new," or, to draw attention to what perhaps is overemphasized about the concept of "invention," what in an "invention" is "invented" by the "inventor."

I suppose the airplane is a paradigm of the invention, and the Wright brothers of the inventor, if the concepts have any instances at all. What exactly did the Wright brothers invent? What did they produce that was new?

Quite simply, the Wright brothers invented—that is to say, physically realized—the first successful heavier-than-air man-carrying powered flying machine. Man-carrying lighter-than-air machines had of course existed since the eighteenth century, in the form of the hydrogen and hot-air balloons, and powered ones since the invention of the dirigible. Non-manned non-powered heavier-than-air machines have, of course, existed since the first kite; for that is what a kite is, after all. The glider is a non-powered heavier-than-air man-carrying machine which pre-ceded the Wright brothers' invention and, in fact, in its later incarnations provided them with the basic design for their aircraft. Nor was the Wright flyer the first powered heavier-than-air flying machine: that honor must go to the ornithopter and the rubber-band-powered "model" airplane.

The theory and design of man-carrying powered heavier-than-air machines were certainly not entirely creations of the Wright brothers but were already to a large degree in place when they came on the scene, although they made contributions to both. The two mechanical devices needed to finally turn the trick were an engine light enough and pow-erful enough to fly its own weight, the weight of a pilot, and the weight of a viable airframe, and a method for stabilizing the aircraft in flight. The powerplant was the internal combustion engine; and although the Wright brothers made improvements in it, it was not their invention. Indeed, it seems that the only mechanical device, not already in existence that the Wright brothers had to contrive for themselves was the device for stabilization of the airplane in flight through the "warping" of the wings—a rather cumbersome method which was soon replaced by the French invention of ailerons, still in use. What in the world, then, did the Wright brothers do in "inventing" the first manned powered heavier-than-air flying machine?

Clearly, the answer is that they put a lot of things together. One is tempted to say that the art of invention is the art of synthesis. But, to beware of generalizing from only a single instance, we can at least say that *some* invention consists in synthesis, the invention of the Wright brothers being a case in point and the invention of opera being another.

What I am driving at, of course, is that historical knowledge of the kind Pirrotta provides no more militates against the concept of opera as an invented art than knowledge of the Wright brothers' predecessors and precedents casts doubt on the propriety of calling them the "inventors" of powered manned heavier-than-air flight. More particularly, it does not, at least as yet, even militate against the belief that Bardi's Camerata played a leading role in opera's invention. For the evidence Pirrotta gives only corrects the mistaken notion that the Camerata's role was innovative. But invention is synthesis as much as, or perhaps more than, it is innovation. And, it seems to me, what the Camerata provided was the bringing together of pre-existent philosophical theory and musical practice into a new, and (for the invention of opera) final synthesis. In a sense, to be sure, the Camerata invented nothing: not the theory of musical *mimesis* nor the practice of it, not the theory of monody nor the practice of it, not the theory of musical theatre nor the practice of it. For all of that, it played a major role in inventing the opera. They also invent who get it all together.

o 7 o   The development of film Panofsky thought to be in a kind of retrograde motion: "it took place," he wrote, "under conditions contrary to precedent"; which is to say, he goes on: "It was not an artistic urge that gave rise to the discovery and gradual perfection of a new technique; it was a technical invention that gave rise to the discovery of a new art."[12] The development of opera, too, seems to have had the cart before the horse; in this case, contrary to the normal course of events, theory preceded practice. We all know that in the arts this is uncommon. The Greek playwrights did not read Aristotle's theory of tragedy and then try to realize it in theatrical practice. Opera was, however, on the contrary, the self-conscious application of theory to practice: the Manhattan Project of music, although with perhaps not quite so dire results.

The theoretical underpinnings of the first operas were, broadly speaking, philosophical, although the framers of theory were not, technically, philosophers. And with philosophy as one of its parents, it is not surprising that opera turned out to be a problem child.

CHAPTER III

Enter Philosophy (in Classical attire)

o 1 o If the musical documents we have consulted thus far are Aristotelian (and to a certain extent Platonic) only implicitly (which is not to deny their philosophical paternity), the ones we are about to consult wear their Aristotelian and Platonic hearts on their sleeves. The Florentine Camerata—the association of noblemen, musicians, and scholars who ushered in the musical genre we know as opera—was provided its philosophical foundations, we now know, by Girolamo Mei, a scholar of considerable accomplishments, who was influenced not only by the older Platonism of Marsilio Ficino, but by the new wave of Aristotelian thought, most notably the *Poetics*.[1] The influence of Mei was not direct but, rather, came through the offices of Vincenzo Galilei, father of the great Galileo, a professional composer, performer, and theorist, who in his *Dialogo della musica antica e della moderna* (1581) translated Mei's aesthetic principles, transmitted to him by personal correspondence, into a practical musical program which resulted, by the turn of the century, in a clearly recognizable operatic medium.

In a moment we shall turn to the work of Mei and Galilei, and to the "philosophical" testament of the Camerata. But it will be useful, first, to confront directly the classical texts that provided, no doubt in a mutilated form, their philosophical first principles. Those texts, referred to quite explicitly in the writings of the Florentines, are principally Book III of Plato's *Republic*, Aristotle's *Poetics*, and Book VIII of the latter's *Politics*. I shall begin, naturally enough, with Plato.

o 2 o In the third book of the *Republic*, Plato is concerned with those aspects of a youth's education that form his character, either for the better or for the worse, and, of course, with the purging from the state of the deleterious ones. It is important to bear in mind, when discussing Galilei and his followers, that Plato's account of music is embedded in this context. In other words, it is assumed from the outset that music, like other such aspects of a Greek youth's upbringing as storytelling, religion, or gymnastics, has an influence over men's souls so powerful that it can make them cowardly or brave, morally upright or depraved: in other

words, good citizens or bad. We have only the Greeks' word for it that
Greek music could do these things, as none of their music survives for us
to hear, and, perhaps, to be thereby convinced. But Mei, Galilei, and the
members of the Camerata were apparently willing to accept this audacious claim sight unseen, or rather, sound unheard. And as their own
music could not perform such feats of moral or psychological behavior
modification, it was their intention, with the help of Greek philosophy,
to reform their music into a kind that could.

It is terribly hard to divine just what Plato was saying about music: as
hard, for example, as it would be two thousand years from now for a
musicologist from Alpha Centauri to try to figure out what Wagner was
saying about music if none of the music of the West survived for him to
hear. Talk about music in the complete absence of music itself is hiero-
glyphics without the Rosetta stone. All I can do here is interpret Plato by
the lights of the music that I know and the tradition of philosophy,
musical theory, and criticism that accompanies it. But that is all the
Camerata could have done either. For our purposes it will suffice.

Two claims that Plato makes in *Republic* III bear scrutiny. The first—
already alluded to—is that music can alter human character. The
second—which is, indeed, the *modus operandi* of the first—is that musical
tones and rhythms can "imitate" or "represent" the characters of men, or
their emotions, or the states of their souls. The second claim is as mysterious and puzzling as the first; and all we can do, through an impene-
trable mist of time and musical ignorance, is to conjecture about both.
Let us begin with the second.

Perhaps the best way to approach this opaque notion of music as an
imitation of human character or emotion or soul—opaque because it is
so difficult to imagine how sounds are to imitate or represent or be like
a character or an emotion or a state of mind—is to begin, *in medias res*,
with some of the more notorious passages and see what we can make of
them.

Plato avers that at least one particular "harmony" can "suitably represent the tones and accents of a brave man engaged in a feat of arms, or
in any violent operation . . ."; that there is "another harmony expressive
of the feelings of one who is engaged in an occupation not violent, but
peaceful and unconstrained . . ."; that there are "plaintive harmonies,"
namely, "Mixed Lydian and Hyperlydian, and such as are like these";
and so on.[2] What are we to make of this?

One very attractive construction that can be put on these passages—
attractive because it is not only intelligible but even plausible—is that
what Plato means by music "imitating" or "representing" human character, emotions, or soul-states is that it can imitate their behavioral man-

ifestations: in particular, the inflections of the human voice. Music, then, does not represent bravery, whatever that would mean, but can "suitably represent the tones and accents of a brave man. . . ." (Other translators, by the way, render this passage in like manner.)

But why should the representation of a brave man's voice make other men brave, or the representation of a coward's make them cowardly? For that is the further claim that Plato seems to have made, and the Camerata to have accepted (more or less). In the eighteenth century, the belief that music was capable of arousing human emotions was coupled either with the Cartesian "physiological psychology" or with the association of ideas, both products of Enlightenment science (or pseudo-science). It would be a mistake, however, to read mechanistic models like these into the Platonic theory of musical affect, even where, at times, it seems almost to invite them. Yet if such quasi-physiological and psychological mechanisms are not appealed to, where else can we turn? Not surprisingly, I think, it is to Plato's "moral psychology": in particular, the belief (shared by Aristotle) that one can take on character traits by imitating the behavioral expressions of them; or, in other words, that one can become moral or immoral through practice. I can, that is to say, become cowardly by pretending or acting the coward, even though cowardice, at the outset, is not a part of my moral makeup, as I can learn to play the piano by playing the piano, even though I *can't* play the piano when I start.

That this may have been what Plato had in mind for music is suggested by the fact that just such an explanation is provided in *Republic* III for the moral effect of narrative, immediately before the subject of music is introduced.

Narrative, of course, Plato is thinking of as a performance. And he distinguishes in *Republic* III between two kinds: the simple description of events, and the kind of narrative where, as he says, the narrator speaks "in the person of" the character whose deeds he relates. Now, "when he delivers a speech in the character of another man," Plato maintains, "he aims at the closest resemblance in style to the person introduced as the speaker." In other words, he imitates that person.[3] And therein lies a danger as well as a benefit. For, Plato continues, "imitations, whether of bodily gestures, tones of voice, or modes of thought, if they be persevered in from an early age, are apt to grow into habits and a second nature." In other words, imitate the coward enough, even if only in voice and gesture, and you will play the coward thereafter. This, then, is the manner in which the "performer" of an imitation is afflicted with the character, emotions, or states of soul that are his objects of imitation. And for this reason Plato is leery of having his citizens—particularly those entrusted with the guardianship of the state—partake of such practices:

"or if they do imitate, let them imitate from very childhood whatever is proper to their profession,—brave, sober, religious, honourable men, and the like,—but meanness, and every other kind of baseness, let them neither practise nor be skilled to imitate, lest from the imitations they be infected with the reality."[4]

But music (by which Plato means here sung poetry, that is, "vocal music") is, like imitative narration, a representation of the behavior, in particular the language, of men; and what a man expresses is what he is: his character, his emotions, the state of his soul. It is clear, I think, that Plato meant the account of narration, and specifically the infectious character of imitating, to spill over into the musical discussion which immediately follows. Thus we can conclude that the singer and composer of "songs" is aroused, moved, formed by his music because music "represent[s] the tones and accents" of men; for that makes the maker and performer of them an imitator of men, with all that that implies, including the deplorable fact that imitating wicked men makes one wicked, and imitating sad men makes one sad, as well as the more felicitous result that imitating good men makes one good, and imitating happy men makes one happy.

But, it might be objected, this explanation of narrative and musical power over the emotions and minds of men applies only to those who perform and compose, not to those (by far the greater number) who only listen and watch. Do narration and music have no power of arousal over audiences, but only over practitioners?

Such a conclusion would not, of course, have seemed so professionally elitist to the Greeks of the fourth century B.C. as it might to us, since there would have been a far greater proportion of performers and "composers" among the educated citizenry than we have today, with the rigid lines that we draw between professional, amateur, and public. Aristotle, in the *Politics*, insisted on musical performance and composition as part of the necessary education of the citizen; and although Plato, for reasons we have already seen, was more or less opposed at least to the guardians taking part in imitative activities, he apparently accepted that such activities would inevitably take place, and had to be satisfied with cautioning against their abuse.

In any case, however, it is clear that Plato saw the contemplation of imitation to be as infectious as its performance. Indeed, it must have seemed even more obvious a phenomenon than the latter; for he everywhere assumes it, and nowhere deems it problematic enough to be flagged. Imitation, after all, is a form of flattery. So what is presented to me in imitation, particularly in the impressionableness of youth, will be taken by me as an example to be emulated. That, of course, is why Plato did not want the gods to be represented as behaving immorally. For what is good (or bad) enough for Apollo or Poseidon is surely good (or bad) enough for me. What should I emulate if not the god-like? And if the god-like is also represented to me as the adulterous, why not emulate *that*? It makes religion not only a duty but a pleasure.

We can fairly assume, then, that Plato thought musical performances imitative of the tones and accents of immoral men would tend to be treated as examples to be followed, as would imitations of the good and the righteous. For this reason, the spectator had as much to gain or lose from a musical imitation as did the composer and performer. Therein lies the power of music for both. The theory is complete.

So much then for the Platonic musical inheritance. I turn now to the Aristotelian.

○ 3 ○   The *Poetics* "was the foundation of Girolamo Mei's musical aesthetics";[5] and Mei's musical aesthetics was the foundation of Galilei's—therefore of the Camerata's. But the *Poetics* really says precious little about music, at least as we understand it and as it was understood in the sixteenth century. Mei and his companions turned, therefore, as we do now, to Book VIII of the *Politics* for futher enlightenment. What the *Poetics* did give them, of course, and this is of supreme importance for the subject at hand, was a well-worked-out, philosophically powerful aesthetics of the drama which assumed, as a matter of course, that the drama of which it treated was a sung drama, a musical drama, in some sense or other of "song" and "music" that was related to their own sense of those words. Further, it subsumed music, as had *Republic* III, under the arts of imitation, which gave that very important and fruitful notion further authority in their eyes.

I have already quoted in Chapter II the passage in which Aristotle catalogues the imitative arts. It is important enough, and relevant enough in this place, to quote again (this time more fully).

> Epic poetry, then, and the poetry of tragic drama, and, moreover, comedy and dithyrambic poetry, and most flute-playing and harp-playing, these, speaking generally, may all be said to be "representations of life." But they differ one from another in three ways: either in using means generally different or in representing different objects or in representing objects not in the same way but in a different manner. . . . [They] all make their representations in rhythm and language and tune, using these means either separately or in combination. For tune and rhythm alone are employed in flute-playing and harp-playing and

in any other arts which have a similar function, as, for example, pipe-playing.[6]

This thought is completed, a bit further on, with the crucial statement—crucial, at least, for the Camerata and the history of music—that "There are certain arts which employ all the means which I have mentioned, such as rhythm and tune and metre—dithyrambic and 'nomic' poetry, for example, and tragedy too and comedy."[7]

Three important points can be—and I think were—teased out of these passages, and they require some scrutiny here. First, it seems apparent that something like "pure instrumental music" was supposed by Aristotle to be an art of imitation. What did it imitate? The answer is not clear (at least to me); but for what answer there is we must turn to Book VIII of the *Politics*.

In *Politics* VIII, Aristotle, like Plato in *Republic* III, expresses the view that music "has some influence over the character and the soul"; and like Plato too he believes that music is (among other things) an "imitation" or "representation" of human character, emotions, states of the soul.

> Rhythm and melody supply imitations of anger and gentleness, and also of courage and temperance, and of all the qualities contrary to these, and of the other qualities of character which hardly fall short of the actual affects, as we know from our own experience, for in listening to such strains our souls undergo a change.[8]

As in Plato, the notion of music (or anything else of the kind) being an "imitation," a "likeness" of an emotion, state of mind, or character trait, is a very murky one. What can it mean? All that the eighteenth-century English translator of the *Poetics*, Thomas Twining, could make of it was a metaphorical reference to arousal. His argument seems to have been: music cannot "imitate," that is "resemble" emotions or states of the soul; it can "arouse" them; so when Aristotle says that music "imitates" emotions and states of mind it can only be a figure of speech for "arouses" them in the listener. Twining writes in his commentary on the passage in hand:

> It appears then, in the *first* place, that Music, considered as affecting, or raising *emotions*, was called imitation by the antients, *because* they perceived in it that which is essential to all imitations and is, indeed, often spoken of as the same thing—*resemblance*. This resemblance, however, as *here* stated by Aristotle, cannot be *immediate*; for between *sounds themselves*, and *mental affections*, there can be no resemblance. The resemblance can only be a resemblance of *effect*:—the *general emotions, tempers,* or *feelings* produced in us by certain sounds are *like* those that accom-

pany actual grief, joy, anger, &c.—And this, as far, at least, as can be collected from the passage in question, appears to be all that Aristotle meant.[9]

That this could *not* be what Aristotle meant, however, is made abundantly clear by his carefully fashioned and persistently held distinction between musical representations and musical arousal, and, indeed, by the claim already met in Plato, that the former is the cause of, the means to, the latter. Thus he says that "when men hear imitations, even apart from the rhythms and tunes themselves, their feelings move in sympathy."[10] I take Aristotle to be claiming here that when men hear imitations, whether they are the kind provided by rhythm and tune, that is, the musical kind, or whether they are some other kind of imitation, appropriate emotions will be aroused in them by sympathy. I do not know whether what Aristotle is suggesting is that if I hear grief imitated I will feel grief, or some other emotion appropriate to grief (say, anger), or perhaps both. But what is perfectly clear is that he distinguishes sharply between music's power to imitate emotions and its power to arouse them, and asserts its power to do both. He cannot, therefore, as Twining suggests, be using "imitate" as a synonym for "arouse." We shall have to look elsewhere for an interpretation of what Aristotle could have meant, then, by music's "imitating" emotions.

It is tempting to believe that he shared Plato's view in *Republic* III (if I understand *that* text correctly) that what music does is to imitate the tones and accents—the expressions, that is to say—of men under the sway of this or that emotion. Unfortunately, that will not wash, as it seems to run afoul of something else Aristotle says. In contrasting the sense of hearing with the other senses, Aristotle maintains:

> The objects of no other senses [than hearing], such as taste or touch, have any resemblance to moral qualities; in visible objects there is only a little, for these are figures which are of a moral character, but only to a slight extent, and all do not participate in the feeling about them. Again, figures and colors are not imitations but signs of moral habits, indications which the body gives of states of feeling.[11]

I do not pretend to understand this strange passage fully. What I do understand is this. Aristotle is contrasting two ways in which an object of the external senses might be an "imitation," a likeness of a feeling or moral character: a literal sense, and an attenuated one. Only the objects of sound (in this context, clearly, musical objects) are literally imitations or likenesses of moral characters and feelings. The objects of sight, figures and colors, can only be imitations or likenesses of these mental traits by proxy; they imitate (in painting and sculpture, for example) the bodily manifestations of these states; they do not imitate the states themselves, which is something only music can do. But if that is what Aristotle believed, then it contradicts what we interpreted Plato as meaning by music's imitating moral character and feelings (in *Republic* III). Plato was saying that music imitates moral character and feelings only in that attenuated sense. It imitates, for Plato, the tones and accents in which men (vocally) express their feelings and characters; it does not imitate the feelings and characters directly (whatever that might mean). But for Aristotle, music is, apparently, not merely a copy of emotive expressions but a direct copy of emotions themselves.

There does not, then, seem to be an easy answer to the question of what Aristotle may have meant by the dark saying that music imitates feeling and character. I don't know if there is any answer at all. I will leave it at that.

The second point that emerges from *Poetics* 1447a—and a crucial one it is for the inventors of opera—is that in Aristotle's time tragedy and comedy were "sung," at least in part, since he insists that they "employ all the means which I have mentioned, such as rhythm and tune and metre. . . ." This point is articulated still more emphatically later on, in a familiar definition of tragedy, where Aristotle says:

> Tragedy is, then, a representation of an action that is heroic and complete and of a certain magnitude—by means of language enriched with all kinds of ornament, each used separately in the different parts of the play: it represents men in action and does not use narrative, and through pity and fear it effects relief to these and similar emotions. By "language enriched" I mean that which has rhythm, and tune, *i.e.* song, and by the kinds separately I mean that some effects are produced by verse alone and some again by song.[12]

That we have very little, if any, notion of what Greek tragedy "sounded" like—how much, if at all, was "music" in any form recognizable to us as such—need hardly be said yet again. That it *was* "music" in the "modern" sense of the word Mei, Galilei, and the Camerata did not doubt. Or, rather, they believed that it was a kind of music that, unfortunately, the Renaissance polyphonists had turned away from much to the detriment of the art, which could not, as a result, any longer work those powers over the emotions and characters of men of which Plato, Aristotle, and a host of ancient thinkers spoke. Mei had convinced Galilei, and through him the rest of the Camerata, no doubt, that Greek music, unlike the music of his time, was completely monophonic: that is, it was not polyphonic in the sense of being contrapuntal, or even in the sense of being chordally accompanied. Tones were not, in other words, ever simultaneously sounded except in unison (or at the octave?). When we turn to Mei, Galilei, and the rest, we will address this subject again. For now, however, it will suffice for us to note that although the members of the Camerata claimed to be reviving in their operas and monodies the kind of musical performance Aristotle spoke of in the *Poetics*, that claim should not be taken quite literally. What they surely must have meant was not that they had recaptured the sound of the Greek theatre, or even had tried to. For *they* never gave up polyphony in either of its two senses: counterpoint or harmony. The *stile rappresentativo* is chordally accompanied, with an independent (if not melodically significant) bass line; and right from the start, at least simple contrapuntal choruses and instrumental ritornelli were an important part of their operatic works. Since they were convinced that Greek music was monodic, they could not have been asserting that it was being revived in the letter, without contradiction. It was, they undoubtedly thought, being revived in the spirit—and that could only mean, one supposes, that its celebrated power over the human mind was being revived with means that a revamped but "modern" music could provide.

The third point to notice in *Poetics* 1447a is that whatever it was Aristotle thought "pure" instrumental music might imitate, the "song" of the drama might imitate that too. One can reasonably assume, I would think, that "instrumental music," like "song," was for Aristotle a representation of character and emotion. Another interpretation is, of course, within the realm of bare possibility. Aristotle might have been saying, first, that "song" sometimes represents human character and emotion, and, second, that "song" and "instrumental music" sometimes represent the same thing, and when they do it is not human character and emotion but something else (unnamed). But this is a tortured reading at best; and I see no reason to give it. When Aristotle refers to music in general, that is, rhythm and melody, he never suggests that they represent anything but human character and emotion; and there is no evidence that "instrumental music" was an exception. In any event, it seems a certainty that Mei, Galilei, and (therefore) the Camerata must have read Aristotle as ascribing the same objects of imitation to "pure" instrumental music as to "song." That is the important point for our purposes.

We now have before us the philosophical passages that must have been the basis for the musical aesthetics of Mei, Galilei, et al., in an interpretation that, I believe, must have been close to their own. What these theorists and musicians, with their practical artistic concerns, made of them we must now discuss.

o 4 o   In discussing the theoretical basis for the invention of the opera, we will want to look both at the makers of the theory and the makers of the opera, for the makers of the opera were makers of theory as well: or, rather, translators of philosophical theory into practical musical precepts. In the following chapter we will then look at the first major product of this theory-making, Monteverdi's *Orfeo*. For, as I had occasion to remark in regard to Plato and Aristotle, the philosophy of music, in the absence of the music itself, is a code without the cipher. First, then, to the makers of the theory.

Five major conclusions were reached by the "philosophers" of opera, in their direct or indirect encounter with the Platonic and Aristotelian texts. Three of them we ourselves were easily able to discern in *Republic* III, *Poetics*, and *Politics* VIII. They are, first, that music exerts a power over the souls and characters of men; that it can change them, morally, for the better or worse, and raise their emotions. Second, that this emotive arousal and moral manipulation is accomplished through the "imitation" or "representation" of human character and emotions. Third, that (as Plato apparently believed) by music's "representing" or "imitating" human character or emotions one can only mean its "representing" or "imitating" human speech and other expressive behavior. Fourth, that Greek drama was a "musical performance" of some kind— that in some sense or other it, or part of it, was "sung." Fifth—but only by inference, as the texts bear no witness here—that Greek music was neither contrapuntal nor chordally accompanied: in other words, completely monophonic.

This whole array—which amounted, indeed, to a complete little musical aesthetics—exists completely intact and interconnected in the letters which Girolamo Mei sent to Vincenzo Galilei between 1572 and 1579, and can be found essentially complete in the passages from these letters which Palisca translates in his seminal article on the subject. The importance of Mei to Galilei and the Camerata, and his intrinsic interest as a musical "aesthetician," suggest that we look here first. I will rely for my exegesis mostly on passages from Mei's first letter to Galilei (8 May 1572) as it appears in Palisca's article. What I hope to show is that the entire position, including the argumentation (sometimes implicit) lurking behind it, can be derived entirely from the propositions above that I have extracted from Plato and Aristotle.

Mei begins, as I suggested he and all of his followers in the Camerata do, with the belief, on the authority of the ancient texts and observation of the contemporary musical scene, that the ancient music had a power over the character and emotions of men that the polyphony of his own day did not possess. He then seems to have concluded that since the most notable characteristic of his own music *was* polyphony, this must be what made the music of his day ineffective, and its absence what gave the other its potency. The ancient music, in other words, must have been monophonic.

> What chiefly persuaded me that the entire chorus sang one identical air was observing that the music of the ancients was held a valuable medium for moving the affections, as can be inferred from the many incidents related by the [ancient] writers and from noting that the music of our composers instead is appropriate for anything but that. Now all this naturally arises from the apposite qualities that are intrinsically characteristic of these two kinds of music: the qualities of ancient music being suitable and by nature apt for achieving the effects they attained, those of the moderns, on the contrary, for hindering them.[13]

Were this all that Mei's argument consisted of, it would be an egregious instance of Mill's method of difference in the service of an absurd conclusion from a false premise: A causes X; B does not; B has *p*; A does not; therefore it is the absence of *p* that enables A to cause X (and Mei, of course, never doubted that A, Greek music, caused X, emotions in the listener). But this is *not* all there is to Mei's argument, and that is what makes it interesting and musically fruitful, although no less a bad argument for all of that.

The more that there is is a very clear idea on Mei's part of what it is about polyphony that defeats emotive arousal, based on the Platonic notion of what it is in music that enhances it. If I am right, that the blood and bones of Mei's—and, by consequence, the Camerata's—philosophy of music was provided directly or indirectly by *Republic* III, *Poetics*, and *Politics* VIII, then we can reconstruct Mei's reasoning process as going in something like the following way. Ancient music had power over the "affections," and modern music does not. Ancient music had this power, both Plato and Aristotle agreed, by virtue of being able to "imitate" or "represent" the "affections"; and for Plato the rather problematic concept of imitating or representing the affections was cashed out in terms of the more intelligible notion of imitating or representing the tones and accents of the human voice when expressing this emotion or that. In short, I arouse sadness with my music by "representing" or "imitating" the characteristic tones and accents of the human voice when, in either speech or inarticulate utterance, it is expressing that emotion. Mei must then have asked himself, given these premises, what it was about modern music that made it a poor likeness, or no likeness at all, of the tones and accents of the human voice in a particular passion; since if it were a good likeness the passion would be raised, which it manifestly was not. The signal feature of the music of his day was, of course, its exceedingly complex polyphonic structure. Once his eye fell on that, as it inevitably and immediately would, the whole theory must have fallen into his lap. For the question would then become: why is *polyphony* a bad likeness, or no likeness at all, of human speech? The answer was clear, as we have seen, and it had already been given by the Council of Trent: *we don't all speak at once.* But Mei was more subtle than that.

The human voice, Mei reasoned, was a naturally expressive instrument, with particular resonant qualities appropriate to particular emotive states.

> Now, nature gave the voice to animals and especially to man for the expression of inner feelings. Therefore it was logical that, the various qualities of the voice being distinct, each should be appropriate for expressing the affections of certain determinate states and that each furthermore should express easily its own but not those of another. Thus the high voice could not properly express the affections of the intermediate and far less those of the low voice, nor the intermediate any of those of the high or low. Rather, the quality of one ought naturally to impede the operation of the other, the two being opposites.[14]

Here, then, is the key to an explanation more detailed than "we don't all talk at once" of why polyphonic music cannot be a reasonable representation of the human voice in any particular passion. For the human speaking voice is different in both range and rhythm, under the influence of different passions: "the tones intermediate between the extremely high and the extremely low are appropriate for showing a quiet and moderate disposition of the affections, while the very high are signs of a very excited and aroused spirit, and the very low, of abject and humble thoughts, in the same way that a rhythm intermediate between rapid and slow shows a poised spirit while a rapid one manifests excitement, and a slow one, sluggishness and laziness."[15] But if I write a polyphonic composition in (say) four real parts, only one (or perhaps two) of the melodic lines can be in the appropriate range (and, because of the exigencies of counterpoint, in the appropriate rhythms) for any given passion. Thus the overall "picture" will be a jumble, rather like the double exposure or superimposition of a sad face and a happy one: both passions are there, but the whole cannot be "read" as anything intelligible. Neither in the music nor in the superimposition of faces do we have a good likeness, or any likeness at all, of a recognizable human expression.

Further, of course, arousal or "moving" of the affections must fail if representation fails; for it is clear that the affections are moved in the souls of others by representing, as if in the presence of these others, affections through objects or recollections that have previously those same affections. Now this cannot be done with the voice otherwise than through that quality, whether low, high, or intermediate, with which nature provided the voice for this purpose and which is a characteristic and natural sign of that which we wish to arouse in the listener.[16]

I must recognize an expressive "object" presented or represented if I am to be aroused by an emotion; and where the object bears no recognizable expressive character, as would indeed be the case if it were a polyphonic composition, no sympathetic emotive reverberations can be set in motion. I can be made sad by hearing a melody that represents the sad aspect of a human utterance, just as I can by seeing a drawing that represents the sad aspect of a human face; but where four different melodies sounding simultaneously present four different emotive aspects, they end up presenting no *recognizable* aspect at all.

Mei compared the effect of modern polyphony on the soul to the vain efforts of several men straining to pull down to the floor a stable pillar by tugging at it with ropes from opposite directions, failing despite all their forces to budge it. Modern contrapuntal music, with its melodies and "tones" of opposing expressive natures pulling in diverse directions, was incapable of conveying any distinct affections.[17]

We have, to sum up, a remarkably well-worked-out application of the Platonic and Aristotelian *mimesis* to music in Mei's epistolary fragments. But it was, essentially, a theory without a subject matter, at least where it spoke of what music ought to be doing as opposed to what it was in fact doing in his time. For the ancient music that he lauded existed only in his imagination—and may never have existed in reality at all. Certainly, it *could not* have existed if we take some of the more extravagant claims that were made for it at face value. Mei's theory, then, had a normative implication to it, a program for action that he was in no position himself to spell out. His was the work of a scholar and something of a philosopher, not someone with musical skills or even musical taste. In Vincenzo Galilei and the composers of the Camerata it found hands to translate theoretical precepts into a musical practice, and a musical practice into musical works.

o 5 o   It would be well to begin this section with a caveat. I have based my account of Mei's musical aesthetics solely on what was made available in Palisca's judicious but necessarily limited selection of passages; and what is to come concerning Galilei et al. will be based on the somewhat longer, equally well-chosen, but nonetheless far from complete selection in Strunk's now-classic *Source Readings in Music History*. So what I am about to say may simply be the result of a false impression derived from a skewed sample. I will venture it anyway, however, because I strongly suspect that what is all but absent from Mei, in Palisca's selection from his letters to Galilei, and what is noticeably present in Strunk's abridgment of Galilei's *Dialogo* would, if it had been in the letters, have, because of its importance, inevitably caught Palisca's very acute scholarly eye and forced its way into his article.

What I speak of is this. Mei, as well as Galilei, was, of course, well aware of the fact that the practical problem facing the composer of music was the setting of words; yet his discussion of the emotional character of music was on a level of abstraction that, at least in the passages Palisca reproduces, precluded any discussion of what gives the composer his emotive cues, namely the text. What makes the *Dialogo*, in spite of its theoretical nature, a theory of potential musical *practice* is that Galilei goes right to the heart of the practical matter: the relation of musical emotion to the expressive qualities of the texts being set. Whenever Galilei is talking about the emotive character of music, it is always in that context. That, therefore, is what we must principally devote ourselves to here, there being no need to recount in the words of Galilei those principles which he merely lifted bodily from Mei.

It is no mere surmise that Galilei thought the problem of text-setting of paramount importance to practical music aesthetics. For when he reaches the topic, it is as the culmination of his argument, the goal of his theorizing; and he does not leave the point in any doubt. Galilei writes: "Finally I come as I promised to the treatment of the most important part of music, the imitation of the conceptions that are derived from the words."[18] What Galilei means by music's being "the imitation of the conceptions that are derived from the words" constitutes, I would suggest, his original contribution, beyond what he took from Mei, to the musical aesthetics of the early monodists and opera composers. Needless to say, Platonic and Aristotelian *mimesis* is still operative here.

The contrapuntists of Galilei's time and of a previous generation, particularly the madrigal composers, were no strangers to musical "imitation." And part of what Galilei means by "the concepts that are derived from the words" are the visual images that can be represented in sound and that such composers delighted in portraying: for example, the representation of ascent or descent, when mentioned in the text, by ascending or descending lines, or the representation of a lame ox by "staggering, wavering, syncopated notes as though they have the hiccups."[19] But this sort of musical imitation is not—as we can gather from the scorn with which these kinds of examples are treated in the *Dialogo*, as well as from what Galilei specifically says—the true path of musical *mimesis* as it was understood by Plato and Aristotle, and as it must be understood if the ancient power of music over the minds of men is to be restored.

One of Galilei's major objections to these so-called "madrigalisms" is that they are often at cross purposes with a variety of "concepts that are derived from the words," namely, the expressive character of the text, its dominant emotive tone at any given point; and it is the latter that must always dictate the representational character of the music because, as the theory has maintained in its various forms, from Plato to Aristotle to Mei, it is through the representation of emotive states recognizable to the listener that by a kind of sympathy, the listener is aroused to those states—and it is, let it be remembered, the emotive arousal, the power of music to alter human character, that is the ultimate goal of music, on the classical view.[20] For the "sole aim" of music that pictorially represents, and ignores the ruling passions of the text, "is to delight the ear, while that of ancient music is to induce in another the same passion that one feels oneself."[21]

The question then arises: How does one divine exactly what the leading passion of a text is? I cannot, for example, assume that simply because the words "fear" and "sadness" occur in it that the leading passions are those; for the words might be "I have no fear, and sadness has departed," in which case the leading passions are just about the opposite. Indeed, it was the madrigalists' fastening on single words rather than on the meanings of sentences that raised the ire of Galilei and others as being musically insensitive to the text. But even reading sentences rather than words will not prove infallible as a guide to the right emotion; for Don Giovanni may say "I love you" to Zerlina but we all know that's not what he means, regardless of what the *sentence* means, and the orchestra tells us as much by giving the Don the horselaugh.

At this point in his thinking (at least as I have reconstructed or imagined it) Galilei had a most fruitful insight that was to serve as the link between theory and practice. What he in fact suggested is not just that the composer must thoroughly understand the words he is to set—although he certainly must do at least that—but that he must also imagine for himself what the situation and character are of the person who utters them. Indeed, even where we are not dealing with a dramatic text in which the *dramatis personae* can be isolated and studied—a lyric, for example, or a sonnet—we are still to understand some kind of textually implied speaker whose utterance the text must be imagined as being, if we are to set it appropriately to its leading passion (or passions). "When the ancient musician sang any poem whatever, he first considered very diligently the character of the person speaking: his age, his sex, with whom he was speaking, and the effect he sought to produce by this means; and these conceptions, previously clothed by the poet in chosen words suited to such a need, the musician then expressed in the tone and with the accents and gestures, the quantity and quality of sound, and the rhythm appropriate to that action and to such a person." And again, some advice to composers:

> when they go for their amusement to the tragedies and comedies that mummers act, let them a few times leave off their immoderate laughing, and instead be so good as to observe, when one quiet gentleman speaks with another, in what manner he speaks, how high or low his voice is pitched, with what sort of accents and gestures, and with what rapidity or slowness his words are uttered. Let them mark a little what difference obtains in all these things when one of them speaks with one of his servants, or one of these with another; let them observe the prince when he chances to be conversing with one of his subjects and vassals; when with the petitioner who is entreating his favor; how the man infuriated or excited speaks; the married woman, the girl, the mere child, the clever harlot, the lover speaking to his mistress as he seeks to persuade her to grant his wishes, the man who laments, the one who cries out, the timid man, the man exultant with joy. From these variations of circumstances, if they observe them attentively and examine them with care, they will be able to select the norm of what is fitting for the expression of any other conception whatever that can call for their handling.[22]

The practical musical program, then, that Galilei's theoretical precepts sanction is one in which music is taken to be a medium for the representation or imitation of the human voice and gesture under the influence of particular passions, those to be determined by what emotions the imagined utterer or actor is supposed to be expressing, or what emotions he intends to convey. What remained was to find specific musical means of realizing this representational goal. That, of course, was the job of the composers, whom we shall hear from now.

 ∘ 6 ∘ Two names are associated with the composition of the earliest operas: those of Jacopo Peri and Giulio Caccini. Both write of a similar goal: to realize the tones and accents of passionate human speech, for the purpose of moving the hearer. I shall return at the conclusion of this chapter to the question of what "moving" the hearer might have meant. Let us first see how they proposed to mint the mimetic theories of Mei and Galilei in genuine musical coin.

In the Foreword to his *Euridice* (published 1601) Peri makes two very revealing observations about what he was aiming at, and what assumptions lay behind it, that deserve to be quoted rather fully.

> Seeing that dramatic poetry was concerned and that it was therefore necessary to imitate speech in song (and surely no one ever spoke in song), I judged that the ancient Greeks and Romans (who, in the opinion of many, sang their tragedies throughout in representing them upon the stage) had used a harmony surpassing that of ordinary speech but falling so far below the melody of song as to take an intermediate form. . . . For this reason, discarding every other manner of singing hitherto heard, I devoted myself wholly to seeking out the kind of imitation necessary for these poems. And I considered that the kind of speech that the ancients assigned to singing . . . could in part be hastened and made to take an intermediate course, lying between the slow and suspended movements of song and the swift and rapid movements of speech. . . .
>
> I knew likewise that in our speech some words are so intoned that harmony can be based upon them and that in the course of speaking it passes through many others that are not so intoned until it returns to another that will bear a progression to a fresh consonance. And having in mind those inflections and accents that serve us in our grief, in our joy, and in similar states, I caused the bass to move in time to these, either more or less, following the passions, and I held it firm throughout the false and true proportions until, running through various notes, the voice of the speaker came to a word that, being intoned in familiar speech, opened the way to a fresh harmony.[23]

Along with those from whom he derived his views about Greek music, Peri shared the view that Greek tragedy was in some sense or other "sung." But what the first passage above hints at is that he must have found difficulty in understanding how a tragedy truly "sung," in the modern (sixteenth-century) sense of the word, could possibly be kept to a reasonable length. For if one imagines (say) the text of Euripides' *Bacchae* (as we possess it) set to music in even so condensed and economical a style as Palestrina's setting of the Mass in the *Missa Papae Marcelli*, the performance for a sixteenth-century audience, anyway, would take too long to be acceptable. (Obviously Bayreuth had yet to be dreamed of by them!) On the other hand, the pace of any kind of music must be slower than human speech. So Peri reasoned that a middle way must be found:

"an intermediate course, lying between the slow and suspended movements of song and the swift and rapid movements of speech. . . ." Thus one of the theoreticians' precepts, "Tragedy must be sung," was to be realized by the invention of a kind of declamatory style, somewhere between speech and florid song—something like but in important respects very different from, what eventually developed into operatic recitative. (Peri and Caccini both claimed to have invented the so-called *stile rappresentativo*. I will not enter into that but leave it to the musicologists to adjudicate.)

Equal in importance to the precept of a sung drama was, of course, the demand for a representational, mimetic music, to fulfill its moral destiny as a mover of men's minds. That was to be achieved, Peri makes clear, following Galilei's advice to mark the character and circumstances of an imagined speaker or dramatic actor, by imitating in the new declamatory style the tones and accents of emotionally charged utterance. Indeed, it is less like imitating than simply "reproducing": hearing in speech the musical tones that lie hidden there, and letting *them* do the composing, as Michelangelo saw the statue already formed in the marble block, merely waiting to be liberated.

The Foreword to Giulio Caccini's collection of monodic songs, *Le nuove musiche* (1602), provides another insight into the new declamatory music and its theoretical underpinnings. About the contrapuntal style Caccini voiced misgivings at least as old as the Council of Trent. His remedy, like Peri's, was a declamatory style, neither speech nor song but something in between, based on the "natural music" of human utterance. "It being plain . . . that such music and musicians gave no other delight than what harmony could give the ear, for unless the words were understood, they could not move the understanding, I endeavored in these my late compositions to bring in a kind of music by which men might, as it were, talk in harmony, using in that kind of singing . . . a certain noble neglect of the song. . . ."[24] The "noble neglect of the song" is, of course, a figure for the halfway house of the *stile rappresentativo*. But apropos of that, it is of interest to note that Caccini does not reject florid melody completely. What he insists on is that melismas be in their proper place: "there being nothing more contrary to passion than they are . . . I introduced them for use in some kind of music less passionate or affectuous. . . ."[25]

Caccini, like Peri, has recognized Galilei's injunction to study the leading passion of a text and realize it in music. But he is less clear, perhaps, on Galilei's very nice distinction (if I have not read too much into it) between the meaning of the words and the emotion of the utterer. For it is the utterance rather than the utterer that Caccini fastens upon, where he writes, for example: "in increasing and abating the voice, and in exclamations, is the foundation of passion, and who doth always use them in every sort of music, not discerning whether the words require it," falls into error; "whereas those that well understand the conceit and meaning of the words, know our defects and can distinguish where the passion is more or less required."[26]

◦ 7 ◦ We have before us, now, at least for present purposes, a fairly clear and thorough picture of the theory of musical representation that motivated the first composers of opera, and at least some idea, though perhaps a murky one, of its Platonic and Aristotelian sources. One loose end remains to be tied before we can move on. It is the question of just what *effect* the theorists and composers of the Camerata thought that their music was to have, to fulfill its destiny as the heir to the music of the ancients.

The members of the Camerata, as well as their spiritual fathers, Mei and Galilei, spoke of the complex polyphony of their time as meant merely to charm, or titillate, or please the aural sense, whereas the music of the Greeks and the music they envisioned was music that was "moving"; that "moved" the listener. Thus, for example, Caccini describes the motivation behind the composition of his first monodic songs in terms of "believing that they had more to delight and move than the greatest number of voices singing together . . . ," whereas many-voiced compositions "gave no other delight than what harmony could give the ear. . . ."[27] There are two benign (and quite compatible) constructions one can put on this claim, and one that is pernicious. Unfortunately, it is clear that at least some of the time it is the pernicious construction that is necessitated by the text.

There seems, to begin with, absolutely nothing wrong with making the claim that a piece of music is (say) "sad" in that it is a really good representation of a human utterance when made under the influence of that emotion, and that it is "moving"—moves the listener—by the excellence of the representation as by the other aesthetically successful features of the music. We are moved by the beauty, the excellence, of works of art, as we are moved by the suffering of others. We are moved by the suffering of others to sadness, perhaps, and what we are moved to by the excellence or beauty of works of art is an emotion, perhaps, without a name; but that is no reason to believe that the emotion we are moved to by the beauty of art is some mysterious or special "aesthetic" emotion, nor is it necessary (certainly not plausible) for us to be driven to the view that what we are moved to by the excellence of "sad" music is sadness. Some human emotions simply cannot be described in terms other than of what it was that aroused them in us; or, in other words, some human emotions can only be described in terms of what their intentional objects are. What we are moved to by the beauty of works of art may very well be just such an emotion: an emotion, that is to say, that is only (and adequately) described by saying "I am moved by the beauty of that," "I am overcome by its beauty," or something of the kind.

Sometimes, however, a Camerata text speaks of moving the *mind* of the listener when it seems that what is meant is that the composer, by the skill of his representation, gets the listener to recognize the emotion being represented, as I recognize that a congeries of lines is—is a representation of—a rabbit or a landscape or a human face. As Galilei put it, the goal of music was (and ought to be) "to express the passions with great effectiveness . . . and secondarily to communicate these with equal force to the minds of mortals for their benefit and advantage. . . ."[28] Again, there is nothing at all unreasonable about this claim, nor is it at odds with the previous one. Sometimes we do indeed recognize (frequently with the help of a sung text) what a piece of music is meant to represent: the composer has communicated this to us, as Galilei says, or, in the words of Caccini already quoted above, he has "move[d] the understanding . . ."; and sometimes we are moved by the beautiful way the representation is brought off (although, needless almost to say, other musical parameters play a far more prominent role in moving the listener than does musical representation, since they play a far more prominent role in making the beautiful in music).

But finally, and unfortunately, what the Camerata texts seem to mean by music's "moving" is that it arouses the emotions that it represents *in* the listener, making him or her sad when a sad expression is represented, happy when a happy one, and so on. As Mei says, "the music of the ancients was held a valuable medium for moving the affections . . .";[29] and by "moving the affections" he clearly means "arousing" them. I say of course that this is an unfortunate conclusion because it seems clearly false. I have treated the by now well-known objections to this "arousal" theory of musical "expression" elsewhere.[30] They can be rehearsed here in brief. (1) What we call "sad" music does not seem to have any consistent tendency to make us sad; we show none of the familiar (or unfamiliar) signs of the emotion when we listen to it. (2) Sadness and other such emotions are aroused by our encounters in the world of people, objects, and events for which some of the arts may present us with facsimiles or simulacra but which music does not to any considerable degree. (3) Unpleasant emotions are to be, and generally are, avoided; yet music which is described in terms of these emotions is, if it is good music, sought after and savoured, which would be difficult to explain if music truly aroused them. (We do not shun "sad" music the way we do the sad-ness-provoking events of life.) (4) Music does, indeed, acquire the power to evoke emotions in us by the association of ideas—the "they're playing our song" phenomenon—so that I may be reminded of a happy incident in my life by Chopin's Funeral March, if I first heard it at that time, and the remembrance might well make me happy. But I would hardly call the Funeral March "happy" on that account. Such associations of ideas are personal and idiosyncratic, whereas the sadness of Chopin's music is "public property."

That a conclusion is false does not, unfortunately, suggest that it was not drawn. But I intend to invoke here the principle of interpretational charity, and take the Camerata texts simply to be saying that music is describable in emotive terms in virtue of its representing the tones and accents of vocal utterance. What is moving about such music I will take to be the beauty of the music and nothing more, a benign and (so I believe) true conclusion. For this is not, after all, an historical treatise but an attempt to develop a valid position (or set of positions) about the philosophical issues surrounding music, drama, and text; and a true conclusion will, in this context, find more favor in my eyes than an entirely correct interpretation. In any event, although the belief that music arouses emotions was an important factor in motivating the early opera composers to write the kind of music they did, because they thought the arousing of emotions an important thing to do, the aesthetic character of the music that they evolved for the purpose, and that we hear when we listen to it, is the *representational*. It is this which endures, which generates dramatic interest, and which excites philosophical dispute. (This was not the first nor the last time that a false theory would produce great works of art.) This is where the matter can be left. It is time now to turn, with this theoretical structure in hand, to its musical result. Only then will we begin to see the conceptual difficulties of opera emerge. And that of course is the real subject of this study. Our true work now begins.

CHAPTER IV

The musical parameters

○ 1 ○ The sheer weight of philosophical theory that Mei and Galilei produced in their attempt to "revive" the effects of the ancient music must have been heavy indeed upon the composers of the late sixteenth and early seventeenth centuries. This for two reasons. First, the theory itself was of unusual age, authority, and substance. It carried the imprimatur of Plato, Aristotle, and antiquity; and it was, after all, a remarkably successful theory, thoroughly worked out. At least with regard to arts other than music—principally painting, statuary, and literature—it seemed to work, to "fit the facts." *Mimesis*, the imitation of nature, was a way of understanding all of these arts. Why not music as well? In other words, the theory of musical *mimesis* that Mei and Galilei presented to their contemporaries was not some pretentious upstart theory but a well-established account of the arts, and a product of genius to boot. Second, as an attempt to give a broadly philosophical account of the art of music—its goal, its effects, its nature—the mimetic theories of Mei and Galilei fell into something of a philosophical vacuum. That there were texts propounding the theory and practice of music I have no wish to deny. What there was not, in the modern sense, was a "philosophy of music." That Mei and Galilei provided; but, of course, they made of music a *representational* art in the process. The composers were given a means of capturing reality, much in the way the painters of the Renaissance were by the theory of perspective. And Galilei, in fact, drew that analogy himself.

> Judicious and learned men, when they regard the various colours and shapes of objects, do not find satisfaction, like the ignorant multitude, in the mere pleasure that sight affords, but in investigating afterwards the mutual appropriateness and proportion of these incidental attributes and likewise their properties and nature. In the same way, I say that it is not enough merely to take pleasure in the various harmonies heard between the parts of a musical composition unless one also determines the proportions in which the voices are combined, in order not to be like the herbalist who in his simplicity knows nothing about simples except their name—and such are most of those who pass for musicians today among the vulgar.[1]

The problem is, needless to say, that music never has been and never will be, at least as we know it, a primarily representational art. Composers since the Renaissance and perhaps before have, indeed, done some "representing" in music, to varying degrees and with varying degrees of success.[2] But music remains, and was in 1600, an art of the most abstract kind. A "theory" of how music "represents" can only account for a very small part of what the art of music is all about. And there was in 1600 no philosophical foundation for the purely abstract in music. Thus five percent of the art had one hundred percent of the theory. The balance of philosophical theory was being pulled entirely to the representational, whereas musical practice pulled in the opposite direction. The philosophical theory was, of course, what gave the nascent opera the only foundation it had. The "problem" of opera, then, was to reconcile philosophical theory with some kind of acceptable musical practice: to, in other words, find an acceptable musical form in which to put the new representational content. By "acceptable musical form" I mean musical form that would make of the opera *music*, and not some other thing. This will require some explanation.

○ 2 ○   Let me take as two somewhat arbitrary boundaries the end of the sixteenth century and the middle of the nineteenth. During that period, we can distinguish certain characteristics, at least some of which most of the art music we know about possessed. Without at least a fair preponderance of these, we might well have art, but not *music* in the full-blooded sense in which that term was understood during the period we are talking about.

(a) *Music has closure.*   By that I mean there is at any given period or in a given style or genre a set of conventions which tells us when a piece of music has begun and when it has ended. It is music's picture frame, its "Once upon a time" and its "Finis." It is what separates a musical entity from the real world of sound out of which it emerges into our experience, and into which it returns again. It is what tells us that the orchestra has stopped tuning and started playing; stopped playing and started packing. It is capital letter and period (with, of course, semicolon and comma in between). It is what makes a given, self-contained segment of musical sound a "well-formed formula."

But, of course, rules for a "well-formed formula" in music are not the inviolable, hard-edged rules of the predicate calculus. If they were, Beethoven could not have opened the *Creatures of Prometheus* Overture with a tonic chord in its second inversion, nor would Mozart's 39th Symphony have ended in the abrupt way that it does, with the first seven notes of the first theme. For the purpose of the conventions of closure is not only to reinforce our expectations by fulfilling them forever, but to build them up for the purpose of (sometimes) frustrating them as well. Aesthetic surprise is as much a part of the musical experience as is aesthetic comfort; and surprise cannot be achieved without expectations. A person without any expectations whatever is not in a position to experience any surprise whatever; for surprise is, by definition, the frustration of expectation. Adam was not in a state of perpetual surprise but was completely incapable of it, as he knew not *what* to expect. (More of this anon.)

(b) *Music has finite duration.* I use "finite" of course in an attenuated sense to indicate that at any given period and in any given style or genre there are constraints on what the length of a musical "sentence" or "paragraph" may be. Aristotle said that a tragic plot must not only have a beginning, a middle, and an end but must be of a certain length; for something that is too small cannot be beautiful because we cannot discern its parts, and, contrariwise, something that is too large cannot be beautiful because we cannot take in the whole.[3]

Moreover, in everything that is beautiful, whether it be a living creature or any organism composed of parts, these parts must not only be orderly arranged but must also have a certain magnitude of their own; for beauty consists in magnitude and ordered arrangement. From which it follows that neither would a very small creature be beautiful—for our view of it is almost instantaneous and therefore confused—nor a very large one, since being unable to view it all at once, we lose the effect of a single whole; for instance, suppose a creature a thousand miles long. . . . [C]reatures and other organic structures must have a certain magnitude and yet be easily taken in by the eye. . . .

It might be well to meditate on Aristotle's restraints on size (and duration) for a moment. This may appear, at first blush, to be a completely unwarranted piece of *a priori* aesthetic constraint-making with no foundation at all except perhaps the taste of its author or the taste of his times. After all, Mozart's operas are longer than *Orfeo*, and *Meistersinger* longer than *Zauberflöte*; and if the length of a Mahler symphony would have been unacceptable to an eighteenth-century audience, it is not to a twentieth-century one. Some Indian ragas are said to go on for many hours, while some of Anton Webern's compositions last but seconds. Surely, the avant-garde will object, the composer in pursuit of his muse may make his work as short or as long as he wishes and as is necessary to achieve his aesthetic ends, whatever they might be, and however unforeseen and unpredictable. For length is relative to those; and it is impossible to foresee what length, however great or small, might be aesthetically acceptable, as it is impossible to foresee what end some future composer might pursue. Who in the eighteenth century could have foreseen the length of *Meistersinger* on the one hand, or of some of Webern's compositions on the other?

But this objection misses the point I am trying to make here, which is a far less expansive one than such an objection implies. I surely lay down no limits on how long or how short a melody, or theme, movement, or section, composition, or part thereof may be. But one can, nevertheless, make certain generalizations, of a non-normative kind, in this regard, about what would be happening if (say) one were to write a "melody" that took eight hours to complete (as whale "songs" are said to do) or an "opera" that lasted twenty-four years from overture to twelfth-act finale. It is not that one could not do such things, or that they could not have even great value. They would, however, be so different, *merely* because of their length, from what Mozart or Gluck was doing as to not so much have solved a problem which a Mozart or a Gluck might be grappling with, but to have simply rejected it: cutting the knot rather than untying it. For "mere length" is not an isolated parameter, as Aristotle clearly saw. If we are to have *closure*, and if, looking ahead, we are to have *form* (with all that that implies), we must have also a duration falling between certain vague limits that enable us to discern the beginning of a formal structure, its parts, and its cessation. Forms are closed; and for us to have them we must have human length.

But, I must emphasize again, I am not denying the possibility of art works that have neither closure, nor form, nor finite duration. What I am denying is that they would solve the problems, or serve the purposes, that composers of opera from Monteverdi to Mozart were concerned with. Indeed, to put bluntly and without argument a conclusion that I hope will emerge from this study after many qualifications and much argument, Wagnerian music drama (for example) represents not a solution to what I am calling the "problem" of opera but an evasion of it. It is a musical non sequitur. (That is not a value judgment.)

(c) *Music has form.*   To speak of form is to raise a host of questions. I hope to avoid undue difficulty by treating the concept of form in a very intuitive way. I shall define "form" not by precept or principle but by example. The minuet-and-trio is a form; the classical symphony is a form; the symphonic sonata-allegro is a form; the classical sonata, the sonata de camera, and the sonata de chiesa are forms; the French overture is a form; the Baroque suite is a form; and (*pace* Tovey) the fugue is a form, albeit a loose one with, consequently, or rather definitionally, fewer and less certain expectations; the rondo is a form, and the ritornello, of which it is a special case, is a form, although the form varies from period to period, while the *principle* of the form remains the same. I hope these examples will suffice; but what I mean will, I think, become clearer as I use the concept of form in what follows.

Now, to a certain extent, the concept of form and that of genre overlap; and in the absence of a theory "from above" to prize them apart—a theory I make no pretense of having or wanting—many artistic productions can be described with equal propriety as the one or as the other. To instance some cases in point, the novel and the classical symphony might be (and are) indifferently referred to as "forms" or "genres," depending, I imagine, largely on what one wants to emphasize about them. What is important to note here, for the sake of avoiding unnecessary disputes, is that it makes absolutely no difference in the argument to follow whether one prefers, in any given instance, the one term or the other. For it is one of the things form and genre have in common that interests me, namely the raising of expectations, inherent in both. In the interest of simplicity of expression, I have used the term "form" fairly consistently. If in any particular case a reader prefers "genre," he or she is welcome to the term and will get no quarrel from me.

Musical forms or genres are patterns that recur. They therefore build up expectations in the listener, whether these expectations are brought to consciousness in the listener or lie below the level of consciousness in the musically "untutored" but not "uncultured" one. Musical forms, then, involve an aesthetic play in which expectations are both reinforced—that is, gratified—and also, of course, frustrated. Any musical regularity of a formal kind can be violated for aesthetic purposes; but, of course, no such aesthetic play, based on the surprise of our expectations, would be possible without a well-entrenched form, in some kind of regular occurrence, to establish the aesthetic "hypothesis" which the composer can disconfirm at his or her pleasure.

But therein lies a problem. If I am hearing a minuet-and-trio by Haydn (say) for the first time, my strongest expectation, if I am a well-educated listener, will be that it will follow something like the most common and most frequently repeated pattern. Haydn, however, surprises my expectations in various ways, by lengthening some of the periods, going into an unexpected key in the trio, and not making the repeats literal. The problem is that if I have an even passable musical memory the effect will only work the first few times I hear the movement. After that, since it is an individual as well as a member of a class, I will expect to hear exactly what has happened in the past hearings, assuming that I am confronted with a correct performance each time. All surprise has been dissipated by familiarity.

> Once one has encountered the work, one knows subsequently what to expect, and so if the work's sole claim to attention is the surprise or shock, then the attention will not be long held. . . . Any work needs to repay repeated inspection, to be rewarding with familiarity, and surprises are the first casualties of familiarity.[4]

I may be surprised by Cyrano's nose the first time I am introduced to him, but cannot be after that. Yet, it will be argued, and quite rightly, music is not meant to be heard only once. And the effect of the "aesthetic surprise" of which I have been speaking does seem to play an important role in Western art music, at least within our stipulated time frame, and does seem to survive rehearing. How can surprise survive the ordeal of familiarity?

The problem of rehearing music has plagued all attempts to build any part of a musical aesthetics on expectation and its frustration.[5] But what musical aesthetics can do entirely without them, as the phenomena seem so ubiquitous in the music of the West? The solution of this problem is in a way quite simple, I believe, although the well-known perceptual experience to which I shall appeal in offering my solution is not at all easy to understand, as it touches very deep issues in the philosophy and psychology of perception.

Consider the familiar illusion known as the Müller-Lyer Lines (Figure 3); or the more complicated Fraser Spiral (Figure 4). The lines in the Müller-Lyer illusion appear to be of unequal length (the right one longer) although they are not; and the Fraser Spiral is not a spiral at all but a series of perturbed concentric circles. Once one is convinced that the lines are equal (by measuring them), and that circles not a spiral are what is before one (by tracing them around with a finger), one ceases, of course, to believe that the lines are unequal or the figure a spiral. Nevertheless, the illusions never cease to be seen as, respectively, two unequal lines and a spiral. One certainly *believes* that the lines are equal and the circles concentric; and any behavior that might be called for in regard to them would be consistent with those beliefs. But in some sense or other the eyes continue to "believe" that the lines are unequal and the Fraser figure a spiral, not concentric circles. Let us call the former two beliefs (that the lines are equal and the thing a series of concentric circles) "epistemic," and the latter two (that the lines are unequal and the thing a spiral) "perceptual." (The terms are introduced merely as terms of art and bear no deep significance.) We can then say that while I epistemically believe that the lines in the Müller-Lyer illusion are equal, I perceptually

Figure 3. The Muller-Lyer Lines

Figure 4. The Fraser Spiral (reproduced by permission of John Wiley and Sons)

believe one is longer; and that while I epistemically believe the Fraser illusion is a pattern of concentric circles, I perceptually believe that it is a spiral.

What I want to suggest now is that in the musical cases with which we are concerned, once we have become familiar with the work through rehearing, although we epistemically believe (and expect) the aesthetically "unexpected" musical event will occur, we nonetheless continue to perceptually believe that the more "expected" (i.e. more common) event will transpire, and therefore are "perceptually" surprised when it does not. This of course does not *explain* how the musical phenomenon takes place. I have no explanation for that (nor is it easy, or perhaps even possible, as yet to explain the perceptual mechanism that gives rise to the Müller-Lyer Lines and the Fraser Spiral). What I offer, rather, is de-mystification by subsuming the unfamiliar under the familiar. For if I am right that being "surprised" by the "expected" is a species of perceptual believing, of which such familiar figures as the Müller-Lyer Lines and Fraser Spiral are paradigmatic instances, then at least it will be seen *that* the same musical event might be epistemically expected and perceptually unexpected, even though it will not be seen *how*. I can conclude, then, I think, that *music has form*, and that part of the aesthetic vocabulary of musical form is the building up and frustrating of perceptual expectations: in other words, "surprise."

(d) *The larger musical forms are atomically constructed.*   By this I mean that the larger musical forms are composed of individual, self-contained, smaller musical forms which themselves exhibit, as do the larger forms they belong to, *closure, finite duration*, and *form*. Now the distinction between "larger" and "smaller" is, of course, a completely relative one. And as in the case of form itself, I shall simply attempt to define by example, with the following added stipulation: the "atomic" pieces of which the larger forms are made up can be—indeed, frequently are—extracted and performed satisfactorily as complete musical compositions (although sometimes, as in the case of an overture that "leads into" the first scene, a "concert version" must be employed to achieve closure). Thus operas, oratorios, sonatas, symphonies, string quartets, motets, suites, cantatas, concertos, settings of the Mass all possess formal shape, composed of atomic, self-contained parts, or "movements," such as minuet-and-trio, aria, chorus, allemande, first movement, slow movement, song, overture, and so on, each one of which can be performed separately, in part because it exhibits the characteristics of *closure, finite duration*, and *form*.

(e) *Music has unity.*   If this has not already been implied by the parameters of *finite length, closure,* and *form,* it deserves mention now. Again, no *a priori* stipulation is made here as to what sound as an art-form requires in the way of organization to merit the status of art. I merely make the observation that, in the period under discussion, Western art-music has required of itself a certain amount of organic unity, achieved by the recurrence of thematic material, harmonic or contrapuntal "tags," rhythmic patterns, tonal qualities (i.e. timbres), and the rest. What degree of such unity is required or tolerated varies, of course, from time to time, from genre to genre. But it is a master that all composers have served, at least since the sixteenth century, and it places certain boundary conditions, albeit vague ones, on what "solutions" to musical "problems" are allowable. These boundary conditions apply to the "problem" of opera no less than to that of any other musical form or genre.

(f) *Music has variety.*   As the thematic, rhythmic, harmonic, contrapuntal, tonal materials of music are expected to exhibit a certain uniformity—a re-use, recycling, transformation of what nevertheless is to remain recognizably the same—so also they are expected to be varied, fresh, interlarded with the novel—in other words, variegated as well as unified. To sum this up in the language of the eighteenth century (of which more anon), music is to exhibit *unity amidst variety.*

(g) *Music is a self-sufficient pattern of sound with "syntactic" but not "semantic" properties.*   In a way this sums up what has been itemized above. Music, in the period from 1600 to 1800, and, indeed, for the most part, to the present day as well, with some notable exceptions, has been understood—whatever its other pretensions to "meaning," "representation," "expression," "handmaiden of the text"—as at least, and perhaps at most, to use Kant's felicitous phrase, a "pleasurable play of sensations"[6] or, in Hanslick's, a "kaleidoscope of sound."[7] This is not to say that it is a random play of sensations as the kaleidoscope is a random arrangement of colored glass. It has, of course, at any given period, what comes very close to a grammar, to the extent that grammar can be separated off entirely from meaning in natural languages (as opposed to formal ones), which it cannot. The only ultimate test of grammatical error, as opposed to metaphorical extension of language, is appeal to meaning. As a last resort, in other words, it must be the yielding of nonsense, not the violation of a syntactic rule, that distinguishes the ungrammatical from an intended departure from accepted usage. Such an appeal is not possible in music, where there is no semantic component. It is therefore not possible, in principle, to tell, apart from musical aesthetics, whether parallel fifths (say) or a "mistake" in harmonic progression is a slip of the pen, a result of ignorance or ineptitude, or a conscious attempt at some daring musical effect. (Brahms made a careful historical study of parallel fifths, sorting them out into "mistakes" and various kinds of bona fide musical uses, the determination, however, being not on the basis of rule-violation—for they all violated the "rule"—but on the basis of the composer's refined aesthetic sensibility.) Nevertheless, music progresses, in any given period, in a way that is not merely predictable but susceptible of judgments as to "syntactic" correctness or incorrectness, however vague and unsure such judgments may of necessity be.

The upshot of this is that Western art music (I make no claim for any other kind), during the period with which we are involved, was supposed to stand on its own as an art of pure, syntactic sound structure, even when it also served other aesthetic purposes: the setting and "expressing" of a text, or (a special case of that) the musical realization of a dramatic work, as in opera and (later) oratorio, or even programmatic symphony or sonata. This is the more obvious in the period before the emergence of pure instrumental music as a significant separate category, when "instrumental" music might simply be vocal music played on instruments. For that kind of "instrumental" music could have been possible only if music was, even when sung to a text, a self-sufficient art-form, with its own "laws" of aesthetic adequacy and correctness. And that requirement survived, more or less intact, although perhaps more freely interpreted, even into the modern period, in which an independent instrumental music arose to rival, and indeed surpass in importance, the musical setting of texts.

o 3 o   It is time now to suggest of what significance the *musical parameters* are that I have enumerated above. They are not, as I have said before, *a priori* limits placed on what can properly be construed as "music" or "art." What I do suggest, however, is that they did indeed, at least implicitly, play that role for the composers of opera from the outset, and for a long time thereafter. The "problem" of opera, then, was to create a musical drama within those limits. The parameters could, of course, be manipulated, even exaggerated for specific purposes. But in some form or other they had all (or most) to stay in place, or the game was lost. It was not, needless to say, that one could not transgress these parameters and still create a work of musical art, as one would cease to be a tennis player if one were to win by wearing roller skates. What I am trying to suggest is that once any one or more of these parameters was transgressed—as of course they *were* in the nineteenth century, and even before—one had something different enough to not count as succeeding artistically in that given form. Wagner's music drama, Debussy's *Pélleas et Mélisande*, and (to take an earlier example) Georg Benda's melodramas are not, as I see it, successful or ingenious "solutions" to the "problem" of opera but, essentially, total rejections of it: rather like what happened when physicists ceased to try to decide whether light was a particle *or* a wave, and rejected the disjunction altogether. So, if you will, going beyond the parameters I have outlined is like choosing an entirely new paradigm or model in science: the old questions are not answered but, rather, new questions are substituted.

I say this was understood implicitly, if not explicitly, by the composers of opera in the seventeenth and eighteenth centuries. But the greatest of them—and, perhaps, the greatest of all, for some people's money—did not leave the axiom unarticulated. In two letters to his father during the planning and composition of *Die Entführung aus dem Serail* (1781-82) Mozart enunciated his attitude toward the setting of dramatic texts in a way that is at once revealing, deep, and yet utterly free of theoretical or philosophical pretensions. I introduce here but one seminal passage; for it sums up and states, as no theoretical document does before or since, the peculiar paradox, problem, and essential nature of opera as a *musical* genre or form. It supplies, for this reason, the epigraph of this book and, indeed, its very argument.

It has been observed many times before that Osmin, the cantankerous harem-keeper in *Die Entführung aus dem Serail*, is Mozart's first great comic character. And it is clear, particularly from the letter to his father of 26 September 1781, that Mozart carefully considered, planned, and executed in music the dramatic persona of Osmin, in direct collaboration with his librettist, Gottlieb Stephanie the younger (with Mozart pretty much calling the tune, Stephanie more or less dancing to it). In regard to Osmin's music, particularly that in which his rage is depicted, Mozart writes in one place:

> The passage "Drum beim Barte des Propheten" is indeed in the same tempo, but with quick notes; but as Osmin's rage gradually increases, there comes (just when the aria seems to be at an end) the allegro assai, which is in a totally different measure and in a different key; this is bound to be very effective. For just as a man in such a towering rage oversteps all the bounds of order, moderation and propriety and completely forgets himself, so must the music too forget itself. But as passions, whether violent or not, must never be expressed in such a way as to excite disgust, and as music, even in the most terrible situations,

must never offend the ear, but must please the hearer, or in other words must never cease to be *music*, I have gone from F (the key in which the aria is written), not into a remote key, but into a related one, not, however, into its nearest relative D minor, but into the more remote A minor.[8]

Mozart's point, here, is clear enough, and admirably put. To stay with the problem-solving paradigm, Mozart set himself the task of "representing" Osmin's rage in music—or, rather, representing in music Osmin's *expression* of rage—while remaining within the limits of the purely musical parameters: parameters imposed upon Mozart by his age, his taste, and his genius. Modulation from one key to another, and the relation of keys more or less "distant"from one another—relations heard as well as cognized—these "syntactic" properties of Western art music provided Mozart with the artistic means of representing the human temperament in its various states of repose, agitation, and, in Osmin's case, almost unbridled frenzy: a convenient representational metaphor in music for change of temperament being change of key, and for "wild" change of temperament "wild" modulation to distant tonal territory. But wildness must have its bounds, since modulation is a "syntactic" concept: grammar can be conventional, innovative, even bizarre; but it cannot go on holiday except at the risk of producing nonsense. The problem for Mozart, then, in representing Osmin's rage, was to use musical "syntax" at the boundaries of grammatical coherence, to represent human expression out of control, while still remaining within those bounds, for to transgress them would be to give up the game: to represent, perhaps, but not represent in music as Mozart understood that art.

That Mozart recognized the problem of dramatic musical representation not only in terms of the internal, "syntactic" parameters but in terms of the external, formal ones as well is revealed just a bit later on in the same letter to his father, where he says of Constanze's aria in the first act,

> I have sacrificed Constanze's aria a little to the flexible throat of Mlle Cavalieri, "Trennung war mein banges los und nun schwimmt mein Aug' in Tränen." I have tried to express here feelings, as far as an Italian bravura aria will allow it.[9]

It comes as no surprise to a student of eighteenth-century opera that Mozart "sacrificed" something musical, in an aria, the better to suit it to a particular singer's vocal equipment. Nor does it surprise—and this is the crucial point here—that he was willing to sacrifice, as the above passage clearly suggests, "expression" to "form." Or, to put it more precisely, he was willing to make his musical representation—in this case, Constanze's emotional state—somewhat less successful *qua* representation, so that he would not violate the defining properties of the musical form he had chosen, namely, the "Italian bravura aria," which made certain musical demands of its own on the composer who wished to employ it. Why Mozart employed it may in part be explained by the taste of his audience, the demands of his singers, the conventions of opera and Sing- spiel, his own musical ends—half a hundred things more. But surely mixed up with all of these pushes and pulls, and essentially behind many of them, was the fact that opera presented itself as a musical form, real- izable and recognizable as such only if the purely musical parameters— *closure, finite duration, atomic structure, unity, variety, syntax*—were accom- modated. And choosing the "Italian bravura aria" in one place, the "aria concertante" in another, the quartet here, the duet there, was, of course, the eighteenth-century composer's way of doing just that. Dramatic rep- resentation was only half of his problem. Putting that dramatic represen- tation in musical form was the rest. Mozart saw this as clearly as anyone ever has: the mature operas themselves would have sufficed to tell us that. It is an added delight to find that he verbalized it as well.

This, then, is the "problem" of opera. By Mozart's day it would be enunciated with some degree of clarity and self-consciousness. At opera's birth it existed no less urgently, but certainly less explicitly. For what the earliest composers of opera—Peri and Caccini in Florence, Monteverdi in Mantua—had was an imperative to realize the spoken drama represen- tationally, in music. Only the attempt, with all of its practical (which is to say musical) problems, could reveal the deep tension that the represen- tational imperative and the demands of the purely musical parameters would generate in their interaction.

First there was the neoclassic vision of a drama re-animated by the co-operation of music. Doubts grew up only later.[10]

CHAPTER V

Enter Orpheus (Philosophy attending)

o 1 o   If Joseph Kerman is right (as I think he is) that "Doubts grew up only later," then it would be in vain for us to search the documents of the early seventeenth century to find there the philosophical debate that so characterized the opera in the eighteenth century and beyond: a debate generated, if I am right (as I think I am), by the tension between a Platonic and an Aristotelian philosophy of music as representation and (later) a growing philosophical foundation for music as an art of pure sensuous, but at the same time "syntactic," aesthetic form. What I propose to do in the present chapter instead, therefore, is to seek this debate, and this tension, not in what was said about the first operas in the seventeenth century but in the twentieth: to see it by a reflected light, as it were, since it then had no light of its own. More specifically, I propose to make some general remarks about early opera, and in particular Monteverdi's *Orfeo*; and thereafter to examine some recent writings on that work which, so it seems to me, reveal, perhaps unbeknownst to their authors, the tension and philosophical debate of which I speak. I shall argue that *Orfeo* can be looked at in two ways: as a noble failure to solve the problem of putting spoken drama in musical form; or, perhaps, as a rejection of the problem altogether—in other words, an attempt, right from the start, to create a non-musical art-form (albeit one with close affinities to the art of music as Monteverdi understood it). These two attitudes toward the work I find inherent, but never made explicit, in the writings which I examine. Perhaps with these attitudes before us we will be better able to understand the writings in question and, more importantly, better understand the work itself.

One further point, in the form of a caveat, before I get to *Orfeo* and its critics. What I offer is not a musician's or musicologist's analysis of the work. I am neither of those, and have nothing new to offer in the way of musical or historical analysis. I wish, rather, to do something else: to look at *Orfeo*, and some of the criticism it has given rise to, through the lens of a particular kind of philosophy I have learned for the most part from American teachers and British books. This is not better than what musicians and musicologists have to say, but it is certainly different. Perhaps it will be of help.

o 2 o   We can reasonably imagine that the early opera composers confronted (at least) two artistic problems. One, obviously, was how to plausibly represent human speech in music. And it is no accident, needless to say, that the story of Orpheus was such a popular subject for opera composers then (and later); for it made an end run around the problem of "talking music" by providing a singing hero. The solution they evolved for musical speech was that of the so-called *stile rappresentativo*, the style of the actor (or declaimer). Their immediate musical goal, as we have seen in our examination of their theoretical pronouncements, was to represent in music, as accurately as possible, the sound of human speech of the more passionate sort. In this very specific musical goal, I think, Monteverdi at least, and perhaps Peri as well, succeeded more fully than any composer since, in any subsequent musical style or genre. But their very success posed a second musical problem for them that, in the end, seems to have proved insurmountable: the problem of giving this musical representation musical form—that is to say, reconciling musical representation with the parameters of pure musical "syntax" and structure.

Why this would be a problem is not very hard to see. For human linguistic expression follows "laws" of logical and psychological progression that are quite independent of the "laws" of purely musical "syntax" and form. And unless linguistic expression is brought into complete synchronization with pure musical form and "syntax," they must needs be more or less at odds. Ordinary language, of course, unlike music, has a semantics as well as a syntax; and, in addition, it pursues (except under conditions of severe artistic constraint) utilitarian goals which dictate in what *manner* a thought is to be expressed: dictates, in other words, the manner of utterance. If I express the thought that it is a very hot day by saying "It is a very hot day today," what I intend to do, what (to use J. L. Austin's terms) the illocutionary force of my utterance is intended to be, will dictate what tone and manner my speech act will take (to appropriate Austin again). If I am a meteorologist merely conveying a piece of not very interesting information, I will say "It is a very hot day today" in a somewhat laconic, laid-back way; but if I am the wife of a sixty-five-year-old man with a history of heart disease, and I want to urgently warn him against continuing to mow the lawn at high noon, I will utter "It is a very hot day today" in a somewhat more elevated tone of voice. The composer who wishes to represent the utterance "It is a very hot day today" in *stile rappresentativo* must reflect in his music the manner as well as the content of it; and if it is the meteorologist whose utterance he is setting, then his music must be subdued and laid-back, rather than *forte* in a high tessitura, even though the latter might be called for on purely musical grounds. Such is the musical price that must be paid for representational fidelity. (The example, needless to say, is nonsensical; but the reader will easily imagine more believable ones, or recall the genuine article from his or her musical experience.)

In *Orfeo*, Monteverdi displayed an unparalleled ability to follow such illocutionary cues musically, as has been universally recognized and frequently remarked upon. "The listener to *Orfeo* is impressed throughout . . . by the easy grace with which it is obviously following every refinement of its verbal text," writes Donington.[1] And Schrade writes in a similar vein:

> Monteverdi adhered to the supreme law: "L'oratione sia padrona del armonia e non serva." He derived his musical form from the spiritual essence of the word, which is nothing more than the *affetto* Monteverdi and his contemporaries had in mind when speaking of the inner meaning of text and music. This responsiveness to the *affetto* results in the unique, tense, dramatic effect which gives the *Orfeo* its supreme quality.[2]

I shall return to these two distinguished musicologists in a moment, in something of a critical stance. But on the extraordinary responsiveness of Monteverdi's music in *Orfeo*, and elsewhere, to all of the emotional, dramatic, and conceptual permutations of his text there can be no disagreement at all.

How then did Monteverdi and, to a lesser extent, his Florentine predecessors try to avoid paying what would seem to be the inevitable price of such representational fidelity: namely, the complete breakdown of musical "syntax" and structure? The problem must be seen at, if you will, both a micro- and macro-level. At the micro-level, it presented itself as a problem of giving each "atomic" part of the work—in this case the individual sections of *stile rappresentativo*, arioso, aria, chorus, and instrumental interlude—a viable musical form. At the macro-level it meant putting these atoms together into an artistically integrated work, which, at the beginning of the seventeenth century, must have seemed an imposing task, as even a text of such modest length as Rinuccini's *Euridice* made, when set, a musical work of greater length than almost anything theretofore attempted.

Aria, arioso, song, chorus, and instrumental interlude presented no new *musical* problems for the early opera composers. For these forms had been practiced before, and their purely musical structure was highly evolved. They were, of course, basically musical forms, even where a text was involved, and they could follow "laws" of musical progression even while meeting textual demands. Polyphony, imitation, ritornello, thematic development, strophic song were all available musical materials out of which to make structurally viable "atoms."

It was the great new invention or discovery, the heart and soul of the new dramatic music, that presented the musical difficulties. For, as Schrade put it,

> The recitative, of course, had no formal structure of its own. From the very beginning of the *stile recitativo* this was its most crucial problem. . . .[3]

But it was the *stile recitativo* that bore the major burden of carrying the story forward, evolving the drama, expressing the thoughts and passions of the characters. And although the individual sections of such musical recitation could be given closure, through formulaic openings and cadences and, of course, correct musical "syntax" in both harmonic progression and polyphonic interplay between singer and basso continuo, it was well-nigh impossible to impart anything to speak of (or sing of) in the way of pure musical form. Because, of course, in this respect, the musical progression was, indeed, the slave of the text: *L'oratione sia padrona del armonia e non serva.* The music had to follow where the text led. For all of its representational success, harmonic expressiveness, and beauty, it was not truly *music*, even in the hands of a musical genius: musical, yes, but not music in the autonomous way that would make it at least minimally self-sufficient without its text and dramatic setting. After a while, the *stile rappresentativo* begins to pall, whether it is by Peri, Caccini, or even Monteverdi. The most vital and ubiquitous, then, of the musical "atoms" that were to make up what was to be a musical genre were seemingly recalcitrant to purely musical success.

But that is not where the problem ended. It has repercussions at the macro-level as well. From the beginning, the early composers of opera hit upon a rather simple expedient for the organization of acts and other sections of that magnitude: that of the instrumental "ritornello," that is, a small, self-contained instrumental interlude, repeated periodically, perhaps on different instruments for variety and mood, and presumably with improvised ornaments to the same ends. The return, re-use, and development of thematic material for unifying purposes is, of course, a ubiquitous feature of Western music (and some other musics as well); and the instrumental ritornello partially fulfilled that function for Monteverdi in *Orfeo* (as it had for Peri in *Euridice*). Unfortunately, the same trick cannot be turned with the *stile rappresentativo*; for the re-use of thematic material there would defeat the very purpose for which it came into being, namely, the direct reflection of every nuance of mood or meaning in the text. (For the same reason, the ritornello is often at cross-purposes with the dramatic and emotional progression of acts as well, since it would be difficult to find an instrumental composition appropriate to the mood or dramatic situation prevailing at the beginning of an act that would be appropriate for the middle and end as well.) It would only be by sheer good fortune or planned textual monotony that a phrase invented to represent an utterance by one character, in a particular dramatic situation in the first act of an opera, could be re-used to represent a different utterance by a different character, in another dramatic situation some point further on, and be representationally accurate at both occurences.

Monteverdi did indeed attempt such an organizational feat in the Prologue to *Orfeo*, with signal success. But it was appropriate there, and worked, only because of the singularly undramatic nature of the Prologue itself, and its more or less uniform emotional tone. It contains only one character—and a "non-person" at that: La Musica, the allegorical voice of music, who introduces what is to come with not surprisingly, given the subject of the story and the aims of Mei and Galilei, a recitation in praise of the powers of music. Every section but one of this brief *scena* is built on a clearly recognizable melodic descent; added thematic unity is given the five discrete passages of recitative by basing the opening of each on a palpably obvious repeated figure in the voice, accompanying each with the same bass line or a slightly varied form of it—a kind of basso ostinato. Of the ten sections which make up the Prologue, five are occurrences of an instrumental ritornello: four repeated literally, the fifth in altered but clearly recognizable form. Thus the whole *scena* is a tightly knit thematic unity, alternating between sections of recitative, all thematically related to one another, and repetitions of the instrumental interlude, thematically identical to one another and thematically related, through the principle of melodic descent, to all but one of the sections of *stile rappresentativo*. The thematic material is given in Example 2.

Monteverdi could get away with this traditional structure of thematic unity, casting the *stile rappresentativo* essentially in the form of strophic

EXAMPLE 2
Claudio Monteverdi, *Orfeo*, Prologue
(a)

(b)

Dal mio permesso a-ma - to   a voi ne   ve - gno

(c)

Io   la mu - si-ca son   ch'ai dol - ci ac-cen - - ti   so far tran-quil-lo

(d)

Io   su   ce - te-ra d'or   can - tan - do so - glio   mor-tal o - rec-chio

(e)

Quin - ci a   dir - vi d'Orfeo   de - sio mi spro - - na,   d'Or-feo che tras - se

(f)

Hor   mentre i can-ti al-ter - no   hor lie-ti hor me - - sti   non so mo - va

song, just because absolutely nothing happens in the Prologue, emotionally or dramatically; no dramatic event occurs to require the breaking of the thematic unity either of the ritornello or the recitative in the interest of representational fidelity. Strophic song will work, representationally, just so long as the text remains dramatically undemanding; but as soon as the trout is caught, the game is up, and the game was up for Monteverdi as soon as the story of *Orfeo* began to dramatically unfold, some short distance into the first act. It is just here that, in my view (but not, as we shall see, in the view of others), the musical structure evaporates, to a significant degree, in the heat of the drama; for the demands of representational fidelity, supported by theory, are just too strident for the purely musical parameters to withstand. Music and dramatic representation had not yet reached a viable compromise. And why should they have? The problem was too new, and the newly found representational theory and practice of music were too enticing—too seductive—to be resisted by purely musical considerations.

This is not to say that Monteverdi simply gave in to musical chaos. The instrumental ritornello was still available as a general principle of organization within each act, and served that function in *Orfeo* as it had in Peri's *Euridice*. But the tight thematic unity that characterizes the five sections of *stile rappresentativo* in the Prologue was just not possible in the drama to come, if the composer was to obey the admonitions of the Camerata theoreticians and his own self-legislated maxim, which was to follow the passions of the text where they led. For linguistic utterance is a law unto itself, as is the fabric of Western music; and in choosing the former as his master of opera, Monteverdi was pretty much obliged to make the latter its slave. Musical "syntax" remains; but musical structure, in the *stile rappresentativo*, is cut to the bone.

This is not so easy for some musical analysts to accept. For Monteverdi's stock is very high these days, and so is the stock of "thematic unity" (although not, perhaps, quite so high as heretofore). But, it seems to me, the very effort that Donington, for example, expends to find thematic unity in the *stile rappresentativo* of *Orfeo* outside of the Prologue, the points that are stretched, the latitude given to the concept of thematic unity itself—all these point up how problematic the pure musical parameters are in this first great attempt to come to terms with the peculiar nature of opera as drama-made-music (if that indeed is how Monteverdi viewed his task). To this (in my view) failed, logically flawed attempt at rescuing *Orfeo* for "pure music" we must now turn our attention.

o 3 o   Donington's quest for thematic unity begins, surprisingly enough, at the very beginning: the *Toccata* (as Monteverdi calls it) that serves as *Orfeo*'s brief overture. Surprisingly, I think, because most people would say that the opera overture did not really begin to have any palpable thematic relation to the opera proper until the late eighteenth century—and then only on rare occasions—and, indeed, frequently had no dramatic or emotive relevance to it either, as late as the *opera seria* of Handel with its at times emotively neutral French overture, as interchangeable as spare parts for a lawnmower. Surprisingly too because the mood of this musical flourish—which is all that it really is—is so utterly at odds with the tragic events to follow, having nothing of tragedy or even melancholy about it. Nonetheless, Donington claims that "The downward scale of the Toccata already provides matter for the first ritornello and for the recitative . . . ,"[4] and provides Example 3 to substantiate his claim.[5] Later on we discover that it is not only the downward scale but the upward one as well that is to be looked to as a source of material (and, indeed, some of the excerpts in Example 3 can only be understood under that further stipulation). Thus, Donington's full claim for *Orfeo* is that "Its thematic material . . . proves to be largely based on the ascending and descending scales first introduced in the opening Toccata and later developed both in the monody and in the ritornellos and sinfonias. . . ."[6] If that were true, *Orfeo* would, indeed, be an extraordinarily unified work, satisfying some of the most severe of what I have been calling the "pure musical parameters." That it is not true—or, more modestly, that Donington has failed to demonstrate its truth—I will now proceed to argue.

To begin with, the Toccata is said to have a "downward scale" which "provides matter for the first ritornello and for [some of] the recitative, . . ." We are, then, meant to see thematic relationships among various descending melodic fragments: they are all, we must presume, examples of a "downward scale." But that is not literally true. Literally, the only downward scalewise passages quoted in Example 3 are (*b*), (*i*), and (*j*), if by a scalewise passage one means an unbroken succession of whole- and half-steps all in the same direction. Even the "downward scale" in the Toccata—which, after all, is supposed to be the source of all the rest—is not that exactly, as each degree of the scale is repeated before the next step down; and this is true of (*e*) to an even greater degree, as each tone of the scalewise passage is repeated *at least* once, the first one three times. Even more liberties are taken in construing (*c*) and (*d*) as scalewise passages for they not only contain repeated notes but skip one degree of the scale as well in their descent, going from C to A and omitting B (or B flat) altogether. Indeed, if we consider the whole phrase to end where the example does, then the "downward scale" not only fails to be a scale; it fails to be entirely downward as well, as (*c*) and (*d*) both rise from A to B flat before finally coming to rest on A. But moreover, the scalewise downward descent in (*j*) occurs not at the beginning of the passage at

EXAMPLE 3
Monteverdi, *Orfeo*

(*a*)

Clarino
Quinta

Alto e basso
Vulgano
Basso

(*b*)

RITORNELLO

(*c*)

PROLOGUE: MUSIC

Dal mio — Per-mes-so a - ma - to   a voi ne ve - gno,

(*d*)

(last stanza)

Hor   men-tre j can-ti al - ter - no,   hor lie - ti, hor me - sti,

(*e*)

SHEPHERD

In que-sto lie - to e for - tu-na - to gior - no

(f)

(g)

(h)

(i)

(j)

all, but somewhere after its very distinctive *non*scalewise and *ascending* beginning.

The two instances of ascending scalewise passages are treated in pretty much the same liberal way. The opening of the chorus (*h*) is an ascending scale only if one ignores the fact that it begins with the leap of a major third and hence skips the second degree of the scale—indeed, it gets as much (or more) of its melodic character from the leap as from the scale. While the recitative (*g*) begins with the wider leap of a fifth downwards, and re-ascends scalewise only later, in a very halting way, the scale interrupted by repeated notes and an eighth-rest, the scale hardly being one of its notable or noticeable aesthetic qualities.

From these observations, which at first may seem niggling and trivially literal-minded, two rather non-trivial conclusions can be reached about the ground rules for this sort of thematic dissection—or, rather, conclusions about the utter lack of any ground rules. First, that in demonstrating that passage *A* is thematically related to passage *B*, one can ignore any notes in either passage that count against the claim; and second, that one can pick *A* and *B* out of any place within a larger melodic structure that one wishes, after the fact, as it were, so that if you have already decided to look for scales (say) you may look for them anywhere you like.[7] The hypothesis of thematic unity, where constraints on evidence are so weak, becomes irrefutable: it always must succeed, at the inevitable cost of becoming vacuous, as we shall see in a moment.

Suppose for the sake of argument—although it is a bit of an oversimplification—that during Monteverdi's lifetime, for a considerable time before, and for a considerable time after, a composer could write a line with the following melodic materials: scalewise passages up, scalewise passages down, leaps (defined as intervals larger than a whole-tone) either up or down, and repeated notes. If the composer is writing music within this style-frame—which is, of course, the framework of tonal music, be it modal or major/minor—these are the choices he or she is limited to. And it is a pretty fair bet that in *any* composition from this period, of the length of Monteverdi's *Orfeo*, I can find an abundance of *any* of these melodic building blocks, just as long as I may choose them anywhere I like and may ignore "extraneous" notes. Add to this the lack of any way of quantifying the result—that is, of knowing when I have found enough examples of whatever I am looking for—and I think that I can substantiate for *Orfeo* any of the following hypotheses: the themes are largely built on upward and downward scalewise passages; the themes are largely built on upward and downward leaps; the themes are built largely on repeated notes. Are all of these hypotheses true? Yes and no. Yes, if all that you mean is that *Orfeo* is made up of the same stuff as any tonal music. But certainly no, if you mean that *Orfeo* has some special, notable, aesthetically significant thematic unity based on these scales or intervals or repeated notes, or that this separates *Orfeo* from any other musical composition from *Three Blind Mice* to the *Missa Solemnis*. Within *Orfeo*, only the Prologue has *that*.

To bring this point home more forcefully still, I cannot help picking up the all but irresistible gauntlet that Donington unknowingly throws down when he writes:

> The recurrence of this modest thematic material [of the Toccata] may be quite an important factor in giving *Orfeo* precisely what earlier extended works in monody lack: an effect of organic growth and uniformity. . . . Monteverdi's music is at least as close to the expression of the words as Peri's or Caccini's; but there is a strength in his composition which theirs does not have, and it can partly be attributed to the taut design and closely braced structure underneath, which the felicitous movement on the surface so misleadingly conceals.[8]

Facsimiles of the first edition of the first extant opera, Jacopo Peri's *Euridice* (1600, new style 1601) are readily available, as is a performing edition of the work by Howard Mayer Brown. How can one, with Donington's claim in mind, resist finding out what closer study will reveal about Peri's work?

Actually, close study is hardly necessary. Even a cursory examination reveals a veritable beehive of Donington-like examples of "thematic unity." I shall concentrate on three swarms: the repeated-note motive, the upward scalewise motive, and the downward scalewise motive, each of which is "prefigured" in a segment of the "overture." The segments are marked (*a*), (*b*), and (*c*) respectively in Example 4.[9] I cannot indulge in the luxury of tracing out and laying before the reader every occurrence of these three easily identifiable melodic fragments. (It would be overkill in any case.) The following brief survey, with a few representative instances, must suffice.

The Prologue, recited by La Tragedia (the obvious progenitor of Mon-

EXAMPLE 4
Jacopo Peri, *Euridice* (ed. Brown), prelude

teverdi's La Musica), consists of seven verses, all sung to the same theme, based on the repeated-note figure (measures 1–3, 29–31, 57–59, 85–87, 113–115, 141–143, 169–171). I have ferreted out (without very much trouble) the following other instances of the repeated-note figure as a major operator in a melodic phrase, almost always constituting its beginning. Because of the profusion of occurrences, I have been obliged to confine myself to only the first of the five scenes (according to Brown's division); and even here my list is by no means exhaustive. The name of the character is followed in parentheses by the measure numbers in which the figure appears: Aminta (measure 1); Euridice (measure 88); Nymphs II, III, Arcetro, Aminta, Shepherd IV (measure 184); Nymph II (measures 199–200); Aminta (measures 235–236) (Example 5).

I have followed the same procedure in regard to the ascending and descending scalewise figures, confining myself again to Scene I. *Descending scalewise figure*: Aminta (measures 3, 13, 32); Nymph II (measures 43, 61, 68); Euridice (measures 95, 97–98); Aminta (measures 121, 140–142); Arcetro (measures 173–174); Nymphs II, III (measures 176–179); etc. (Example 6). *Ascending scalewise figure*: Aminta (measures 5–8,

EXAMPLE 5
Peri, *Euridice*
(*a*)

(*b*)

(*c*)

(*d*)

(*e*)

5. Vo - stro, _ Re - gi - na, fia _ co -

(*f*)

6. Tal _____ per _ voi _ tor - no, e con

(*g*)

7. Men - tre Sen - na _ Re - al ____ pre -

(*h*)

AMINTA

Nin - fe, ch'i bei crin d'o - ro Scio-glie-te

(*i*)

EURIDICE

Don - ne, ch'a' miei di -

(*j*)

NYMPHS I II

ARCETRO Al - le bel - l'on - d'e

AMINTA

(*h*)

NYMPH II

Sel - vag - gia Di - va,

(*l*)

AMINTA

Bel - la ma - dre d'A - mor, dal -

EXAMPLE 6
Peri, *Euridice*

(*a*)

lie - te al - lo scher-zar de' ven - ti,

(*b*)

Tut - te ve - ni-te o Pa - sto - rel - le a-man - ti;

(*c*)

Pur vi con - giun - se il ciel,

(*d*)

vol - gi in - tor -

(*e*)

crin d'al - me vi - o - le,

(*f*)

si - mil par

(*g*)

Tut-to ras-sem-bra il mio gio - ir rac-col - to, Deh come lie-ta a - scol - to I dol - ci

(*h*)

Pre - gio d'o - gni bel - lez - za,

(i)

AMINTA

De' vo - stri dol - c̣i̯a - mo - ri.

(j)

ARCETRO

pas - se - rem con lie - to can - to.

(k)

NYMPH II

Al can - to͜al bal - lo, al can - to͜al bal - lo͜al -

NYMPH III

Al can - to͜al bal - lo, al bal - lo͜al -

28); Nymph II (measures 39, 41, 56–57, 66–67); Arcetro (measure 76); Nymph III (measures 107, 112–113); Aminta (measures 137–138); Euridice (measures 143–145); Nymph II (measures 270–273, 277–280); etc. (Example 7).

If thematic interconnections are as profusely distributed as this, there is something very wrong. Indeed, as the reader of Brown's introduction to his edition of *Euridice* will have immediately realized, the situation is even worse than might appear to the reader unfamiliar with it; for the "overture" is not by Peri at all (there being no known prelude to the work of his authorship) but is an addition of the editor's. It is by Girolamo Fantini; and except for the title, "La Renuccini," and the fact that "This Fanfare was undoubtedly composed as an act of homage to some member of the librettist's [i.e. Ottavio Rinuccini's] family . . . ,"[10] it has absolutely no relation to the opera at all, and was certainly never intended to be any part of the work by Peri. Any thematic relationship between it and *Euridice* must be purely fortuitous. What is more, it would be equally appropriate, "thematic relationships" and all, to Monteverdi's *Orfeo*; and I dare say there is as much (or as little) resemblance between its ascending and descending themes and the musical material of *Orfeo* as that which Donington perceives between *Orfeo* and the Toccata with which that work begins.

Overture aside, have I simply shown, by this little exercise in tune detection, that Peri is a better composer than we heretofore thought? I

EXAMPLE 7

Peri, *Euridice*

(*a*)

voi,   ch'al - mo te - so - ro   Den - tro chiu - de   -   te a' bei ru - bi - ni ar - den -

(*b*)

Av - ven - tu - ro   -   so Or - fe   -   o,

(*c*)

Al   me - mo - ra   -   bil   gior - no,

(*d*)

ch'il   car - ro   d'or

(*e*)

Va   -   -   ghe Nin   -   fe a - mo - ro -

(*f*)

Non   ve   -   de un

(*g*)

Non   ve   -   -   de un

(*h*)

Qual   in si roz - zo   co - re

(i)

NYMPH III

Che di si bel - l'a - mor   l'al   -   ta ven-tu - ra

(j)

AMINTA

me   e   lie   -   ti,i   co - ri

(k)

EURIDICE

E   mil - le gui-se,e mil - le

(l)

NYMPH II

Cor - rin di pu-ro lat - te,e   ri   -   -   -   -   -   vi,e _ fiu   -   mi,

(m)

NYMPH II

O - gni sel-vag - gia   can   -   na: Ver - sa - te,am-bro   -   sia

think not. What, then, has gone wrong here? Surely I can't be arguing that the attempt to find thematic resemblances in musical works by looking at scales and such is misguided, either methodologically or musically. (I think I hear the same things in the first movement of Beethoven's Fifth as Professor Donington.) It must be the *way* the thing was done that has led us (and Donington) astray. Somehow Donington has gotten some kind of cart before its horse. Let me suggest what the cart is, and where it belongs. Imagine the following two possible scenarios.

(a) I am listening to the first movement of a symphony by Michael Haydn that I have never heard before. It conveys to me a very palpable (and unexpected) sense of unity, but I can't quite put my finger on the reason. So I acquire a score, examine it closely, and discover that all of the themes are related to one another by the use in each of a distinctive ascending scalewise passage. This, I satisfy myself, is what is responsible for the palpable sense of unity the work conveys.

(b) I am listening to the first movement of an early symphony of Mozart's that I have never heard before. It conveys to me no particularly compelling sense of unity at all, although I find myself quite entranced by its beauty. Convinced that a composer of Mozart's stature could not have failed to impart thematic unity to his works, particularly the ones I find especially fine, I acquire a score and examine it closely. I discover in it an abundance of ascending and descending scalewise passages, which I take to demonstrate the thematic unity of the work.

The first scenario I take to be a valid mode of procedure. The second more often than not leads directly to error; for it is simply the musical version of finding bad reasons for what one already believes. It is the difference between attempting to verify an hypothesis you initially have some antecedent empirical evidence for (in this case the aesthetic experience of unity on first hearing), and attempting to establish a hypothesis that you have no reason at all for believing in the first place. That Donington has followed the second scenario is clear. He all but says so in admitting that *Orfeo* gives "the appearance of inconsequence"; that

> The listener to *Orfeo* is impressed throughout by its evident freedom, and by the easy grace with which it is obviously following every refinement of its verbal text. The music sounds, as it was meant to sound, spontaneous in the complete service of the words.[11]

In other words, *Orfeo*, in Donington's view as in mine, gives, for the most part, no initial impression of unity at all (except for the Prologue and the junction of the Prologue with the first scene); in fact, its impression is quite the reverse. Why, then, assume that the appearance is at odds with reality? Given Monteverdi's over-arching goal in the work, the "following [of] every refinement of its verbal text," music "in the complete service of the words," we have every reason to expect just what our initial response to the work is: a feeling, at least in the passages of *stile rappresentativo*, of palpable lack of thematic unity.

Clearly, there is one very deep motive at work here: to distinguish a work of genius from the many works of talent (or worse) that abounded in its time. "Organic unity" has, since time out of mind, been believed to be such a distinguishing mark. (Recall the *Poetics*.) Further, picking out scales, ascending or descending, and intervals of one kind or another is a neat, hard-edged, unproblematic decision procedure. Something either is or is not a descending scale or an ascending leap of a fifth. Whereas the initial judgment that a work conveys a palpable sense of unity is far from hard-edged, or mechanically made, although I do not for a moment suggest that it is "subjective," or (not the same thing) "non-condition-governed" (to use Frank Sibley's well-known phrase).[12] But it is an "aesthetic" judgment that there is a temptation to try to avoid (especially if one sees oneself as doing "scientific" musicology); and if all thematic unity in music consisted in were the kinds of "cobbler's patches" that Donington offers us in his analysis of *Orfeo* and that I have offered in my pseudo-analysis of *Euridice*, such problematic judgments would be circumvented. They cannot; and the result of trying is to discover a kind of "unity" tantamount to the kind one would discover by coming to the realization that the whole of the *Oresteia* is written in Greek.

What Donington has turned up, in his thematic fishing expedition, is, from the authorial point of view, thematic relationships at the level of chance. This is not to say that they are "chance" occurrences in the sense of lacking an adequate explanation for their having taken place. But that explanation does not lie, as Donington would have it, in Monteverdi's compositional intentions; rather, what we are seeing are merely the most general symptoms of the fact that Monteverdi's music is part of a tradition, with a history and a future. Even Donington is prepared to admit at least the possibility of Monteverdi's intentions in this regard being *unconscious*, and even must concede a certain element of seeming unintentionality, if nothing more.[13]

I will not raise the question of whether unconscious intentions are fullblooded intentions in the sense required here; nor will I raise the equally perplexing one of whether full-blooded intention to impart thematic unity to a composition is a necessary condition for its presence. (Certainly it is not a *sufficient* condition, as the attempt can always fail.) What I do want to argue—a claim completely independent of these two—is that the impression in the work of intentional, planned-for thematically unifying relationships is indeed a necessary condition; and that is what large portions of *Orfeo* and Peri's *Euridice* lack, in spite of the common thematic building blocks that can be found in each. One cannot prove to the reader, *a priori*, that these works are not thematically unified. Once such materials as those that Donington turned up in *Orfeo* are called to one's attention, one then has to return again to the work and listen with these in mind. If one can in fact hear them as constituting intended thematic unity, Donington has won his point. But my own ear hears them, as it does the thematic "relationships" in Peri's *Euridice*, only as the background noise of Western tonal music. And that is the acid test for me.

Whether the impression of consciously intended thematic unity is sufficient as well as necessary is a nice question. My own view is that it is necessary only. For the subsequent discovery of thematic resemblances, as in scenario (a), can then be seen as the discovery that the appearance is the reality after all. Failure to discover such resemblances might or might not dispel the initial impression of unity. In either case what we would have is apparent rather than actual unity.[14] But under no circumstances would we say that unity existed in the continued absence of the sense of intentional, non-accidental thematic structure that I have spoken of above. And that, it seems to me, is where scenario (b) and Donington's analysis of *Orfeo* must fail.

o 4 o   Donington has essentially attempted to demonstrate that *Orfeo*, despite its adherence (at least implicitly) to the representational aims of the Camerata, has a kind of pure musical form: which is to say that it falls into recognizable formal structures. "Its forms are of an almost academic strictness."[15] If I am right, he has failed, and so has *Orfeo*, in that particular regard, at least as far as that most vital element, the *stile rappresentativo*, is concerned.

But surely, it will be argued, to show that *Orfeo* has not achieved a "pure musical form" in the sense of "academic strictness of form" is not to show that it has failed to achieve a "pure musical form" at all. There can be other forms in music besides the ones sanctioned by the academy—the ones with the names. Is it not a conservative, inflexible, and (in the pejorative sense of that word) "academic" posture to construe "pure musical form" in such a way as to recognize as such only those that are canonized in textbooks? Something like this sort of reasoning must lie behind Schrade's claim that

> Monteverdi did not treat musical form as an unalterable preconceived scheme or pattern as did the later opera, where the *da capo* aria prevailed as a more or less fixed form. Such a conception of form occurs in very mature, even overripe, phases of historical development, and is the one usually adopted by a classic artist. The other and opposite conception occurs where the artist is not bound to an established scheme but creates a new form each time, according to the special conditions and by interpreting those conditions. All musicians who are born dramatists have taken form to be something flexible and responsive to the action of the drama.[16]

Schrade is surely not the first to develop this view of musical form in opera, but he has stated it in a particularly clear and felicitous way. It is an at least initially compelling view and requires our careful scrutiny.

The problem of musical form, for the composer of opera—or, for that matter, for the composer of any musical setting of a text, if he has embraced the representational paradigm—is to both reflect in his music the expressive and cognitive content of the text and impart to his music some kind of intelligible form *qua* music. Occasionally that turns out to be easy; where, for example, the poet has written a refrain as

> Meine Ruh' ist hin,
> Mein Herz ist schwer;
> Ich finde sie nimmer
> Und nimmermehr,

giving the composer the opportunity of perfectly matching his music to a segment of the text that, in the nature of the case, will be bound to recur a number of times. The poem, having a musical form to begin with—rondo, ritornello, or whatever you choose to call it—can be perfectly "expressed" in music without sacrifice of musical form. But this will seldom happen at all—certainly never in any text expansive enough to serve for an opera, even where librettist and composer are in cahoots.

Yet every sequence of words has some form or other, however complicated it might be. And if the composer lets the form impart itself to the music, then the music cannot fail to have form; but, of course, it will be a different form for each text: or as Schrade puts it, "the artist is not bound to an established scheme but creates a new form each time, according to the special conditions and by interpreting those conditions." All the composer need do, then, to achieve musical form in setting his text is to grab hold as tight as he can of one horn of his dilemma, and to reflect in his music as faithfully as he can the content of his text; for where musical representation is the function, musical form will inexorably follow it.

I said that this view seems initially compelling. But surely there is something amiss here. And I think we can see what it is by uncovering what seem to be two very different senses of "form" in the contrasting views of Donington and Schrade which are being systematically equivocated upon in Schrade's account.

There is one sense of "form" in which we might want to say that nothing is formless. It is the sense, I think, embodied in the following passage from Leibniz, where he defends the notion of a universal order in nature.

> [N]ot only does nothing happen in the world which is absolutely irregular, but one cannot even feign such a thing. For let us suppose, for example, that someone makes a number of marks on paper quite at random, as do those who practice the ridiculous art of geomancy. I say that it is possible to find a geometrical line, the notion of which is constant and uniform according to a certain rule, such that this line passes

through all these points, and in the same order as the hand had marked them.

And if someone drew in one stroke a line which was now straight, now circular, now of another nature, it is possible to find a notion or rule, or equation common to all the points on this line, in virtue of which these same changes must occur. And there is no face, for example, the outline of which does not form part of a geometrical line and cannot be traced in one stroke by a certain movement according to rule. But *when a rule is very complex what conforms to it passes for irregular.*[17]

If Leibniz is right—and at least in the realm of "ordinary affairs" he would seem to be—there is no visible shape without an intelligible, which is to say describable, form: conforming, in other words, to some mathematical equation or formulation rule. And when I say, for instance, that the building which houses the Department of Defense has a definite form, whereas clouds tend to be formless masses, what I am literally saying, on Leibniz' view, is that the Pentagon has a shape conformable to a simple rule, whereas clouds never do, for *when a rule is very complex what conforms to it*—a cloud (say)—*passes for irregular.* The same, one can reasonably assume, is true of audible patterns too. So, if we apply Leibniz' argument to them, we can conclude, for example, that when we say the Minuet-and-Trio in Mozart's *Eine kleine Nachtmusik* has a clearly outlined form, and the *stile rappresentativo* in Monteverdi's *Orfeo* is a shapeless thing, we can be understood to be saying that the sound pattern of the Minuet-and-Trio is stateable in a simple rule whereas the sound pattern of the recitative in *Orfeo* conforms only to a complex one—but has a "form" nonetheless in virtue of that. The day has been saved for *Orfeo* as a musical work with a real, if complex, musical form.

But so, of course, has the day been saved for Peri's *Euridice*, the "songs" of whales, and the noise my furnace makes during the month of January. And isn't that merely a Pyrrhic victory for *Orfeo*? If nothing lacks form, it hardly pays *Orfeo*, or Monteverdi, a compliment to say that the work has form or that the composer is responsible. It hardly marks *Orfeo* or Monteverdi out as unusual, if my furnace has it, and whales do it.

The problem is that we can be satisfied with this restoration of form to *Orfeo*'s *stile rappresentativo* only if we adsentmindedly think the old sense of "having form" into the new Leibnizian definition. That is where the equivocation lies. And the reason for it is clear: for what we used to call "formless"—and now are licensed to think of as having "form," but only in so far as conforming to an extremely complicated description or rule—

still lacks all of the *relevant* features whose perceived absence led us to call it formless in the first place, prior to our Leibnizian enlightenment.

When I perceive that a musical work has form, I cannot do it independently of understanding it under some formal description: I must perceive it as a form of a certain kind. To perceive that something has form is to perceive (at least dimly) at the same time what that form is. If I cannot do that, I will perceive it as formless. This does not mean that I must know the name of its form, or even that its form must have a name; nor need I be completely aware of what its form might be. I might perceive that a piece has form by immediately being able to place it in the category "French overture." But perhaps I merely recognize it as that familiar pattern, which I have heard before, of a slow, stately section followed by a fast one in which the instruments come in a few at a time, chasing each other. Or there may be no name to the form at all. Mozart's Fantasia for piano in D minor (K.397) has a clearly perceivable form—a readily describable pattern of themes and sections—that has no musical name and fits into no ready-made musical niche; which, of course, is precisely why Mozart called it "Fantasia." But it does have a formal structure which indeed complies with a simply, easily grasped formation rule. And it is by placing it under this rule, or under the numerous formal sub-descriptions appropriate to it, that I perceive its formal character. I may not get the whole picture at first hearing but only be dimly aware that it follows some sort of pattern I do not yet completely grasp. But until—or unless—I can do at least that, I will perceive only formlessness.

It is, of course, *at least* the minimal sense of form that the composer relies upon, and that makes form, as I understand the concept here, function aesthetically in music. Were it not for the listener's ability, at least minimally, to place a minuet-and-trio into a formal category, the composer could neither organize his music by its use nor ring the changes on it that play with the realization and (at times) frustration of our expectations.

We can now see, I think, with this in mind, why the Leibnizian sense of form, which Schrade seems to be drifting toward, offers no consolation to those who might find the *stile rappresentativo* of *Orfeo* "formless." For the form which they have in mind, and which they seek but do not find in *Orfeo*, is just that kind of form I have been describing above, with all that it implies in terms of recognition, description, and expectation. The composer who, as Schrade would have it, "creates a new form each time," even if that form were a "simple" one, would not be able to make use of either expectation or its frustration—provided, of course, the form were really new. For if a form is entirely novel, we can, of course, have no expectation whatever about it and (by consequence) no surprise. And if, into the bargain, the form were of the complicated, Leibnizian kind, as it pretty much would have to be in the case of *Orfeo*'s *stile rappresentativo*, with the music completely responsive to the exigencies of the text, all of what can be thought of as the aesthetic function of musical form would be up the spout: we would have "form" in name only. To offer one consolation that *Orfeo* really has musical form, because, after all, as Leibniz has shown, nothing is formless, would be about as helpful as assuring someone with religious doubts that "yes, there is a God," and then referring him or her to Spinoza's *Ethics* for the particulars.

Now of course it does not follow from what I am saying that composers cannot invent "new forms"; but in actual fact that happens, even in the most extreme cases, by the partial alteration of a form already pre-existent. (Musical forms have an amazing resiliency, witness the survival in dodecaphonic music of such old favorites as the crab canon.) The *Eroica* and *Symphonie fantastique*, certainly on everyone's list of "revolutionary" works, still stand recognizable under the description "symphony"; and although the sonata-allegro takes a pretty bad beating (particularly in the latter), it does survive intact—different, to be sure, but the same nevertheless. And, we might add, the same game was afoot in that most revolutionary of musical revolutions, the invention of opera itself. For where there *is* form there, it is recognizable as a pre-existent one or a variation thereof. The choruses, instrumental interludes, and strophic songs all are in well-established idioms; and the ritornello, which is, of course, put to new use as an organizational principle in opera, is nothing new as a musical principle.

What I think must be concluded from all of this is that where there *is* form in *Orfeo*, it is form as we all know it: falling more or less into pre-existent paradigms. That is just what we mean by musical form, as opposed to the musically formless. Where there is not *that*, there is not form in any other than a remote, metaphysical sense that may be of great significance in theodicy but does very little for musical analysis. Where Monteverdi has succeeded in giving musical form to *Orfeo*, he has succeeded in the usual way. Where he has failed, as in much of the *stile rappresentativo*, he has failed in the usual way. To say that his failures are really successes in some philosophical way unknown to musicians is to pay him no compliment at all.

○ 5 ○   Failure, of course, can be only relative to a task undertaken. I suggested at the outset of this chapter that *Orfeo* might be regarded in two ways: as an attempt to put spoken drama in musical form or, alternatively, as an attempt at a dramatic work with prominent musical elements—but not a musical work in the sense of its time, in Monteverdi's sense, or in ours. I have argued that as an attempt at putting drama to music *Orfeo* is in an important respect flawed. But if that was not the task Monteverdi set himself, the judgment is misapplied. It may well be that he saw himself as pursuing the latter goal, in which case the failure of musical form and, perhaps along with it, the failure of *Orfeo* to be fully "music" is no failure at all. Furthermore, and not without significance in this regard, this "non-musical" interpretation of *Orfeo* is very like the one Brown puts on Peri's *Euridice*, which he seems reluctant to place squarely in the musical camp but locates somewhere in the *terra nullius* between music and literature. "The composer took such pains to make his music reflect precisely both the form and the content of the Italian words," he writes, "and was so successful in this attempt to create a music whose chief *raison d'être* was the heightening of dramatic speech, that *Euridice* is as much a literary as a musical work."[18]

That both Donington and Schrade are at least drawn toward this latter view of *Orfeo*, in spite of their spirited (if unsuccessful) defenses of the work's pure musicality, is revealed by their frequent and telltale use of the phrase "music drama" and its relatives far too seriously for it to be accidental. Thus Schrade remarks that "Technical, stylistic, and expressive preparations combined to make the *Orfeo* the first musical drama in history."[19] And Donington, in a Schrade-like passage, remarks upon *Orfeo*'s "musical structure responding effortlessly to dramatic development," adding that therein "lies the true art of *dramma per musica*, of music drama."[20]

Now I do not want to suggest that the terms "opera" and "music drama" are used in any kind of strict or mutually exclusive way. Rather, they tend to point in different directions: the former toward drama in musical form, with the musical parameters more or less intact; the latter toward an art-form-cum-music, but in various respects (depending upon the work) free of the constraints of pure musical considerations. The way these terms are used is indicative of this distinction, even when they are not deliberately used to make it. To call an "opera"—that is to say, an unequivocally musical work—a *dramma per musica* is to give it credit for being, in spite of its inherent musicality, faithful to the dramatic text. (This is the spirit in which we tend to call Mozart and Verdi great musical dramatists.) And to call something an "opera" that technically is not—say, a Broadway show—is to pay it the compliment of elevating it from the level of "merely" musical theatre to that of "real music." When, however, a work is problematical—when it is a question, as in the case of *Orfeo*, of what the work *is*—the temptation to call it *dramma per musica* rather than opera, a temptation that both Schrade and Donington succumb to, clearly signals a reluctance to see the work as a bona fide musical one. Nor are Schrade and Donington the only commentators to feel such reluctance.

In running over the *Orfeo* literature, one comes across an article by Domenico de' Paoli with the unlikely title " 'Orfeo' and 'Pelléas' "—unlikely, I think, because at least on first reflection the comparison seems about as apt as one between a hatrack and a halibut. But whatever the musical gap between the two works, there is method as well as madness here. For Debussy's *Pelléas et Mélisande*, like *Orfeo*, is one of those problematical, text-bound works that seem to have gone beyond the bounds of the purely musical into the *sui generis* territory of musical drama. And that in fact is de Paoli's major point. He writes, "the only two music-dramas, in which poetry and music are really indissolubly fused, are 'Orfeo' and 'Pelléas' "[21]—a fairly extreme claim, given the other candidates at least in the running. However, he obviously means it, for the assertion is repeated later on, even more emphatically. "Thus, at a distance of three centuries, in Italy and in France, we find the same principles ruling the conception and the realization of two veritable music-dramas—the only music-dramas the musical theatre possesses, if it be true that the guiding principle of music-drama is that poetry and music should not encroach upon each other, but together form an indissoluble whole."[22]

The way in which Paoli spells out this claim is of some interest, for it sheds further light on the distinction, as it is usually seen, between opera and musical drama. That *Pelléas* is not opera in the traditional sense seems altogether clear. That it is music drama Paoli has already affirmed in the strongest possible terms. But now the same disturbing doubts arise as to its musical claims that arose, for Schrade (and for us), with regard to *Orfeo*:

> In Debussy the notes exactly followed the intonation of the words as they are spoken in real life. From that it was only a short cut to the question whether Debussy's vocal writing was musical at all—and more than one critic was forced to ask it. It has been seen even in recent criticism by writers who hesitated to answer it in the affirmative.[23]

The response Paoli gives to these critics seems to me to be very perceptive. The question could have been quickly reduced to a purely evaluative one, with no descriptive content at all; but Paoli foresees this possibility and does not allow it to occur. There can be no doubt that the critical charge of "unmusicality" directed at *Pelléas* was simply an adverse value judgment, thinly disguised as a judgment regarding the character of the work: "unmusical" being a transparent code-word for "bad music." But Paoli does not fall into the trap of replying in kind by insisting that, on the contrary, *Pelléas* is indeed "musical" after all. Had he done so, the "argument" would have been no more enlightening than a name-calling match. Rather, Paoli disarmingly acquiesces in the charge of "unmusicality" and, in the process, calls attention to just that unique, musico-dramatic element that he is arguing for in Debussy's work. He writes:

> One might reply that the musical, the admirably musical outcome of Debussy's vocal style leaves not a twinge of doubt in those of unbiased sensibility who are free from preconception; but it may be preferable to ask the question—a question never to be forgotten where opera is concerned—whether the vocal style of a work for the stage may even be considered from a purely musical point of view, or whether we should not rather study the problem of a more particular point of view, namely that of a kind of poetic text (and it is only in this respect that it is no longer "pure" music) while its own nature and very structure are conditioned by that text.[24]

There is, doubtless, a bit of the high-wire act here, with Paoli teetering on the edge, between an outright admission that Debussy has produced, in *Pelléas*, a wonderful work of art but not a musical one—and so what?— and the familiar, less daring compromise to the effect that the text has given the work a musical form of its own. This impression of indecision is reinforced by Paoli's comparison of *Pelléas* with "verist" opera, where a view quite like Schrade's is at least dimly outlined. That *Pelléas* does not have "musical form" in the traditional operatic sense he readily admits. The question is, does it have "musical form" at all? And here Paoli is less clear. "Form" it has, but we are left in some doubt as to what the cash value of the claim really is. "Needless to say there is no question of arias enthusiastically vociferated by tenors or sopranos; . . . but if there is a music-drama which circumscribes and throws into relief perfect form and harmonious architecture, that music-drama is surely 'Pelléas et Mélisande.' "[25]

The waters are muddied still further by Paoli's discussion of "recitative" in *Pelléas* and *Orfeo*. That it is not "melody" in the familiar sense of the word seems obvious: indeed, the early opera composers were consciously avoiding melismatic song in the *stile rappresentativo*, and said as much quite explicitly. But melody would seem, after all, to be a musical *sine qua non*, and so must have seemed to Paoli.[26] How could we have *music* without it? He rescues it for both works by the familiar method of the attenuated sense:

> . . . in connection with both "Orfeo" and "Pelléas" the word "recitative" has been decidedly overworked. . . . [F]or both composers' procedures one might usefully claim "continuous melody" as a definition.[27]

Now the notion of "continuous melody" need not be taken literally: an "endless" journey on the Long Island Railroad does, after all, come eventually to an end. But if *closure* and *finite length* are parameters of music, at least as we normally understand it, stretching the notion of "continuous melody" too far, as Paoli surely does in describing the *stile rappresentativo* of *Orfeo* that way, leads, I think, to absurdity. Whether it is stretched too far as well in reference to *Pelléas et Mélisande* is a question I will not go into here, as that is not my present concern. I tend to think that with regard to the latter work it is a useful and intelligible extension, for *Pelléas* is, it seems to me, "melodic" in a way that the *stile rappresentativo* in *Orfeo* clearly is not. And the phrase "continuous melody" calls our attention here, more appropriately indeed than in Wagner, to the fact that melodic closure and length have perhaps been pushed to their outer limits, and that, therefore, we must expand our perceptions accordingly. Being pushed to the outer limits, however, is not being pushed beyond.

But to call the *stile rappresentativo* in *Orfeo* "melodic" even in an attenuated sense of the term does seem to me to go beyond what the concept of melody will permit. A "continuous melody," like an "endless sentence," may just be unusually long. (Some of Milton's sentences seem almost "endless.") A truly continuous melody, however, would not be a melody, any more than a truly endless sentence would be a sentence. They would both fail to be well-formed formulae in their respective domains. Nor need we take "continuous" and endless" literally to get this absurd result. An English sentence that took eight hours to enunciate in a normally paced speaking voice would not, in fact, be endless; nor would an eight-hour melody be literally continuous. For us, however, that is what it would amount to. It is as little comfort to reassure us that *stile rappresentativo* really is melody after all—that is, "continuous melody"—as to reassure us that it has "form" in the minimal, Leibnizian sense of conforming to an enormously complex rule or description (for it is, I think, a thinly disguised special case of that very fallacy).

Vagaries aside, however—or, perhaps, vagaries very much to the point—what Paoli strongly suggests with regard to both *Pelléas* and *Orfeo* (the point, of course, of comparing them) is that, at the very least, it takes considerable intellectual effort and the putting aside of scruples to see them as fully musical works: considerable intellectual effort, and a large dollop of fallacy into the bargain. In Paoli's braver moments the suggestion is, rather, that in calling *Pelléas* and *Orfeo* music dramas instead of operas he is placing them in another category of art-work altogether—one, doubtless, that has strong family ties to music proper, but that is, in crucial respects, *sui generis*. The latter is the view of *Orfeo* that I have wished to bring to notice here, and that is perhaps vaguely suggested by Donington and Schrade as well.

○ 6 ○   What, then, is *Orfeo*? A work of music? Or something else again? I will conclude this chapter with a brief consideration of the nature of this question and, more important, of its significance for the present study. What I will not consider is its answer (which I do not know anyway).

I have spoken of Monteverdi's *intentions*. Is the question a matter of intentions? And can we answer it by determining what they were?

Some would say that Monteverdi's intentions in the matter are quite irrelevant. Whatever Monteverdi might have intended, the work is what it is and must be judged by its character alone. "You can't expect that after a poor fellow has written a book he should also understand it."[28]

But even those who may not take such a hard line on authorial intentions are bound to admit that, as a practical matter, authorial intentions are seldom available for our inspection anyway and so cannot be relied upon to answer interpretational questions. Certainly that is the case with Monteverdi; for his extant letters and writings tell us nothing about the question of whether he intended *Orfeo* to be a musical work, or something else, or whether, in fact, he was even able to frame such a question at all.

To complicate matters further, there are those who would deny that the question has an answer at all, if you mean by an answer the assigning of a truth value either to the statement that *Orfeo* is basically a musical work or to the statement that it is not. On such a view it might be more or less plausible, or a better or worse way of looking at things, to think of *Orfeo* as a *dramma per musica*; but it could not be true or false.

A softer line in this regard might be to see *Orfeo* as falling under a wide range of interpretations, some number of which could be dismissed as false, leaving a smaller sub-set of possible readings, which might be determined to be more or less plausible, better or worse, but not true or false, and in addition (therefore?) not completely eliminable.

Even, however, if we take the softer line, it seems to me that the question of *Orfeo*'s citizenship—music or merely musi*cal*, opera or music drama—is an ineliminable one, in the sense of its being able to be assigned a true value. Further, it can be plausibly argued that even if a truth value were assignable, the criterion whereby we would do so would turn out to be the same one—the only one available—for determining better or worse, more plausible or less. That criterion is, simply (or not so simply), under what description the work becomes most relevantly rewarding. Even if one were convinced that it is a matter of hard fact whether *Orfeo* is an opera or a music drama, a work of music or a work of something else, the compatibility of both interpretations with the known historical facts, the known (or, more likely, unknown) intentions of the composer, the perceived features of the work itself (in so far as they can be ascertained neutrally as between the two interpretations), leaves no further recourse than an appeal to which reading rewards the listener more, or, to put it another way, which reading yields a better work of art. In other words, all other things being equal, that interpretation would be counted as true which yielded the best or most rewarding reading, under the (perhaps fallacious) principle of charity to the effect that it would be highly unlikely for a false interpretation to (by accident, as it were) be aesthetically optimal. But if those who believe that interpretations are either true or false must ultimately resort to the principle of charity when (as is likely) all other criteria will be exhausted before all readings save one are eliminated, those who believe that interpretations can only be plausible or implausible, better or worse, good or bad, must resort to it straightaway, since it is the only criterion available to them, the others being criteria only under the rejected assumption of interpretational truth values.

Since the principle of charity is the only interpretational criterion ultimately in the running, whatever your interpretation of interpretation might be, we can ask here, without taking a stand on theories of interpretation, Which interpretation of *Orfeo* is the more artistically rewarding one, the optimal one in terms of artistic value? *Orfeo* as opera, or *Orfeo* as music drama, as a drama *with* music but not a musical work *per se*? My answer—which may only be subjective—is that it is a tossup: that understanding *Orfeo* under either description has its own payoffs and its own debits, but that the positive sums come out about the same.

Each interpretation would, of course, have different implications for appreciation, because each would call attention to, emphasize more or less strongly, different features of the work. And what might be a fault on one interpretation—the ignoring of music for dramatic veracity on the musical interpretation, the sacrifice of drama for music on the interpretation of *Orfeo* as *dramma per musica*—would be a merit on the other. (Needless to say, which interpretation one plumped for would also, if one were a director or conductor, have implications for performance: whether one wanted primarily singers or actors, a static or a dramatically busy production, and so on. And this, in turn, would affect what interpretation the listener would be more likely to give the work.)

Now if, indeed, there is no choosing, by the principle of charity, between these two descriptions of *Orfeo*, it brings into even sharper focus the problematic character of the work. That it can be understood equally well as a flawed opera or a non-opera drives us to the inevitable conclusion: *Orfeo* poses the "problem" of opera, it does not solve it. As an opera it fails (although magnificently) to bring true musical form to the drama; fails to make of the drama *music*. And although it cannot fail to solve the problem of opera if seen as a music drama since something cannot fail to solve a problem it does not address, *Orfeo* as music drama nevertheless fails to be a solution to the "problem" of opera (for something can be a solution to a problem even if the solution of that problem was not the reason for its coming into being).

Orfeo fails. Is that because the "problem" of opera—of making drama truly music—is completely intractable? I do not think so; for solutions, although always controversial, were to come. The problem was insoluble in 1607. What made it ripe for a solution was, I shall argue, the development of a new psychology, peculiarly amenable to musical representation with the musical forms then available, and a new philosophy, peculiarly amenable to musical purism and, thus, a counterbalance to the overweening influence of representational theory that kept the Camerata, and even the great Monteverdi, from being musically airborne where opera is concerned. To understand this is to understand the true "aesthetics" of the opera. All of this will be argued in the second part of my book.

PART II

Solving the problem

CHAPTER VI

Philosophy and Psychology
(in early modern dress)

o 1 o   Hegel, in the *Lectures on the Fine Arts*, characterized the artist as one whose peculiar role it is to "display the depth of the heart and the spirit"; and, he warned, "these are not known directly but are to be fathomed only by the direction of the artist's own spirit on the inner and outer world."[1] The goal of the artist, on Hegel's view, the "display [of] the depth of the heart and the spirit," is, not surprisingly, redolent with the aroma of Romanticism. But Hegel, in spite of that, does not give us the rest of the expected package, namely, the artist as gushing forth the display of spirit in an unconscious, unstudied burst of inspiration, he knows not how from he knows not where. On the contrary, the artist does not fathom this depth of heart and spirit directly: "only [rather] by the direction of the artist's own spirit on the inner and outer world"—in other words, "it is study whereby the artist brings this content into his consciousness and wins the stuff and content of his conceptions."[2]

Art requires, then, even where its goal is the revelation of the self rather than of the world, knowledge wrested from study of both. But, Hegel goes on to say, the arts are not equal in the demands they put on knowledge and experience; and music is, in a way, a counterexample, or at least the limiting case.

> Of course, in this respect, one art needs more than another the consciousness and knowledge of such content. Music, for example, which is concerned only with the completely indeterminate movement of the inner spirit and with sounds as if they were feeling without thought, needs to have little or no spiritual material present in consciousness. Therefore musical talent announces itself in most cases very early in youth, when the head is empty and the heart little moved, and it may sometimes attain a very considerable height before spirit and life have experience of themselves. Often enough, after all, we have seen great virtuosity in musical composition and performance accompanied by remarkable barrenness of spirit and character.[3]

Goethe evinced similar views on music, though philosophically less articulate ones, in response to a comment of Eckermann's.

"It is remarkable," said I, "that of all talents the musical shows itself earliest, so that Mozart in his fifth year, Beethoven in his eighth, Hummel in his ninth, already astounded their immediate neighbourhood by their play, and compositions."

"The musical talent," said Goethe, "can well show itself earliest, while music is entirely something innate, inward, which required no great nutriment from outside and no experience drawn from life."[4]

Hegel was thinking, we must assume, mainly of instrumental music, of which (we learn later on in the *Lectures*) he had a rather low opinion (in spite of the fact that Haydn, Mozart, and Beethoven had already raised it to equality in musical society); for it was the text that, on Hegel's view, gave music the ideational content a major art-form requires. But that is not the point I wish to dwell upon here. Rather, it is the picture of music and the musical intellect that the above-quoted passages from Hegel and Goethe imply. That picture is one of a self-contained game for the intellect, with its own unique definitional and procedural rules, susceptible of mastery and application by someone completely innocent of experience, either of the world outside or within. Mathematics and chess immediately come to mind as comparable employments, as does Hermann Hesse's *Glasperlenspiel* which, perhaps, was meant to be a literary evocation of them all. And, therefore, just as music has its Mozart, mathematics has its Gauss and Galois, chess its Bobby Fischer.

But if one can "know the rules," master the discipline, innocent of experience, working only with the materials of the craft, often "in the head," then there seems no room here for the kinds of influence on the historical development of the discipline or craft that one is wont to adduce for such things as sculpting, painting, poeticizing, and the like, where a "content" may be dictated by societal, religious, philosophical, moral, political, or other such "outside" influences and may, reciprocally, reflect back upon the "rules." It is hard to imagine Bobby Fischer's endgame being influenced in its style by his cultural surroundings, or Boris Spassky's by Marxism. Nor is it plausible to think that the nature of Galois' mathematical discoveries was influenced by the political climate of his time and place and by his own very strong political principles. Surely, chess and pure mathematics are influenced almost entirely by the internal histories of those two disciplines: the problems facing the contemporary practitioner being those bequeathed by the generations before. Personality, of course, is there: an aggressive person might well (for all I know) make an aggressive rather than a defensive chess player; a fastidious dresser perhaps has a different mathematical style from a rumpled slob. But such things are imponderables.

There is some reason to believe that pure music, if it is, indeed, analogous to chess and mathematics in the other ways stated above, may be analogous in this respect as well. That is to say, music, more perhaps than any of the other arts, follows an historical development motivated almost entirely, or at any rate in large measure, from within.

This rather circuitous train of thought has not been pursued for its own sake, interesting though it undoubtedly is, but is meant as a rather baroque introduction, apologia, and (perhaps) warning for what will follow in the next two chapters, and at least in some of the chapters thereafter. For I shall be drawing some connections between music and the intellectual life of the seventeenth and eighteenth centuries that may seem as remote as the ones I rejected pretty much out of hand between chess or pure mathematics and their intellectual milieu. Of course I shall be talking here not of pure instrumental music but of opera and other musical settings of texts; and surely that kind of music will have a more direct connection to the literary and even philosophical currents of its time than will the trio sonata or string quartet. Yet even here the ice is thin. For composers, until the nineteenth century, tended to be neither literary nor philosophical personalities. They were trained in the organ loft and opera house, seldom having the benefit of what might be thought of as a "liberal education." And when I try to draw connections, as I shall before long, between Handelian *opera seria*, Cartesian psychology, and the newly forged philosophical discipline of "aesthetics" I might be thought to have about as much chance of success as someone who tried to connect Willie Mays's unique style of catching a fly ball with the development of quantum mechanics. Anyone who knows something of the life and personality of Handel, as they come down to us in contemporary accounts, will know that he had neither the time nor (doubtless) the inclination to read Descartes' *Passions of the Soul* or Francis Hutcheson's *Inquiry into the Original of our Ideas of Beauty and Virtue*, even if he had heard of them (although he did have the education to do so, having attended the University of Halle for a time). To come closer to home, I doubt that he took the time even to read his friend Johann Mattheson's *Der vollkommene Capellmeister* or any of that prolific writer's other works on the theory and practice of music.

These very plausible considerations to the contrary notwithstanding, there is a palpable congruity between the nature of the *opera seria*, in its full Handelian flowering, and the intellectual climate of its times: most notably, I shall argue, between it and that climate as constituted by the Cartesian psychology, and the new philosophy of art which, I have suggested before, gave promise of a philosophy of "pure" music at least comparable in philosophical stature and power to the theory of music as representation that provided the only philosophical foundation for the first generation of opera composers. No one, I think, can give the bill of particulars for precisely how these influences transpired. Certainly there is no direct connection, as there is between Mei and Galilei and the first composers of opera. All I hope to be able to show here is that the congruence is palpable, and that it helps to reveal something about the aesthetics of the opera. I leave it to others, if they can, to uncover the network of historical connections which, I have no doubt, are there. I turn first to the Cartesian psychology.

∘ 2 ∘   *Les Passions de l'âme—The Passions of the Soul* (1649)—is certainly not the work on which Descartes' reputation as a thinker now rests; and few consult it today outside of the narrow precincts of the history of seventeenth-century thought. But it may not be too much of an exaggeration to say that it was one of the most influential books of its time. It affected and formed (and indeed reflected) people's views of their psychology and projected them well into the eighteenth century. More important for our purposes here, it was itself reflected in the arts of painting, literature, and music, and helped to determine what was to be the predominantly psychological makeup of the soon-to-be-born discipline of philosophical aesthetics in general, musical aesthetics in particular. The Cartesian psychology, then, is hardly in the nature of a detour for the argument of this book but, rather, is right on the high road.

The most significant aspect of Descartes' treatment of the emotions is its distinct mechanistic character. This is not to say that the emotions themselves are mechanistic properties. For the machinery of a man is his body, while the emotions are creatures of the mind; and it is the very definition of Cartesianism that what can be a property of mind cannot be a property of body as well (and vice versa).

Thus, Descartes reiterates in *The Passions of the Soul* what he had maintained right along in his preceding philosophical works, *The Discourse on Method*, *The Meditations*, *The Principles of Philosophy*: that "everything we experience as being within us, and which we observe to be capable of occurring in wholly inanimate bodies, must be attributed to our body alone, whereas everything that is in us, and which we cannot in any way consider às capable of appertaining to a body, must be attributed to our soul."[5] But "because we cannot conceive of the body as thinking in any way, we are right in assuming that all of the various kinds of thoughts within us belong to our soul. . . ."[6] And emotions, being a species of thought, must therefore be predicated of mind alone; "there remains nothing in us that we must attribute to our soul except our thoughts, which are of two kinds: those which are the actions of the soul, and those which are the passions."[7] So what is mechanistic about the Cartesian psychology, much to its own confusion and subsequent confounding, is not that the passions *are* something mechanical, which was contrary to Cartesian metaphysics, but that they are *caused* by a special kind of bodily mechanism, which proved refractory to the best efforts of technical philosophy to unravel, as it is an aspect of the notorious mind-body problem (a problem which, I am thankful to be able to say, will not directly concern us here).

I shall come to the bodily mechanism Descartes proposed for the cause of the emotions in a moment. Prior to that we had better get some idea of how, in general, he viewed our emotive life: that is to say, what the pre-systematic view of the emotions was for which he offered a mechanistic explanation. Most important—and particularly important for the purposes of my argument—it is a view of the emotions as discrete, name-bearing "set pieces": hard-edged and rather sharply distinguished from one another—so much so that a catalogue of at least qualified "completeness" could be made of them. This is not to say that Descartes thought the inner universe was completely bounded and finite. On the contrary, he was at pains to make clear that the passions which he enumerated were "only . . . the principal ones, for it is possible to distinguish other more particular ones, and their number is indefinite."[8] Nevertheless, that having been said, the picture that emerges is one of "pragmatic" completeness; for if theoretically "the number [of the more particular passions] is indefinite," in practice there are, on Descartes' view, exactly "six primary passions which are, so to speak, genera of which all the others are species."[9] These six are: "wonder, love, hatred, desire, joy, and sadness, and . . . all the others are either composed of some of these six, or are species of them."[10] Presumably, not only are all of the more particular passions that Descartes enumerates and explains in *The Passions of the Soul* "either composed of some of these six, or . . . species of them," but those of which he does not speak, whose "number is indefinite," are so as well. Thus the infinite universe of the emotive life reduces in the end to a very finite one after all: indeed, a universe of six.

This constricted view of the emotions would suggest, as a more expansive, contours-blurred view would not, the possibility of a one-to-one reduction of emotions to bodily states, and this indeed was what Descartes attempted: not, be it remembered, an identification of emotions with bodily states, which would amount to a concession to materialism, but a one-to-one identification of emotive states with discrete bodily states as their causes. These bodily states were states of what Descartes called the "animal spirits" (*esprits animaux* in the French text of *The Passions of the Soul*), which he imagined to course to and fro throughout the body, via pathways provided by the nervous system: "the nerves, which are like little tubes which all come from the brain, and like it, contain a certain very subtle air or wind which is called animal spirits."[11] It is the discrete and particular states of this material fluid—this "certain very subtle air or wind"—that, on Descartes' view, cause the passions of the soul in a very nearly one-to-one correspondence: one emotion, one state. "Having considered how the passions of the soul differ from all its other thoughts, it seems to me that we may generally define them as those perceptions, sensations or emotions of the soul which we refer specifically to it, and which are caused, maintained and fortified by some movement of the animal spirits."[12]

Now, the idea that mental states are caused by the agitation of some subtle material substance in the body is by no means the invention of Descartes, nor indeed does Descartes present it as such. The view is at least as old as Cicero, and Lucretius' version of Greek atomism. What Descartes brings to the view, besides a systematic thoroughness not theretofore attempted, as far as I am aware, is a real knowledge of human anatomy, no doubt derived not only from reports of the direct observations of others but, very likely, from his own adventures in dissection as well. It seems as if Descartes actually knew something about what goes where in the nervous system, even though he did not have even a vague idea of how nervous tissue does its very subtle and complicated work, and had to make do with the only mechanical model available to him: nothing more sophisticated than miniaturized plumbing. It was surely this up-to-date scientific knowledge of anatomy that lent plausibility to the Cartesian psychology and helped to give it the considerable influence that it subsequently obtained—that and, of course, the considerable reputation of Descartes and his philosophical system.

To be sure, the guts of the scheme, the *esprits animaux*, could no more be the direct-observation report of Descartes than could a treatise on the feeding habits of unicorns. But that is not to say, either, that the animal spirits were "unscientific" or woven out of whole cloth. They represented, rather, an attempt at making an explanatory "model" no less or more "scientific" than seventeenth-century atomism, which in the event proved enormously fruitful, and the theory of the ether, which did not (except in an indirect way). Neither the ether nor Dalton's atoms nor Descartes' animal spirits was (or could have been) observed. They all, of course, were invented to "save the appearances."

That said, we can look a little further into the purported workings of the *esprits animaux*, although there is no need to give an exhaustive account of Descartes' "physiological psychology." We need only know just enough to understand the musical aesthetics—more particularly, the theory of musical "expression"—which called itself Cartesian (or, in some cases, was Cartesian without, perhaps, its proponents realizing it).

Let us take as our exemplar Descartes' "Definition of joy":

> Joy is an agreeable emotion of the soul in which consists the enjoyment it has of the good which the impressions of the brain represent to it as being its own. . . . [F]rom this impression follows the movement of the animal spirits which arouses the possession of joy.[13]

We notice in this "definition" the following components. There is, to begin with, a belief. We cannot feel joy unless we believe that we possess (or will possess) some good to ourselves. One must be joyful *about* something; and (as opposed, say, to sadness) it must be about something perceived to be good. Secondly, this belief manifests itself to us in an "impression of the brain"—that is, a physical brain state. This physical impression, thirdly, causes a particular movement of the animal spirits—for each emotion a particular motion. And, finally, this physical motion gives rise to the mental entity or "thought" which we feel as, and call, the emotion of "joy." That there is a particular motion of the animal spirits not only for each of the six primary passions but for each of the particular "mixed" and "derivative" species of them as well is made clear in the discussion of them that occupies Descartes in the final part of *The Passions of the Soul*. I instance a few examples pretty much at random. Thus: "Hope is a disposition of the soul to persuade itself that what it desires will come about, and it is caused by a particular movement of the animal spirits, namely, by that of joy and desire mingled together."[14] Again:

> Veneration, or respect, is an inclination of the soul not only to esteem the object it reveres, but also to submit itself to it with a certain fear, in order to try to make the object more favorable to it. . . . And the movement of the animal spirits which arouses this passion is composed of that which arouses fear. . . .[15]

Or, finally:

> Similarly, what I call disdain is an inclination of the soul to despise a free cause in judging that although it is by nature capable of doing good and evil, it is nevertheless so far beneath us that it can do neither to us. And the movement of the animal spirits which arouses it is composed of those which arouse wonder or confidence or boldness.[16]

And so on.

We might close this account of Descartes' psychology by emphasizing once again, since it will be of the utmost importance in the argument to come, that each discrete, prefabricated, "at-the-ready" emotion—and that is certainly what the passions of the soul were for Descartes—had, on the Cartesian view, a particular motion of the *esprits animaux* as its proximate cause and necessary condition. This is brought home all the more emphatically where Descartes argues from the *absence* of an appropriate motion of the vital spirits to the conclusion that a given candidate for "passionhood," no matter what its other (perhaps long-standing) credentials might be, cannot properly be an emotion. Thus, although Descartes is prepared to admit that gratitude is an emotion, "a species of love aroused in us by some action on the part of the person for whom we feel it,"[17] he concludes that: "As for ingratitude, it is not a passion, for nature has not placed in us any movement of the animal spirits which arouses it. . . ."[18]

o 3 o   That Descartes envisioned, at least dimly, the musical use to which his theory would be put is not clear, although certainly not impossible either. At least it is not ruled out by any evidence of lack of interest on Descartes' part in matters musical; on the contrary, he corresponded with Mersenne on the subject and wrote, in 1618, a *Compendium musicae* (first published, shortly after Descartes' death, in 1650). The *Compendium of Music*, although dealing primarily with the mathematical and physical aspects of music, contains at least some suggestions as to what Descartes' view on musical "expression" might have been. Certainly he shared the view of the Camerata that music could arouse emotions and that that was one of its major goals, observing, in passing, that intractable paradox of such "arousal" theories: namely, that if music is expressive in virtue of arousing the emotions it is expressive of, it must arouse unpleasant emotions but somehow make us enjoy them as well. Thus he begins:

> The basis of music is sound; its aim is to please and to arouse various emotions in us. Melodies can be at the same time sad and enjoyable; nor is this so unique, for in the same way writers of elegies and tragedies please us most the more sorrow they awaken in us.[19]

How Descartes thought music performed its function of arousal is not clear. He had already observed differences in mood between major and minor, remarking that "the major third and major sixth are more pleasing than the minor third and minor sixth . . .";[20] and he prefaced this with a most enticing hint that he knew more than he had time to say:

> We should now discuss the various powers which the consonances possess of evoking emotions, but a more thorough investigation of this subject can be based on what we have already said, and it would exceed

the limitations of this compendium. For these powers are so varied and based on such imponderable circumstances that a whole book would not suffice for the task.

Unfortunately, it is not obvious how "what we have already said" can explain this ever-puzzling phenomenon, and, unfortunately again, Descartes never wrote that "whole book [which] would not suffice for the task" but which would certainly have been of enormous interest. (Or was the young philosopher only whistling in the dark?)

Another rather enticing hint, again never followed up, relates musical expression to poetics: "poetry is supposed to arouse the emotions in the same manner as music," Descartes says.[21] But what that manner might be he keeps to himself.

I have saved for last Descartes' most extended comment on the *modus operandi* of emotive arousal, although "extended" is, in this case, a rather misleading term, considering its brevity. I have saved it for last because it will help make my transition to the more elaborately worked-out accounts to come. This is, it must be conceded, merely an intriguing hint and requires, perhaps, more imagination than is consistent with sound textual exegesis to yield the reading which I am about to give. Nevertheless, it does seem to me that the passage of which I am now speaking, braced up with a healthy dose of historical hindsight, suggests, at least tentatively, something of the views of musical expression to be constructed on Cartesian psychological foundations in the eighteenth century.

The telltale passage occurs in the midst of Descartes' discussion of rhythm and meter, and begins with an account of how and why we are roused to motion by music, either in time-beating or, more elaborately, in dancing. Descartes says:

> at the beginning of each measure the sound is produced more distinctly; singers and instrumentalists observe this instinctively, especially in connection with tunes to which we are accustomed to dance and sway. Here we accompany each beat of the music by a corresponding motion of our body; we are quite naturally impelled to do this by the music. For it is undoubtedly true that sound strikes all bodies on all sides. ... Since this is so, and since, as we have said, the sound is emitted more strongly and clearly at the beginning of each measure, we must conclude that it has greater impact on our spirits, and that we are thus roused to motion.[22]

The crucial words to note here are: "it [i.e. musical sound] has greater impact on our spirits, and ... we are thus roused to motion." Now although the reference here is only in passing, and the subject is never taken up again, I think we can conclude nothing else but that the "spirits" referred to are the *esprits animaux* of later fame, and that at least the bare bones of the Cartesian psychology were already in place at this early point in the philosopher's intellectual development. What Descartes must be saying, then, is that music is capable of rousing us to motion—as evinced in time-beating, and swaying, dancing, and the like—by, as it were, short-circuiting the normal process in the course of which human activity results. In the ordinary sequence of events which terminates, let us say, in my running away from a mad dog or a bill collector, I first perceive the fearful object; a belief forms itself to the effect that the object is a potential danger to me; that, in turn, in the form of an imaginative impression, puts my animal spirits into that particular motion of them which always arouses fear; the fear then sends the spirits coursing through my nervous system to the appropriate muscles; and, finally, if I have not already been dunned or bitten while enmeshed in this Rube Goldberg physiology, the legs do their work. Music, Descartes is suggesting, can enter this process *in medias res*, so to speak, to directly impinge upon our vital spirits and give them the same motions which, in the ordinary course of things, would eventuate in purposive bodily activity: running, sitting, grasping, and so on. (For, be it remembered, the vital spirits are not only the proximate cause of the passions but the medium by which the passions perform their function of activating the human machine. "For," as Descartes puts it, "the sole cause of the movements of the members is that certain muscles contract while those opposed to them are extended . . . and the sole cause of one muscle's contracting rather than the one opposed to it is that it receives a slightly larger amount of animal spirits from the brain."[23])

Right after this discussion of how music can cause the human body to move, Descartes reverts to a brief discussion of the relation between musical meter and music's arousal of human emotions; and this thought sequence, I am convinced, is no coincidence. Descartes writes:

> As regards the various emotions which music can arouse by employing various meters, I will say that in general a slower pace arouses in us quieter feelings such as languor, sadness, fear, pride, etc. A faster pace arouses faster emotions, such as joy, etc.[24]

Why do I say that this passage from motion to emotion can hardly be accidental? Because, of course, the theoretical connection, not to mention the commonsensical one, between the two is so intimate. Further, to get to the real, underlying substance of the sentences just quoted, it is absolutely implied by Descartes' theory that if music moves my body by moving my vital spirits, it must (not just can) *ipso facto* move my emotions as well. For the vital spirits are like a stretched string: pluck it in the middle and it must vibrate at both ends. At one end of the plumbing system which the vital spirits inhabit is the muscle that twitches: at the other end is the psyche that emotes. Create a turbulence anywhere between by playing *Melancholy Baby*, and the waves can but propagate in both directions, causing swaying at one end, sentiment at the other.

But more: we now have a model which can also tell us why, as Descartes claims, "a slower pace arouses in us quieter feelings such as languor, sadness, fear, pride, etc.," while "A faster pace arouses faster emotions, such as joy, etc." Although Descartes does not quite give us the explanation—indeed, to be perfectly honest, he does not give it at all—it veritably thrusts itself out of the text. Surely, if music arouses emotions in us, as it rouses us to motion, by imparting motion to the animal spirits, "a slower pace arouses in us quieter feelings" because it is capable of imparting only a slow or moderate motion to the animal spirits which, in their turn, are capable by reason of their sluggish motion of raising only sluggish, quiet passions, whereas "A faster pace arouses faster emotions" because it has more energy to impart to the vital spirits which, in their turn, can impart more energetic emotions to the soul. It is strictly a matter of "mechanics": the greater the velocity I impart to the cue ball, the greater velocity it can impart, on impact, to the eight ball. With, of course, the added and seemingly insuperable difficulty that since the mind is for the Cartesian not a material object, it is impossible to explain how mechanical motion can have any effect at all on it or why, *a fortiori*, violent motion should have a violent effect.

This is, at any rate, the bare outline of the musical theory that was to be made out of *The Passions of the Soul*. And if I am correct in believing that at least an ur-version of the Cartesian psychology was already implicit in the *Compendium of Music*, then there seems strong reason to believe that the musical theory was implicitly there as well.

o 4 o   What the Cartesian psychology provided for the philosopher of music was another emotive "medium," besides human utterance, that could be plausibly thought of, as the "ineffable" emotions themselves could not, as an object of musical representation. Early on, it will be recalled, we found difficulty in interpreting the Platonic and Aristotelian texts on music just because we were troubled by the notion contained therein of music as "imitating" the emotions, moods, and states of mind. What could that possibly mean? We concluded, as, apparently, did Mei, Galilei, and the early composers of opera, that it could only mean imitation of human vocal utterance, in the expression of emotions. For why could sound not imitate sound?

The Cartesian psychology considerably broadened the musical canvas. For there is a limit, after all, to what the musical imagination can accomplish if it must restrict itself, in its representational or "imitative" capacity, to the human speaking voice alone: the limited musical interest of the *stile rappresentativo*, even in the hands of a Monteverdi, clearly illustrates that. But if the representational object is the great variety and intricacy of motion which one can imagine a subtle physical medium like the *esprits animaux* to have—plenty of room for imagination here, after all, as the *esprits animaux* are factitious objects anyway—the musical imagination has almost free rein in its representational task. (A unicorn, unlike a rhinoceros, can be blue!) And this new representational freedom is indeed reflected, in part, by the wide range of very florid instrumentally conceived melodies that are construed, in the eighteenth century, as emotive icons and depictions.

This is not to say, by the way, that the theory of music as, in part, a representation of passionate human utterance fell completely by the wayside. It continued to flourish, especially in non-musical circles, alongside of the newer Cartesian model. To cite but one example, from an author of whom we shall speak in detail in a little while, Francis Hutcheson writes, in the *Inquiry Concerning Beauty, Order, Harmony, Design* (1725): "The human voice is obviously varied by all the stronger passions: now when our ear discerns any resemblance between the air of a tune, whether sung or played upon an instrument, either in its time, or key, or any other circumstance, to the sound of the human voice in any passion, we shall be touched by it in a very sensible manner, and have melancholy, joy, gravity, thoughtfulness excited in us by a sort of *sympathy* or *contagion*."[25] As both a theoretical precept and a musical practice, the representation of the human voice "in a passion" managed to co-exist with the modern Cartesian precept and practice. But the latter was to be the major musical ideology of the late Baroque: the so-called "doctrine of the affections"—the *Affektenlehre* (to display forth its largely German lineage in the eighteenth century)—that was to provide Bach and Handel with their distinctive, instrumentally conceived emotive "vocabulary."

The *Affektenlehre*, in my view, took two divergent paths in the eighteenth century that I think it philosophically important to distinguish between, although they result in the same musical practice: the representation of the vital spirits.[26] (And it is the practice, after all, that is the important consideration in our discussion of the opera—which is the subject of this book.) The first of these paths led in the direction of what I shall call the "arousal" theory: the theory which, if I am correct in my reading of the *Compendium of Music*, was already prefigured there. The second—the path, I believe, of philosophical respectability—went in the direction of what I shall call the "representational" account. And although we already have at least a proto-version of the arousal theory before us, I think we must look at a more elaborate and mature version of the thing to do it justice. After that a long look will be given to the representational account developed (I shall argue) by Johann Mattheson, composer, performer, critic, theorist, and friend of Handel's youth: one of the most distinguished figures in Baroque music and, I believe, an unfairly neglected and misunderstood "philosopher" of the musical art.[27]

o 5 o The text that I want to examine, in connection with the arousal theory, is a somewhat *fin de siècle* one: Daniel Webb's *Observations on the Correspondence Between Poetry and Music* (1769). Britain was, both in musical theory and in musical taste, *fin de siècle* about a lot of things; and thus it is no real surprise that in 1769, with Haydn already in his young maturity, and the classical style not just beginning but beginning to flourish, the Baroque doctrine of the affections was still being propounded by the British as if it were at the cutting edge of musical speculation. It is, then, a bit of an anachronism to be talking about Webb's book here, with our argument barely on the threshold of the late Baroque and with Webb writing ten years after the death of Handel and nearly twenty after the death of Bach. But for a brief and in many ways very well-brought-off account of the *Affektenlehre* in its arousal version, the opening pages of Webb's little book cannot be surpassed; so in spite of its historical dislocation I feel no compunction about injecting it into the argument at this point. (After all, if the British were still listening mainly to Handel and Boyce, why shouldn't they still be reading the theory that went along with that kind of music?)

The premise with which Webb begins is, needless to say, that music arouses the emotions: "the influence of music over our passions is very generally felt and acknowledged. . . ." This, he thinks on very Cartesian grounds, is somewhat baffling and mysterious: "we find ourselves embarrassed in our attempts to reason on this subject, by the difficulty which attends the forming a clear idea of any natural relation between sound and sentiment."[28] I say the grounds are Cartesian because there is at least a vague suggestion here of the mind-body problem: sounds being perturbations of a *physical* medium, sentiments things of the *mind*, it would, for Descartes, of course be difficult to form "a clear idea of a natural [i.e. causal] relation between" them. But if the reader is skeptical of this rather flimsy evidence for the presence of Cartesianism, there is a much

more certain sign to come: our old friends the *esprits animaux*, suitably
Anglicized. To be sure, the name of Descartes does not occur anywhere
in Webb's text; and we are referred, rather, to Cicero when Webb's version of the vital spirits is introduced to us.[29] But by this time the Cartesian
psychology was common coin—in advanced circles, indeed, Confederate
money.

Webb's brief account of the animal spirits—and, particularly, his
description of their theoretical function—is not without sophistication. I
will quote it fully.

> As we have no direct nor immediate knowledge of the mechanical
> operations of the passions, we endeavour to form some conception of
> them from the manner in which we find ourselves affected by them:
> thus we say, that love softens, melts, insinuates; anger quickens, stim-
> ulates, inflames; pride expands, exalts; sorrow dejects, relaxes: of all
> which ideas we are to observe, that they are different modifications of
> motion, so applied, as best to correspond with our feelings of each par-
> ticular passion. From whence, as well as from their known and visible
> effects, there is just reason to presume, that the passions, according to
> their several natures, do produce certain proper and distinctive
> motions in the most refined and subtle parts of the human body. What
> these parts are, where placed or how fitted to receive and propagate
> these motions, are points which I shall not inquire into. It is sufficient
> for my purpose to have it admitted, that some such parts must exist in
> the human machine: however, as in our pursuits after knowledge, it is
> discouraging to be reminded every moment of our ignorance, I shall
> take advantage of the received opinion touching this matter, and assign
> the functions in question to the nerves and spirits. We are then to take
> it for granted, that the mind, under particular affections, excites cer-
> tain vibrations in the nerves, and impresses certain movements on the
> animal spirits.[30]

The "received opinion touching this matter" must, references to
Cicero notwithstanding, be the Cartesian *Passions of the Soul*. And Webb
expresses it with some insight into its theoretical niceties. The animal
spirits are not, of course, entities we know by observation: "we have no
direct nor immediate knowledge of the mechanical operations of the passions. . . ." What we do observe directly is how our passions *feel* to us, that
is to say, their subjective phenomenology, and how they manifest themselves in action, their behavioral phenomenology; and from these observations we can infer or postulate (if you prefer) the mechanism of their
operation: "we endeavour to form some conception of them from the
manner in which we find ourselves affected by them. . . ." We observe

that "love softens, melts, insinuates; anger quickens, stimulates, inflames; pride expands, exalts; sorrow dejects, relaxes . . . ," and all of these seem to be forms of subjective or behavioral activity: "they are different modifications of motion, so applied, as best to correspond with our feelings of each particular passion." And so we postulate or infer that underlying them is some mechanical motion or activity, namely, the motion or activity of the animal spirits: "from their known and visible effects, there is just reason to presume, that the passions, according to their several natures, do produce certain proper and distinctive motions in the most refined and subtle parts of the human body"—that is to say, "We are then to take it for granted, that the mind, under particular affections, excites certain vibrations in the nerves, and impresses certain movements on the animal spirits."

Emotions, then, are motions, and reduce themselves to mechanical motions. But music too it is common to think of as motion (although we know, or ought to know, that this is *literally* false). And so it appears plausible to Webb, as it had been for Descartes, to think that musical motion can set the animal spirits into the motions that are both the effects and the causes of the passions of the soul.

> I shall suppose, that it is in the nature of music to excite similar vibrations, to communicate similar movements to the vital spirits. For, if music owes its being to motion, and if passion cannot well be conceived to exist without it, we have a right to conclude, that the agreement of music with passion can have no other origin than a coincidence of movement.
>
> When, therefore, musical sounds produce in us the same sensations which accompany the impressions of any one particular passion, then the music is said to be in unison with that passion; and the mind must, from a similitude in their effects, have a lively feeling of an affinity in their operations.[31]

Webb, however, is not altogether sanguine as to how exactly "pure" music can delineate the specific emotions. It can get into the ballpark, as it were, but not to first base. For the kinds of motions in the animal spirits that the various kinds of musical motion can impart are, each one of them, although incompatible with some emotions, compatible nevertheless with more than one and (hence) cannot uniquely determine any one particular emotion. Webb writes:

> music cannot, of itself, specify any particular passion, since the movements of every class must be in accord with all the passions of that class.—For instance, the tender and melting tones, which may be

expressive of the passion of love, will be equally in unison with the collateral feelings of benevolence, friendship, and pity; and so on through the other classes.[32]

Nevertheless, closer tolerances can be achieved, Webb thought—and this was a common belief in his time—by the intrusion of a text.[33] (It should be borne in mind always, in talking about seventeenth- and eighteenth-century theories of musical expression, that vocal music reigned supreme, "pure" instrumental music merely a sideshow: so that it is usually safe to assume "music" means "music with a text," unless otherwise specified.) A text brings with it that specificity that music alone lacks. Music gets us into the ballpark; poetry gets us around the bases. "But, let eloquence co-operate with music, and specify the motive of each particular impression, while we feel an agreement in the sound and motion with the sentiment, song takes possession of the soul, and general impressions become specific indications of the manners and the passions."[34]

Webb's arousal theory inspires both an observation and a question. The observation, which I have made before in a more general context, is that theories linked to the Cartesian psychology broaden the canvas of musical expression beyond the representation merely of human utterance. This is made abundantly clear in Webb's account because of his recognition that the animal spirits, which musical motion is meant to model, themselves model both the subjective and behavioral manifestations of human emotions, including in the behavioral not merely utterance but gesture and action as well.

The question suggested is this. Granted that music arouses the emotions by aping the motions of the animal spirits, why should the arousal of the emotions be a desirable or pleasurable thing (which it is assumed that it is), especially as some of the emotions aroused are such inherently unpleasant, even painful ones as anger, fear, melancholy, and the like? There was indeed an answer to this question, imbedded in the general theory (or theories) of philosophical aesthetics that were generated in the first half of the eighteenth century; and I shall get to that in the closing sections of this chapter. First we must see the Cartesian theory of musical expression in its finest and fullest flower.

○ 6 ○   The Baroque *Affektenlehre*, as the term suggests, is a product of German thought. Its roots are in theories of musical rhetoric that took the ancient rhetorical figures as exemplars for analogous musical ones. With the advent of the Cartesian psychology this essentially literary theory of musical expression was transformed into a "scientific" account of how the musical figures could really be made to work. This is thoroughly in keeping with the spirit of rhetoric which is, after all, the art of influencing men's thoughts not by logical persuasion but by psychological—which is to say, "emotional"—manipulation. The rhetorical figures are supposed to "play upon the emotions": the *Affektenlehre*, allied with Descartes' *Passions of the Soul*, told the composer why and how—and how to do it.

The *Affektenlehre* was given its most complete and definitive treatment in Johann Mattheson's encyclopedic *Der vollkommene Capellmeister* (1739). And if the figure of Descartes is only a shadowy and lurking presence in Webb's *Observations*, Mattheson allows him to step out and take the bows he deserves: concerning "The doctrine of the temperaments and emotions . . . especially Descartes is to be read . . . ,"[35] Mattheson adjures his readers. And it becomes perfectly clear as Mattheson's account of musical expression unfolds that he has certainly followed his own advice. A more or less faithful version of the Cartesian psychology is in place, and Mattheson is insistent that the composer be conversant with it. "The experts on nature know how to describe the manner in which our affections actually and so to speak physically function, and it is of great advantage to a composer if he also is not inexperienced in this."[36] Clearly, Mattheson has bought into the new "scientific" account of the passions, offered by the "experts on nature," and he correctly surmises that such explanations are mechanistic, telling us "the manner in which our affections actually and so to speak *physically* function. . . ." How can such knowledge be useful to the composer?

Like Webb, Mattheson thought that the composer must pay close attention to the animal spirits: the mechanical causes of the emotions. They were, indeed, to be represented by music; and Mattheson offered far more detailed advice than Webb on exactly how this was to be done. This detailed advice was made possible for Mattheson by, in effect, an amplification of Descartes' theory: he went well beyond Descartes in describing the specific motions that characterize the *esprits animaux*. Although Descartes referred on numerous occasions to the "particular movement" of the spirits vis-à-vis this emotion or that, he never attempted, in any specific instance, to say what the exact nature of one of these "particular movements" was, or how and why the "particular movement" associated with one emotion differed from the "particular movement" associated with another. When he did go into detail, it was in regard to the particular pathways the animal spirits took, the particular organs they visited or emanated from, and (occasionally) the *quantity* of material involved in any particular emotive state. And were it not for the frequency with which Descartes referred to the "particular movements" of the animal spirits as if they were qualitatively different for the different emotions, one might be tempted to interpret him as offering an explanation merely in terms of quantity, pathways, and organs involved: a more elegantly reductionist view. Be that as it may, Mattheson, unlike Descartes, offered rather explicit qualitative descriptions of how the animal spirits are supposed to move in arousing some of the particular passions with which a composer would be most concerned. Whether these descriptions are his own, or derive from some other Cartesian writer, I do not know.[37]

The best way to see what Mattheson is up to is to quote in full his little "catalogue" of emotions (five in number), his descriptions of them and of their causes, and his advice to composers as to the proper way of realizing them in music.

> Since for example joy is an expansion of our soul, thus it follows reasonably and naturally that I could best express [ausdrücken] this affect by large and expanded intervals.
>
> Whereas if one knows that sadness is a contraction of these subtle parts of our body [i.e. the animal spirits], then it is easy to see that the small and smallest intervals are the most suitable for this passion.
>
> If we consider further that love is in fact essentially a diffusion of the spirits, then we will rightly conform to this in composing, and use similar relationships of sounds (intervallis n. diffusis & luxuriantibus).
>
> Hope is an elevation of the soul or spirits; but despair is a depression of this: all which are things which can very naturally be represented [vorstellen] with sound, especially when the other circumstances (tempo in particlar) contribute their part. And in this way one can form a sensitive concept of all the emotions and compose accordingly.
>
> Describing each and every affection here could easily be too tedious; only we must not let the most important ones remain unmentioned. Now here love quite reasonably is to be placed at the top of them all; as it occupies far greater space in musical pieces than the other passions.
>
> Now it is of primary importance here that a composer would carefully distinguish which degree, type or kind of love he takes up or chooses as his subject. For the aforementioned expansion of the spirits from which usually and principally this sentiment arises can happen in a variety of ways, and one cannot possibly treat all love in the same way.[38]

To this basic catalogue Mattheson adds, as the discussion progresses, an assortment of other emotions, such as jealousy, anger, ardor, vengeance, rage, fury, pity, fright, horror, despair—the whole emotional repertoire of opera, cantata, and oratorio in his day—with appropriate, although not so detailed, recipes for their musical embodiment.[39]

The first conclusion we can draw from all of this is that Mattheson thought of music as being structurally isomorphic, more or less, with the animal spirits in motion: more exactly, to make music appropriate to any given emotion, one was to make one's music as structurally isomorphic as possible with the particular motion of the vital spirits that causes that particular emotive state. Thus, since it is the expanding motion of the vital spirits that causes joy, music appropriate to joy must use large, "expanded" intervals—that is, leaps. Sadness, however, is a contraction of the *esprits animaux,* and so "contracted" music, music using the smallest intervals—that is, half-steps—is what is wanted here for a proper fit: an obvious attempt to explain on Cartesian grounds the prevalence of chromaticism, particular chromatic lines, in "sad" music. And so on for the other emotions, although the argument becomes more tenuous. (What is the musical structure that is analogous to *diffuse* animal spirits?)

It seems clear, then, that Mattheson is trying to show us something about the proper relationship between music and the animal spirits: where you want your music to be "sad" music (say), you must musically represent, by way of structural analogy, the "shape" of the animal spirits that causes sadness. The relationship of music to the vital spirits is artistic *representation.* And, indeed, Mattheson uses that very word in more than one place. Thus the elevation of the *esprits animaux,* which is the cause of hope, as well as the depression of them, the cause of despair, "are things which can very naturally be represented with sound. . . ." (the German word is *vorstellen*).

But what, one wants to know, is the relation of music not to the causes of the emotions—that is, the animal spirits—but to the emotions themselves? For Webb, and for Descartes, as we have seen, it was the relation of cause to effect, through the mediation of the animal spirits: music represented the animal spirits in order to arouse the emotions appropriate to them. Is that also the case with Mattheson? Notice, to start with, that if there is a relation of cause and effect between music and the emotions, this does not preclude there being other relations as well. To instance a relevant case in point, Locke thought our ideas of perception were caused by an external world; but he also thought (at least, he was read that way for a long time) that some of these ideas also represent the external world by way of resemblance. So if we should conclude that Mattheson believed music to be a stimulus to emotion, it does not follow that cause and effect is the only significant relationship between them.

To determine what relationship (or relationships) Mattheson thought might hold between music and emotion, perhaps we should ask ourselves first *why* he thought music should be made to represent the motions of the vital spirits at all. If the answer is: In order to raise the corresponding emotions in the listener—Descartes' and Webb's answer, at least in part— then we will have found one purported relation between music and emotion, and a common one at that: the causal one. Mattheson, so far as I can see, never gives that answer, except in a very different and most indirect way. Nowhere, in speaking of music representing the animal spirits that cause sadness or joy, hope or love, or whatever, does he say that this is in order to arouse joy or sadness, love or hope in the listener. What he does think the composer should be arousing in the listener is love of virtue and hatred of vice; for the composer is (or ought to be), on Mattheson's view, a moralist, who will

> present the virtues and vices in his music well, and arouse skillfully in the feelings of the listener a love for the former and disgust for the latter. For it is in the true nature of music that it is above all a teacher of propriety.[40]

And although Mattheson never says so in so many words, part of the reason why the composer does everything he does, including representing the animal spirits, is to the end of presenting to his audience a convincing moral lesson in music. But this still does not tell us what the relation is between music and emotion, where emotion is construed not as moral approval or disapproval but as such garden-variety emotions as love, sadness, hope, joy, and the like.

The answer is that music reflects just those things in the emotive life of a person reflected by the animal spirits. The animal spirits are supposed to be isomorphic with both the behavioral and the subjective phenomenologies of the human emotions. And as musical motion is supposed to be isomorphic with the motions of the animal spirits, it must, since isomorphism is a transitive relation, be isomorphic with these emotive phenomenologies; and although, strictly speaking, representation is *not* transitive (that is to say, if A is a representation of B and B is a representation of C, it does not follow that A is a representation of C), the intent here is such that I think we can correctly describe Mattheson as construing music not only to be isomorphic with the two phenomenologies of human emotion but to be representations of them as well.

Now, if one were at least a partial behaviorist with regard to the emotions—if, that is to say, one thought that the behavioral manifestation of emotion is really part of the emotion itself, rather than merely an expression or a symptom of it—one could interpret Mattheson's view as one which construed music to be the representation of emotions themselves, since it is a representation of how emotions "feel" and how they are behaviorally manifested: for, remember, the animal spirits are representations of both these things. Even, however, if one is not any kind of emotive behaviorist, one must grant that in representing the subjective phenomenology of emotions—their inner "feel"—music is *ipso facto* representing emotions (in something like the way Susanne Langer thought it did). In any case, the relation between the animal spirits and the emotions is such an intimate one in views like Mattheson's that language becomes almost indifferent to whether music represents emotions or the animal spirits which cause them. Certainly Mattheson himself is just as likely to say that music represents emotions as that it represents the animal spirits which cause them. And so, in describing his view, one might just as well let the middle term, the animal spirits, drop out, and say that Mattheson thought music represents emotions and their behavioral expressions, or, more simply (if you are an emotive behaviorist), that he thought it represents emotions pure and simple.

This is not to say that the waters are completely untroubled: there are passages sprinkled throughout *Der vollkommene Capellmeister* which at least seem to suggest an arousal account rather than a representational one. I have examined these passages elsewhere in some detail, and tried to show that very nearly all of them can be brought into conformity with a representational account, while the few that cannot are quite justifiably seen as minor lapses.[41] There is, however, no need to repeat this exercise here; for our argument only requires, as I have said before, that the representation of animal spirits or (what amounts pretty much to the same thing) emotions be a compositional task, not that it be an end in itself rather than a means to emotive arousal. And that much it surely was, whatever else the composer thought its purpose might be. So we can leave it at that.

Of course there remains, for either the representation or the arousal theory, a further question. For the arousal theory it is, as we have seen: Why is it a good thing—a sensible artistic goal—to arouse emotions with music? For the representation theory it is the analogous question: Why is it a good thing—a sensible artistic goal—to represent emotions musically? Philosophers in the early eighteenth century did indeed try to give answers. These answers are embedded, as are the theories of musical expression we have been examining, in a general aesthetic theory that attempted, in the light of the new philosophy, to give a comprehensive account of the arts. This attempt must be our next line of inquiry.

o 7 o   What began to take shape in the first quarter of the eighteenth century, and culminated in Kant's third *Critique*, was a bifurcated "philosophy of music" that tried to do justice philosophically—as the basically

Platonic and Aristotelian theories of Mei and Galilei had not—both to the demands of pure musical "syntax" and structure and to the demands of musical representation. There were at least desultory attempts, as well, to bind these two seemingly disparate musical goals together into one unified philosophical theory. But most important for us is the existence of the two theoretical branches themselves; for they had the effect of impelling operatic practice—as, again, the theories of Mei and Galilei had not—in two directions at once: toward satisfying both the demands of musical representation and those of the pure musical parameters. It was the filtering down of this bifurcated musical philosophy that, I shall argue, made the musical ground fertile for the growth of the first truly viable solution to the problem of opera.

The seeds of the bifurcated theory are already evident in Descartes' *Compendium of Music* where, it will be recalled, a two-part "definition" of music was given: "The basis of music is sound; its aim is to please and to arouse various emotions in us." Descartes did not, of course, think that the aim of music to arouse emotions was essentially incompatible with its aim to please, for he adds straightaway: "Melodies can be at the same time sad and enjoyable. . . ." Thus the juxtaposition of giving pleasure and arousing emotions must be taken as short for giving pleasure *by* arousing emotions and giving pleasure some other way; and it becomes apparent, soon, that the "other way" of giving pleasure is through some of what I have been calling the pure musical parameters of "syntax" and structure.

The art of "pure" musical pleasure is laid out in some of what Descartes calls the "Preliminaries":

1. All senses are capable of experiencing pleasure.

2. For this pleasure a proportional relation of some kind between the object and the sense itself must be present. . . .

3. The object must be such that it does not fall on the sense in too complicated or confused a fashion. . . .

4. An object is perceived more easily by the senses when the difference of the parts is smaller. . . .

7. Among the sense-objects the most agreeable to the soul is neither that which is perceived most easily nor that which is perceived with the greatest difficulty; it is that which does not quite gratify the natural desire by which the senses are carried to the objects, yet is not so complicated that it tires the senses.

8. Finally, it must be observed that variety is in all things most pleasing.[42]

The same kind of musical "dualism" can be found in one of Leibniz' intriguing passages on music, where he writes:

Everything that emits a sound contains a vibration or a transverse motion such as we see in strings; thus everything that emits sounds gives off invisible impulses. When these are not confused, but proceed together in order but with a certain variation, they are pleasing. . . . Drum beats, the beat and cadence of the dance, and other motions of this kind in measure and rule derive their pleasurableness from their order, for all order is an aid to the emotions. And a regular though invisible order is found also in the artfully created beats and motions of vibrating strings, pipes, bells, and, indeed, even of the air itself, which these bring into uniform motion. Through our hearing, this creates a sympathetic echo in us, to which our animal spirits respond. This is why music is so well adapted to move our minds, even though this main purpose is not usually sufficiently noticed or sought after.[43]

We observe straightaway that Leibniz connected the pleasure which music gives with a physical vibration of some kind: periodic motion in some part of the sounding instrument. These motions, he opines, are pleasurable when they are not "confused," that is, when they have some perceivable order but "a certain variation" as well: in other words, organized without being so orderly as to be boring; or (as it was soon to be put by another philosopher) having *uniformity amidst variety*.

How or why the perception of such vibrations can be pleasurable is not altogether clear. A quasi-physiological explanation was frequently forthcoming in the eighteenth century; there are hints of that in the passage under discussion, as we shall see in a moment. But another vagrant passage on music, in the "Principles of Nature and Grace," which has fascinated many and been quoted often, suggests something else with a tinge of Pythagorian number-mysticism. In this familiar formulation Leibniz has it that:

even the pleasures of sense are reducible to intellectual pleasures, known confusedly. Music charms us, although its beauty consists only in the agreement of numbers and in the counting, which we do not perceive but which the soul nevertheless contrives to carry out, of the beats or vibrations of sounding bodies which coincide at certain intervals.[44]

If we interpret the phrases "intellectual pleasures known confusedly" and "the counting . . . which the soul contrives to carry out" literally, with all of their mentalistic connotations in place, rather than as elaborate metaphors for some kind of purely physical process, the picture we get is of a musical homunculus busily at work in the deep structure of the mind, getting (and somehow conveying) the same pleasure from "counting" the musical "numbers" as I might get from consciously following some ordered pattern. That this suggestion poses more questions than it answers is palpably obvious. For present purposes it points up, in its clearest formulation, the "pure" side of the Leibnizian music aesthetics: the "pure," "intellectual" pleasure that is taken in "pure" musical form *per se.*

But there is another side to Leibniz' musical philosophy, as there is to Descartes': the emotional side. And so intertwined, in Leibniz, are the "pure" and the "emotional" parts that it is not clear whether they are, indeed, separate musical entities, whether the "emotional" is really an explanation of the "pure" or, vice versa, the "pure" an explanation of the "emotional." In any event, what is distinctive is the attempt to bring the two together under one philosophical umbrella.

For Leibniz, as we have seen, musical vibrations gain their pleasurableness from their order. To this precept he adds that it is because "all order is an aid to the emotions." Does this mean that the musical homunculus gets pleasure from counting the musical "numbers" because that raises emotions in him (or her, or it)? If so, we are pressed to ask *why* the raising of emotions, particularly nasty ones, is pleasurable. Further on, Leibniz trots out the Cartesian *esprits animaux* to, regrettably, muddy still more these already muddy waters. The perceiving of musical vibrations (however that is done) is now said to create "a sympathetic echo in us, to which our animal spirits respond"; and "This is why music is so well adapted to move our minds [emotionally, one presumes]. . . ." Is it, then, that orderly vibrations are the ones best suited for imparting to our animal spirits those particular motions responsible for the particular emotions? That certainly seems to be the most obvious interpretation, in which case we now have a purely mechanistic explanation for the propensity of music to arouse emotions, and we can dispense with our homunculus altogether in this regard. We still, of course, are stuck with the question of why the arousing of emotion, which Leibniz calls "this main purpose" of music, is at all worthwhile or desirable.

Perhaps there *is* a completely bifurcated theory here: pure musical pleasure raised by the counting of the mentalistic homunculus, emotions and their consequent (but still mysterious) pleasure raised by the mechanical operation of musical vibrations on the Cartesian *esprits animaux.* Or perhaps, as it sometimes seems, there is an attempt to join the separate threads, either under the concept of subliminal counting—in which case we have a thoroughgoing mentalistic explanation—or under the concept of emotive arousal through the animal spirits—in which case we would appear to have a completely mechanical one. Beyond suggesting these alternative interpretations, I do not think more can be done to unravel the Leibnizian "philosophy of music": the texts are just too fragmentary. Nor is it necessary for present purposes. What we can fairly conclude on the evidence is that in Leibniz, as in Descartes, we find a two-pronged theory of music—music as pure form, with a resultant pure musical pleasure; music as emotive arousal, with a resultant emotive pleasure—and, further, in a departure from Descartes, at least hints or suggestions of an all-embracing explanation for them both. But we must look to the first quarter of the eighteenth century to find any fulfillment of these as yet vague promises.

o 8 o   Three systematic works ushered in what can be thought of as the modern discipline of philosophical aesthetics: in France, Jean-Baptiste (L'Abbé) Du Bos' *Réflexions critiques sur la pöesie et sur la peinture* (1719); in England, Francis Hutcheson's *An Inquiry into the Original of our Ideas of Beauty and Virtue* (1725); in Germany, the work which gave us the word for the deed, Alexander Baumgarten's *Meditationes philosophicae de nonnullis ad poema pertinentibus* . . . (1735), where the term "aesthetic," in something like its current use, was coined.

It is now customary in philosophical circles to think of "aesthetics" in the sense of a self-contained philosophical discipline, on a par with the traditional "logic," "ethics," "epistemology," "metaphysics," as having come into being in the period we are speaking of;[45] and this in response to the gathering together of all of the arts into a "system" which required a philosophical accounting.[46] However useful this way of thinking has been in reviving our interest in early Enlightenment philosophy of art, I have come to believe it is literally false in its first claim, and exaggerated in its second. For certainly, to begin with, Plato and Aristotle gave "the arts" a philosophical examination, and a thorough one at that; nor did they treat "the arts" as in any way insignificant. Plato thought they were dangerous, Aristotle useful, but neither thought it possible to discuss them summarily. It is of course true that "modern aesthetics" gave "the arts" their "autonomy"—a special role of their own rather than one parasitic on morals or politics or knowledge. But that can be read as only a substantive claim *within* the discipline of aesthetics itself and not a claim *about* its origins, unless one simply has a theory to the effect that aesthetics cannot be an autonomous discipline unless it construes art as an autonomous practice—a claim for which I can see no justification whatever.

Secondly, I would suggest that the "modern system of the arts" is not so much an invention of the eighteenth century as a recapturing of something like the classical ideal, after a long fragmentation process in which music in particular came to be considered a thing apart. Music is the pivot on which the "modern system" turns; for with regard to it alone, I think, the "modern system" represents a significant departure from the ancient. When Plato and Aristotle talked about "the arts," they did indeed talk about what translators render into English as "music." But it is clear that when we think of music we think of something quite distinct from any of the other arts, even when it is the setting of a text (we can have "songs without words," after all); whereas music and text were an inseparable whole in classical antiquity (when Socrates' voice told him, on the threshold of death, to study "music," Socrates responded by writing poetry, not composing symphonies). Indeed, if I were to define the "modern system of the arts," I would say it was the system that first gathered into it music as a species of the genus rather than as an aspect of a species. (This, by the way, did not happen until well into the eighteenth century.)

What we can say with confidence, however, is that there was in the first quarter of the eighteenth century, an unparalleled heightening of theoretical interest in the arts that can be described as basically philosophical, and that it endured, indeed accelerated, as the Enlightenment wore on. We can say, too, that it is to this work that, at least in the Anglo-American tradition, philosophers of art turn for their philosophical beginnings, much as epistemologists turn to Descartes or to Locke, to Hume or to Berkeley for their problems. And in this respect it is truly the origin of the discipline.

The German tradition—principally Leibniz, in the early period—will not concern us at all at this point, and the French only peripherally. Rather, I shall turn to the British, and to what I take to be the first systematic and self-contained "philosophy of art," Francis Hutcheson's *Inquiry Concerning Beauty, Order, Harmony, Design*—the first of the two treatises that make up his *Inquiry into the Original of our Ideas of Beauty and Virtue*. It will serve well enough as an example of the philosophical background onto which I will later project the Handelian *opera seria*.

Following Locke's theory of knowledge, at least as it was commonly construed at that time, Hutcheson saw the problem of aesthetics as the problem (obvious from his title) of tracking down the "origin" of our idea of beauty (and any other idea that might be construed as, in Addison's phraseology, one of the "pleasures of the imagination"). On the traditional interpretation of Locke, this left Hutcheson with three possible choices as real options. The idea of beauty might be the simple idea of what Locke had called a "primary quality," like shape or solidity. In that case, the idea would have been given in perception by a quality that somehow "resembled" or was "like" the idea which it raised, the idea being construed as a kind of "representation" or "picture" of the quality. If that were so, then the word "beauty" (or "beautiful") would be the name of that quality in the external world that caused the idea of beauty to arise. Or the idea of beauty might be the simple idea of a "secondary quality," like redness or heat. If that were so, then the idea would have been raised not by some special quality of "beauty" in the external world which the idea of beauty resembled, but by a congeries of primary qualities that merely had the "power" to raise that idea, the idea no more resembling any quality in the external world than (the Lockean thought) did the ideas of colors, tastes, or hot and cold. The word "beauty" (or "beautiful"), in that eventuality, would be not the name of any external quality in the world, but merely a name for an idea. Finally, the idea of beauty might be a creation of the mind itself, a complex idea constructed out of simple ideas of primary and secondary qualities, like the idea of a nation, or an army, God, or the Devil. This, apparently, is the kind of thing that Locke himself took the idea of beauty to be.

Hutcheson chose something like the second option, beauty as the idea of a secondary quality, as is immediately evident in his "definition" of the word. "Let it be observed that in the following papers the word *beauty* is taken for *the idea raised in us*, and a *sense* of beauty for *our power of receiving this idea*." He adds immediately, apropos of musical beauty: "*Harmony* also denotes *our pleasant ideas arising from composition of sounds*, and a *good ear* [i.e. the sense of musical beauty] (as it is generally taken) a *power of perceiving this pleasure*."[47]

I say that Hutcheson chose *something like* the idea of a secondary quality for the idea of beauty because there is one very crucial difference: no one in Locke's day would have claimed that we could possibly know what exactly it is in the micro-structure of matter that produced in us (say) the sensation of redness, whereas Hutcheson did claim to know—by induction, one presumes—what gross properties in matter were the ones that caused the idea of beauty: "The figures that excite in us the ideas of beauty seem to be those in which there is *uniformity amidst variety*."[48] This implied another crucial disanalogy between the idea of beauty and the ideas of secondary qualities: the claim that something is "beautiful" was defensible in a way that the claim that something is "red" (say) was not. For if one knew that *uniformity amidst variety* was *the* cause of the idea of beauty, then one could check up on someone who said something was beautiful—i.e. claimed to have the idea of beauty—by seeing if that thing did indeed have *uniformity amidst variety*, whereas one could not check up to see if something that was said to be "red" had what it was that causes sensations of redness, since the cause was unknown. This is not to say that one could be judged "incorrect" for having the idea of beauty in the absence of *uniformity amidst variety*, only that one was "abnormal"—for since "the word *beauty* is taken for the *idea raised in us*," and the relation between that idea and its cause, *uniformity amidst variety*, is a contingent one, it is at least logically possible for the idea to exist in the absence of the quality. Of course judgments about colors and other secondary qualities were also defensible, on the Lockean view, but in a weaker sense, since the appeal could only be to such things as normal conditions of perception and normal perceivers, not to the known causal properties of objects. So we get the somewhat paradoxical result that, for Hutcheson, judgments of beauty are more "objective" than judgments of secondary qualities, which is why, in one place, he seems to put the "pleasures of the imagination" somewhere *between* the ideas of primary and the ideas of secondary qualities, averring that "The ideas of beauty and harmony . . . may have a nearer resemblance to objects than these sensations [i.e. the ideas of secondary qualities], which seem not so much any pictures of objects as modifications of the perceiving mind. . . ."[49]

The beauty that is caused by the purely sensual patterns of *uniformity amidst variety* Hutcheson called "original" or "absolute" beauty, to distinguish it from the beauty of representations, which he called "comparative" or "relative": that is, the representation well made, accurate, beautifully rendered, which would, of course, account for a great deal of what is beautiful in works of art. "Comparative or relative beauty is that which we perceive in objects commonly considered as *imitations* or *resemblances* of something else."[50]

This division of beauties into pure and dependent caused a good deal of trouble not only to Hutcheson but to later Enlightenment thinkers as well, including (notoriously) Kant. Hutcheson must have been aware of the danger here that the theory would fall into two irreconcilable parts; for he did try to knit them together into a formalist whole, under the umbrella of *uniformity amidst variety*, in effect seeing representation merely as another instance of that causal property. Thus he writes of relative or comparative beauty, "that which is apprehended in any object commonly considered as an *imitation* of some original": "this beauty is founded on a conformity, or a kind of unity between the original and the copy."[51] The problem is that the idea of "original" or "absolute" beauty is caused non-epistemically, that is to say, without our necessarily knowing or believing that the object possesses *uniformity amidst variety*, much in the way the micro-structure of matter, without our knowing what it is, causes us to have the sensation of redness, whereas I must know that—perceive that—X is a representation of Y for the idea of "comparative" or "relative" beauty to be raised in me: in other words, I must *perceive that* this kind of "unity" is present. How these two ways of construing aesthetic perception can be brought into conformity with one another I do not comprehend, and Hutcheson does not explain.

For Hutcheson, as for Kant, music provides a ready example in art of the purely formal aesthetic properties.

> Under *original beauty* we may include *harmony*, or *beauty of sound*, if that expression can be allowed, because harmony is not usually conceived as an imitation of anything else. Harmony often raises pleasure in those who know not what is the occasion of it; and yet the foundation of this pleasure is known to be a sort of uniformity.[52]

There is, of course, nothing in Hutcheson's theory to preclude a representational part; and he does, after all, say merely that "harmony [for which read *music*] is not *usually* conceived as an imitation of anything else"—not that it never is, which would have been apparent to Hutcheson if he had had even a passing acquaintance with the music of his time, abounding as it did in representations of various kinds. But he says nothing at all about it, and, like many other philosophers of his time, including Kant, construes the non-formal part of music to consist in the arousal (not the representation) of emotional states.

The doctrine of the affections hangs on to most philosophical accounts of music like an extraneous barnacle; and this is as true of Kant at the end of the century as it is of Hutcheson at the beginning. The reason, I suspect, is a combination of things: lack of interest and technical knowledge on the part of philosophers; a generally low place accorded to music in the pantheon; the apparent willingness, therefore, to accept the music theorists' word for it, without spending much time in trying to figure out how musical arousal might (or might not) jibe with the rest of the philosophical theory being touted. There is more of an effort in this regard (as in all regards) in Kant than in Hutcheson; in the latter, it takes up no more than a passing aside. I have quoted part of it previously. I will quote it now in full.

> There is also another charm in music [besides, that is, its purely formal "charm"] to various persons, which is distinct from harmony, and is occasioned by its raising of agreeable passions. The human voice is obviously varied by all the stronger passions: now when our ear discerns any resemblance between the air of a tune, whether sung or played upon an instrument, either in its time, or key, or any other circumstance, to the sound of the human voice in any passion, we shall be touched by it in a very sensible manner, and have melancholy, joy,

gravity, thoughtfulness excited in us by a sort of *sympathy* or contagion. The same connection is observable between the very air of a tune and the words expressing any passion which we have heard it fitted to, so that they shall both recur to us together, though but one of them affects our senses.[53]

To be noted, at the outset, is Hutcheson's claim that only "agreeable passions" are raised by music or, at least, that only "its raising of agreeable passions" has to do with this particular "charm in music." And the reason for this seems clear: it anticipates the question of why the raising of disagreeable passions should be musically pleasurable by simply restricting music to pleasurable ones. However, this seems to be contradicted very soon afterwards by the list of musical emotions Hutcheson gives, which includes the distinctly unpleasant emotion of "melancholy" as well as the not very much more enjoyable "gravity." Charles Avison, for perhaps related reasons, restricted music to the arousal of what he called the "*sociable and happy passions*."[54] But he too seems forced to allow some pretty doubtful cases; and he provides a hint at what reply Hutcheson might have given to the charge that melancholy is far from an "agreeable" passion when he writes that "by the musician's art we are by turns elated with joy, or sunk in *pleasing sorrow*, rouzed to courage, or quelled by *grateful terrors*, melted with pity, or tenderness, and love, or transported to the regions of bliss, in an extacy of divine praise."[55] The suggestion is, of course, that apparently unpleasant emotions like sorrow and terror have grateful and pleasing manifestations or varieties as well.

Whether true sorrow can be pleasing or true terror grateful remains very doubtful, however; and, in any case, the natural question would be *How?*, since if these emotions *can* be enjoyed it is not clear that they can, and some justification is certainly required. In fact, there was a stock answer to this question throughout the eighteenth century; and if it did not originate with Du Bos, his version of it was widely disseminated and would have been available to Hutcheson.

○ 9 ○ Du Bos begins this account with the following reflections, which both state a fact and at the same time pose the relevant question for the philosopher of art:

> That a sensible pleasure arises from poems and pictures, is a truth we are convinced of by daily experience; and yet 'tis a difficult matter to explain the nature of this pleasure, which bears so great a resemblance with affliction, and whose symptoms are sometimes as affecting, as those of the deepest sorrow. The arts of poetry and painting are

never more applauded, than when they are most successful in moving us to pity.[56]

The underlying assumption, which begins to emerge at the end of this passage, is that the "sensible pleasure" which "arises from poems and pictures" is a form of, or the result of, the passions being raised. The problem, for the philosopher of art, is how this can be so, since some of the passions raised are "sometimes as affecting, as those of the deepest sorrow" and bear "so great a resemblance with affliction": in short, are, at times, it would seem, distinctly unpleasant, at least were they to be experienced in the raw.

Du Bos' answer is based on the psychological premise that the mind requires exercise, as it were, to relieve it from the unpleasant state of inactivity.

> The soul hath its wants no less than the body; and one of the greatest wants of man is to have his mind incessantly occupied. The heaviness which quickly attends the inactivity of the mind, is a situation so very disagreeable to a man, that he frequently chuses to expose himself to the most painful exercises, rather than be troubled with it.[57]

The answer that starts to take shape, then, is essentially this: "unpleasant" emotions are pleasant at least to the extent that they are a release from a state even more unpleasant, that of mental ennui. What would not, in other words, be sought after in itself, or under one set of conditions, might well be sought after and on that account be "pleasant" under another set which made it at least a release from something worse: the lesser, that is, of two evils.

Were this all there was to say, the answer would hardly be convincing. For although we may take risks, as Du Bos points out, and court danger to relieve lives of boredom, we do not after all (except the masochists among us) *cultivate* pain; we may climb Everest, knowing full well the undesirable consequences that might eventuate, to escape from a dull spouse or a tedious job—but we do not *seek* the undesirable consequences; rather, we seek to avoid them (that is why we take ropes). So it still is not clear why, if we need exercise that passions provide, we do not seek the ones without the pain and shun the ones of darker hue. Furthermore, there does seem to be something implausible about equating the terror aroused when a homicidal maniac points a loaded pistol at you and the "terror" aroused by reading a ghost story.

To these anticipated objections Du Bos provides a response by amplifying his "exercise" theory with what one might call the "weakened virus" effect. There is, of course, an obvious difference, on Du Bos' view, between watching an old man have his eyes put out and seeing it in a play: the former is a real event of blinding, whereas the latter is an "imitation" of that event (although, of course, a real event of "imitation"). And so, Du Bos argues, the emotion aroused in the latter must be a weakened form of the emotion, with fewer and weaker deleterious effects. This weakened form of the emotion is sometimes described in just those terms, and sometimes as an "imitation" of the passion rather than the passion itself. The following passage is typical:

> those imaginary passions which poetry and painting raise artificially within us, by means of their imitations, satisfy that natural want we have of being employed.
>
> Painters and poets raise those artificial passions within us, by presenting objects capable of exciting real passions. As the impression made by those imitations is of the same nature with that which the object imitated by the painter or poet would have made; and as the impression of the imitation differs from that of the object imitated only in its being of inferior force, it ought therefore to raise in our souls a passion resembling that which the object imitated would have excited. In other terms, the copy of the object ought to stir up within us a copy of the passion which the object itself would have excited.[58]

But, Du Bos argues, these weakened or imitation passions are more shallow than the real thing, because the impression of an imitation upon the senses and the mind cannot be as strong as the impression of the original; and, hence:

> The pleasure we feel in contemplating the imitations made by painters and poets, of objects which would have raised in us passions attended with real pain, is a pleasure free from all impurity of mixture. It is never attended with those disagreeable consequences, which arise from the serious emotions caused by the object itself.[59]

Music, too, Du Bos (unlike Hutcheson) construes as a *wholly* imitative art. It differs from painting and poetry only in being dependent rather than autonomous: that is to say, Du Bos thought of music only as an aid to poetry, and even instrumental "symphonies" were not envisioned as possible works of art in their own right but merely as parts of operas, where they served either to express the appropriate emotion or to imitate some natural sound supposed to occur in the drama, as "the symphony which imitates a tempest in the opera of Alcione by Monsieur Marais."[60] Thus, Du Bos writes of vocal music, "as the painter imitates the strokes and colours of nature in like manner the musician imitates the tones, accents, sighs, and inflexions of the voice; and in short all those sounds, by which nature herself expresses her sentiments and passions."[61] And of music for instruments: "tho' this kind of music be merely instrumental, yet it contains a true imitation of nature"; that is to say, "The truth of the imitation in symphonies consists in their resemblance with the sounds they are intended to imitate."[62]

Du Bos leaves no doubt that he thinks vocal music, though imitative of passionate utterance, raises the emotion and pleases thereby.

> The natural signs of the passions, which music collects and employs with art, in order to increase the energy of the words she sets, ought to render them more capable of moving us, because these natural signs have a surprizing power over us. This they have from nature herself. . . . By this means the pleasure of the ear is communicated to the heart.[63]

What the effect of instrumental music on the passions is Du Bos does not state explicitly. But there seems reason to believe that, since it imitates natural objects for Du Bos, it must, on his view, raise those passions that the objects imitated would raise, just as in the cases of poetry, painting, and vocal music. Further, one must presume, although (again) Du Bos does not make it explicit, that, like painting and poetry, music raises those counterfeit, weakened emotions, benign enough to be pleasing exercise even in their dark and painful incarnations.

I dare say this is just about as good an explanation for how painful emotions can be pleasant when aroused by art as any other that has been given—which is certainly damning with faint praise. It is never altogether clear whether Du Bos thought that the "emotions" raised by art are the real thing, and imitations only in the sense of being raised by imitations of the world, or whether he literally meant that they were "imitations" of emotions, in which case they would not *really* be emotions, since it is a matter of logic that an imitation of an *x* cannot be an *x*. (An imitation pearl, sad to say, is not a pearl.) But in either case his account runs into serious trouble.

If the emotions raised by art were really emotions, then, even though they might be very weak ones, they would still have to be painful, if their non-art-produced counterparts were. For I take it that it is an essential property of sadness that it be at least minimally unpleasant, as it is an essential property of joy that it be minimally pleasant. Pleasant pain or painful joy are not merely oxymorons; they are (if literal) logical howlers. But if that is the case, then Du Bos' notion of emotion as mental "exercise" fails to explain why we should seek out art works which arouse unpleasant or painful emotions. If I need mental exercise, why should I choose *King Lear* if *School for Scandal* is available? If Du Bos is correct in believing mental ennui to be more unpleasant than the exercise provided by painful emotions "weakened" by art, then I would have reason to choose art works productive of painful emotions if those were the only ones available. Except on desert islands, however, I have a choice; and it is difficult to understand why I should choose a painful cure when a wholly painless or even pleasurable one would do just as well. I choose a painless dentist every time.

If, on the other hand, the emotions raised by art are not really emotions at all but "imitations" of them,[64] either there is no problem at all, or the same problem arises that I have alluded to above. To begin with, there can be no problem of how painful *emotions* can be pleasurable, if it is not really emotions we are talking about, which would indeed be the case if they were "imitations." So our problem would have to be restated as how an imitation of a painful emotion can be pleasurable. But since imitations do not possess all of the properties of the things they imitate, there would be no problem here if imitations of painful emotions were not themselves painful (which seems entirely possible: an "imitation" of a pig need not be dirty). And if they were painful, then we would still not have an explanation of why we should seek them. For that the pain of "imitations" of sadness might be less than the pain of the real things, as we have seen, provides no reason for us to choose a work of art which aroused sadness, as we could perfectly well choose one that aroused "imitations" of non-painful or pleasurable emotions. That in certain circumstances painful emotions or imitations of painful emotions might be the lesser of two evils, and in *that* sense "pleasurable," is no decent account of how artistic emotions of the painful sort can be pleasurable, since those circumstances hardly ever seem to obtain. And that is really what Du Bos' explanation comes down to. It can explain why I should read *King Lear* rather than do nothing; but as most of us have other alternatives, it provides us no insight into the still perplexing existence of the art of the unpleasant, unless you can accept the even more perplexing notion of painless "imitation" emotions. And the choice between "pleasing pain" and "imitation emotion" hardly seems an easy one to make—both concepts are equally unattractive because just about equally unintelligible.

o 10 o   Whether Hutcheson would have bought into this explanation for the pleasure of passion, with all of its vagaries, one cannot say, nor need one for present purposes. What is important to see here, as in the more sketchy accounts of Descartes and Leibniz, is the bifurcation of musical theory into formal and emotive parts, and the cashing in of the emotive part, compositionally, in representational coin: in Hutcheson's rather backward theory, the representation of the passionate human voice.

It is important not to be fooled by the brevity of Hutcheson's (and other Enlightenment philosophers') remarks on music into underestimating their importance in the history of musical thought. Considering the peripheral position music held, from the beginning of the seventeenth century to the end of the eighteenth, in an "educated" man's humanistic studies, it would be too much to expect a philosopher of Hutcheson's (or Kant's) stripe to have had any real technical or practical knowledge of the art. (It is frequently too much to expect even now.) Nevertheless, in his account of original beauty, with its "formal" property of *uniformity amidst variety* as the central idea, Hutcheson provides a potentially powerful theoretical foundation for the "pure" musical parameters, and at least perceives that potential clearly enough to provide some account of the "yet to be" *art* of music. Indeed, what he says is not half so important as that he says it, and how. For Leibniz and Descartes, music, although of theoretical interest, *qua* art form is a thing deserving only casual mention. For Hutcheson, however, both in its formal and emotive parts music *qua* art form is an element in the system; and if the spaces are not filled in, at least the connections are made.

Thus Hutcheson, later Kant, with many others in between, provided a philosophical account of music pulling in two separate directions. There was, on the one hand, the first modern attempt at a philosophical grounding for the purely formal elements in music; and whether it was cause, or effect, or a little bit of both, it is no accident, as I suggested early on, that this was also the century in which pure instrumental music moved from sideshow to center ring. Nevertheless, while the formalist music aesthetics was in the making, the emotive "content" was never forgotten. And although, at least in philosophical circles, it hung on in the far from plausible form of the "arousal" theory, arousal was seen as being accomplished through musical representation—either, as in Hutcheson's case, the representation of the human voice in passionate speech, or, in the case of others, the representation of the Cartesian *esprits animaux*, gesture, and even the very emotions themselves.

What filtered down to the composers of opera, then—I do not suggest that they were readers of philosophy—was a philosophically mixed message: make beautiful patterns that follow their own laws of musical "syntax" and structure; represent in music the emotive lives of human beings. The composers of early opera received only a single order of the day from philosophy: represent the passionate utterances of men and women. The rest was musical practice, without philosophical sanction. The composers of *opera seria*, in the late Baroque, got the full philosophical treatment. The connections between philosophy and music may have been tenuous and remote in the eighteenth century. Nevertheless, I am convinced that the new philosophical message, in concert with the new Cartesian psychology, was of profound importance in the formulation of what, as I shall try to show in the following chapter, was a thoroughly successful solution to "the problem of opera." It is not the solution modern audiences seem to prefer. But when a problem has more than one solution, it is sometimes merely a matter of taste which solution one favors. And this is true in physics and mathematics as well as in music—which, I hope, will suggest to the initially skeptical reader that in regard to Handelian opera it is possible, useful, and important to distinguish between what one likes and what, on something like objective grounds, can be shown to be aesthetically successful and even "correct."

CHAPTER VII

The irrational entertainment as rational solution

o 1 o It has been called "one of the greater ironies of musical history that opera, born in northern Italy during the closing years of the six-teenth century partly as the result of antiquarian interest in the musical dramas of ancient Greece, evolved so rapidly into a theatrical spectacular so different from the ideals it had set out to emulate." The high purpose of Mei, Galilei, and the Florentine Camerata seems to have been entirely forgotten, in practice at least, if not in principle. "In place of a serious combination of poetry and music intended for the moving of souls and the improvement of human society, there quickly emerged an entertain-ment featuring virtuoso display and fantastic scenic effects for an audi-ence primarily concerned with the externals of performance."[1]

The so-called "reform" of the Italian opera libretto by Apostolo Zeno and Pietro Metastasio in the late seventeenth and early eighteenth cen-turies both simplified and formalized these operatic spectacles, a process of refinement that resulted in a remarkably stable and long-lived "solu-tion" to the problem of opera that we know as the *opera seria*. But what-ever improvements in operatic taste this much-abused musical genre may have effected, it has never been able, after its own time, to withstand critical scrutiny or elicit the enthusiasm of a modern audience. The ver-dict of Edward J. Dent pretty much sums up the judgment of posterity: in the period of which I speak, "The Italian opera became just a concert in costume."[2]

But one man's charge is another man's defense: interestingly enough, the damning judgment that *opera seria* is merely a concert in costume originated with, or at least can be traced back to, Charles Burney, who wrote in *answer* to the criticism-cum-ridicule of Addison and Steele: "let it be remembered by the lovers of Music, that an opera is the *completest concert* to which they can go; with this advantage over those in still life, that to the most perfect singing, and effects of a powerful and well-dis-ciplined band, are frequently added excellent acting, splendid scenes and decorations, with such dancing as a playhouse, from its inferior prices, is seldom able to furnish."[3]

Were this the best defense that could be put up for *opera seria*, it would hardly merit serious attention. Surely we have a right to ask more of opera than that it be just a concert more pleasing to the eye than the usual run of such things. Opera is drama in musical form. If *opera seria* is not that, however defensible it may be as music, it is not defensible as opera and probably, on that account, is not defensible as art.

Andrew Porter has contrasted this approach to Handel's *opera seria* (unfavorably) with ". . . Winton Dean's declarations that Handel 'was not only a great composer; he was a dramatic genius of the first order' and that 'the music of no other dramatic composer comes closer to Mozart in its detached but penetrating insight into human nature.' "[4] But Porter has, I think, done Burney a considerable disservice by quoting him out of context. What he said, more fully, is this:

> An opera, at the worst, is still better than a concert merely for the ear, or a pantomime entertainment for the eye. Supposing the articulation to be wholly unintelligible, we [still] have an excellent union of melody and harmony, vocal as well as instrumental, for the ear. . . .
>
> No one will dispute that understanding Italian would render our entertainment at an opera more rational and more complete: but without that advantage, let it be remembered by the lovers of Music, that an opera is the *completest concert* to which they can go; with this advantage over those in still life, that to the most perfect singing, and effects of a powerful and well-disciplined band, are frequently added excellent acting, splendid scenes and decorations, with such dancing as a playhouse, from its inferior prices, is seldom able to furnish.

The defense, then, is not of *opera seria*—least of all Handel's—but *opera seria* "at the worst": that is to say, *opera seria* under the worst possible conditions. The issue here is the unintelligibility of Italian words to an English audience. What Burney is saying is that even when we cannot understand the words or have not perused them beforehand—when, in other words, we are in the worst possible position to really appreciate the *opera seria*—we can still gain considerable enjoyment from it because it is at least, even at worst, the completest concert. Clearly, he thinks that *at most* it is something more than that; and since the issue is that of whether the text is understood, it is equally clear that Burney thought the understanding of the text a *sine qua non* for *opera seria* at its best.[5] What more is it, then, than the completest concert when the words as well as the music are taken in? I venture to suppose that, for Burney, just as for Dean and Porter, it is *musical drama*, especially when the composer is Handel. Why else emphasize the understanding of the text as the pivot on which the experience of the thing turns from worst to best? That the *opera seria* was both charged with being and defended as being a "concert with costumes" in Burney's day, as in ours, I have no doubts. But Burney, I am sure, thought better of it than that; and we should think better of Burney than to put either the defense or the charge in his mouth.

○ 2 ○ Burney defended *opera seria* "at the worst" as "still better than a concert merely for the ear." As the issue which elicited this defense was principally the intelligibility of the words, we are at a loss to say what else exactly Burney may have meant by *opera seria* at the best besides *opera seria* in which the words are properly understood, either through a thorough understanding of the language and a faultless declamation or through a prior perusal of the "book." But we can certainly make a fair surmise that by *opera seria* at the best Burney meant *opera seria* optimally performed in every respect—singing, acting, staging, scenery, orchestral accompaniment—and, needless to say, well composed. Nor can there be any doubt that in the latter department he ranked Handel as the highest point yet attained.

Handel, of course, was not the "typical" composer of *opera seria*, nor were his operas "typical" examples of the genre. A German trained in the organ loft until the age of eighteen, who spent by far the largest part of his life and creative energy writing Italian operas for English audiences, he could hardly be thought to the manner born. Is it plausible, then, to offer a "defense" of the *opera seria*—which, indeed, I propose to do here—with this atypical anomaly as my principal witness?

Surely Handel was the greatest composer ever to make *opera seria* a central focus of creative attention. Both Haydn and Mozart have an equal if not greater claim to compositional greatness, and both, to be sure, did compose in the genre. But neither *seria* nor *buffa* was, taken all in all, at Haydn's vital center; and certainly *buffa*, and not *seria*, was where Mozart directed his greatest energies as a composer for the stage.

In any case, to be the greatest composer ever to set *opera seria* or make the setting of it nearly a life's work is not enough to assure that Handel's operas are the best of the lot. Schubert was the greatest composer to put his hand to early Romantic opera; yet no one would rank his operas with *Freischütz*, any more than one would rank Weber, as a composer, an equal of the man who wrote the C Major Quintet. Furthermore, the awesome magnificence of Mozart's *Idomeneo* gives it, I would think, the title of "greatest" in the *opera seria* department, Handel's claim notwithstanding. And present scholarship may yet lift our evaluation and appreciation of Haydn's *opere serie*—at least the best of them—if not to the level of Mozart's masterpiece (for who can stand comparison to that?), then at least to the level of Handel's best.

Nevertheless, such considerations do not, I think, drive us from the position that if at least the best of Handel's operatic corpus cannot be defended as works of art, the genre of *opera seria* itself is without any adequate defense, in spite of the isolated case of *Idomeneo* and (perhaps) one or two of Haydn's operas. For when *opera seria* was a going concern, Haydn was surely as yet not up to the mark. Nor are Mozart's early ventures in the field, marvelous though they may be as intellectual phenomena, anything but juvenilia. And when Haydn and Mozart were in their maturity, *opera seria* was certainly on the wane. Even *Idomeneo* is slightly *fin de siècle* around the edges; and *Tito* is *fin de siècle* in fact as well as in spirit.

Handel, then, represents, when all is said and done, the highest achievement of the *opera seria*. Not the typical or paradigm; but genius, after all, never produces that. And were we to damn *opera seria* as a nonsolution to the problem of opera by confining our attention only to such typical paradigmatic cases as Caldara, or even Alessandro Scarlatti, that would be tantamount to damning *opera buffa* by confining ourselves to such paradigms of the genre as the operas of Paisiello while ignoring the composer of *Figaro*, another of those foreign poachers on Italian turf. Anomalous or not, it is Handel's *opere serie* that can bear critical scrutiny today if any can at all. They are the best; and if they are not a solution to the problem of opera, no other examples can possibly be.

o 3 o   Criticism and outright rejection of the *opera seria* are not merely the products of succeeding generations, rebelling, as generations do, against the outmoded artistic conventions of their recent or distant past. They are that too; but *opera seria* was detested in its own time by many, as all opera has been in all times. "While *opera seria* seems ridiculously stilted and stereotyped to many twentieth-century critics, we should remember that there were many to whom it seemed patently absurd during the 1720s and 1730s."[6] I venture to say that no criticism of the genre known to us was unknown to the contemporaries of Handel; and, indeed, the devastating lampoon of opera with which Tolstoy opens his essay on aesthetics, *What is Art?*, could just as well have been written by Benedetto Marcello in 1720, without benefit of a time machine to Bayreuth. It is not merely of historical interest, then, to examine eighteenth-century criticism of *opera seria*; it is of the essence that we answer it, if our defense of *opera seria* is to stand. The time has come, therefore, to return to my starting-point.

"When Dr. Johnson characterized the opera as an 'irrational entertainment,' he unknowingly tapped a vein of musical thought that ran through the entire history of the art-form to that date, and continued beyond." What he knowingly did was to characterize the opera of his own time and place, which was for the most part (and the best part) Handel's.

The "irrational" tag is frequently alluded to. More fully, what Johnson said, in the "Life of [John] Hughs," is this: "In 1703 his *Ode on Musick* was performed at Stationers' Hall; and he wrote afterwards six cantatas, which were set to music by the greatest masters of that time, and seem intended to oppose or exclude the Italian opera, an exotick and irrational entertainment, which has been always combated and always has prevailed."[7] Johnson was not, needless to say, a careless user of the language. It behooves us, therefore, to take his distinction between "exotick" and "irrational" as a real one, not merely a rhetorical flourish, and see where it leads.

It seems to me that if one cuts eighteenth-century criticism of the *opera seria* with the razor of Johnson's distinction, what falls on the side of the exotic is the tasteless but inessential customs that had come to surround the Baroque opera house, particularly but not exclusively in its more spectacular manifestations. I say that it is not exclusively the spectacle of opera that falls under the rubric of the "exotick" in Johnson's mind partly because of that most exotic of all the elements of the *opera seria* (and the most tasteless, at least to an English critic), the castrato singer, who was such an integral but not, fortunately, indispensable part of it. And when I say that what, in general, Johnson thought of as the exotic aspect of Italian opera was, to a large degree, the inessential encrustation of the tasteless I do so with some trepidation, because it is notoriously hard to distinguish, in any art-form of another age, between what is essential to it (and *seemingly* tasteless because unfamiliar to us, and misunderstood into the bargain) and what is truly in bad taste, loathed perhaps by the artist himself and by the better part of his public. I take it, though, as hard as this distinction is to make out in practice, that it exists in principle: that there is an essential difference between Sir Thomas Beecham's "correcting" Handel's "bad taste" in orchestration on the one hand, and on the other the understandable reluctance of musical conservatories to reinstitute the noble art of the castrato, conductors, in the pursuit of "authenticity," inserting organ concertos into performances of *Saul*, or singers demanding extra arias in operas where they do not belong (to make their parts more commensurate with their egos). Handel's spare orchestration, the castrato, dropping instrumental compositions into dramatic performances to please audiences, the domination of composers by singers—all were part of the eighteenth-century musical scene: only the first, I presume, is an essential part, the others being tasteless and inessential aspects of the very human and so corruptible institution of music-making.

As for the charge of irrationality: here, I think, the issues run deeper; here is the nub of the matter. Johnson does not give us a bill of particulars; but others have, which we shall see in a moment. And what is at issue in the presumptive irrationality of the *opera seria* is no trivial excess of eighteenth-century taste but the very possibility of sung drama, at least *this* sung drama, as a form of art.

What we are talking about here, essentially, is whether *opera seria* can withstand critical scrutiny of the kind we expect a true work of art to undergo. Clearly, Johnson thought it could not: unlike (say) the spoken drama, it was an irrational entertainment—"the *understanding* having no part in the pleasure we receive at an opera . . . ," as Burney put the view.[8] It may indeed be a pleasing spectacle for the eye and ear, an elaborate (and expensive) confection; but what the charge of "irrationality" carries with it is an adverse judgment on opera as a serious art-form. Unlike the charge of exoticism, the charge of irrationality goes to the very heart of the enterprise: not merely the inessential artifacts of tasteless performances and mediocre scores, but the very rationality of the institution at its best. The charge of irrationality, then, is the charge that a defense of the *opera seria* must answer. But Johnson has merely given us the opening argument: the general nature of the indictment. We must now acquaint ourselves with the details of the prosecution brief, making sure to distinguish, where we can, between the "irrational" and the "exotick"—which is to say, between that evidence which is material, and that which is merely circumstantial.

◦ 4 ◦   It would be pointless, obviously, to thoroughly canvass the circumstantial evidence adduced by the contemporaries of *opera seria* (and it would be difficult, if not impossible, as well). For if the evidence is immaterial, what need does the defense have of answering it? But there might be some purpose nonetheless in at least producing representative examples, if only to prove, in the most convincing possible way, that they exist, and also to better demarcate the line between those that are and those that are not immaterial to the discussion.

Contemporary criticism of the *opera seria* aimed, naturally enough, at two separate targets: the works themselves, and the manner of their performance. It would be tempting to think that the distinction between immaterial and substantial criticism of the genre could be drawn along just those lines: criticism of performance practice being ephemeral, since performance practice can be reformed; criticism of the works themselves being to the point, since the works are what they are, and changing them, whatever its other aesthetic dangers and pitfalls, is not an answer to criticism of the genre but the creation of another genre, in all probability worse than the worst examples of the one being criticized.[9] But although that might have some validity as a first approximation, it will not really wash. For there are, I shall point out in a moment, aspects of performance that are, in a sense, essential and not ephemeral, being "implied" by the genre itself; and there are, likewise, qualities of the works themselves that are not essential to the genre, being merely qualities of individual, flawed instances, not of the genre at its best.

That the performance of *opera seria* in the eighteenth century was frequently absurd and tasteless cannot I think be denied. No one was more sensitive to this (and less sensitive to what really mattered: the music) than Joseph Addison; and no one was, needless to say, more spectacularly funny in pointing it out: even Burney had "to laugh . . . as heartily as any one. . . ."[10] When Handel mounted his first smash hit, *Rinaldo*, at the Theatre in the Haymarket (1711), it drew an oft-quoted sally from *The Spectator*:

> An opera may be allowed to be extravagantly lavish in its decorations, as its only design is to gratify the senses, and keep up an indolent attention in the audience. Common sense, however, requires, that there should be nothing in the scenes and machines which may appear childish and absurd. How would the wits of King Charles's time have laughed to have seen Nicolini exposed to a tempest in robes of ermine, and sailing on an open boat upon a sea of pasteboard! What a field of raillery would they have been let into, had they been entertained with painted dragons spitting wildfire, enchanted chariots drawn by Flanders mares, and real cascades in artificial landscapes! A little skill in criticism would inform us, that shadows and realities ought not be mixed together in the same piece; and that the scenes which are designed as the representations of nature, should be filled with resemblances, and not with the things themselves.[11]

That Addison had the good eye for bad taste can scarcely be gainsaid. Nicolini on a pasteboard sea must have indeed been a sight to see; opera is well rid of waterworks and ought to be, if it is not, of live animals. (Dragons, I am afraid, are indispensable.) But, of course, all of this falls under the head of spectacle in bad taste, no more an essential part of *opera seria* than of any other genre into which it obtrudes.

Two asides might be made, here, however, before we grant Addison his entirely valid but not very damaging point. The first is to remark on the premise with which he begins: that opera's "only design is to gratify the senses. . . ." That of course is Johnson's "irrational entertainment." That *opera seria* is more than that—that it is an aesthetically rational solution to the problem of realizing drama in musical form, and that that project itself is an aesthetically, which is to say artistically, rational one—is the argument of this chapter, and of this book. If Addison is right, at least this chapter must be wrong, and perhaps this book as well.

The second aside has to do with the general principle of "common sense" and criticism from which the *Spectator*'s specific strictures against the staging of *Rinaldo* are supposed to follow. For although the strictures themselves seem to be warranted, the principle must surely be invalid. If it were, indeed, always in bad taste to mix "shadows and realities" together on the stage, if dramatic performances were to "be filled with resemblances, and not with the things themselves," it would follow, I believe, that puppets, not people, would be the only allowable "performers," since when a man performs King Lear he is a real man, not a "shadow" or "resemblance" of a man (although he is a "shadow" or "resemblance" of King Lear). And even if one could find (I cannot see how) some valid metaprinciple to make an exception from Addison's rule of the *dramatis personae*, I cannot see how, on Addison's view, we could countenance King Lear's sitting on a real chair or drinking from a real goblet: they would have, by parity of reasoning, to be made of the same pasteboard as Nicolini's sea. It is not as if we can "define" bad taste in staging even partially as the mixing of the real with the representational; all we can say is that some instances of this mixing are in bad taste and some are not, the waterworks in *Rinaldo* perhaps being an example of the former, Don Giovanni's mandolin of the latter. But in any case, eighteenth-century bad taste in the staging of *opera seria* (which cannot possibly be worse than the rare examples of the twentieth-century variety) is an indictment of performance practice, not of *opera seria*; and the former, one presumes, can be reformed.

I spoke previously of my conviction that not every aspect of performance practice is *inessential* to the integrity of the *opera seria*. Let me conclude this section with what appears to me to be a case in point: the following observations on the performance of the great castrato Farinelli.

> What a pipe! What modulation! But heavens! What Clumsiness! What Stupidity! What offence to the Eye! . . . If thou art within the environs of St. James's thou must have observed in the Park with what ease and agility a cow, heavy with calf, has rose up at the command of the milkwoman's foot: Thus from the mossy bank sprang up the divine Farinelli. Then with long strides advancing a few paces, his left Hand settled upon his Hip, in a beautiful bend like that of the handle of an old fashioned caudle-cup, his Right remained immoveable across his manly Breast, 'till Numbness called its Partner to supply the Place; when it relieves itself in the position of the other handle of the caudle-cup.[12]

Now, to the extent that this is the indictment of a great singer who happened also to be an unusually poor actor, it no more goes to the heart of the *opera seria* than would the same observation, at another time, cast doubt upon the viability of *opera buffa* or Wagnerian music drama. By all accounts, even Addison's, Nicolini was a good actor. And that there were bad as well as good actors and actresses engaged in the performance of Handel's operas is only to be expected, just as there was bad as well as good scenery. No essential flaw here.

But perhaps there is something more at stake than first meets the eye. Farinelli jumps *clumsily* up from the mossy bank, and stands *awkwardly* when he sings. Nicolini was less awkward and clumsy in both departments, let us assume. Yet there is the suggestion here that it is not merely Farinelli's awkward stance while singing that is objected to; it is, rather, that there is a stance in the first place. Opera singers, after all, are personages in a drama. When they sing, they express their thoughts, feelings, intentions, decisions. And if any kind of verisimilitude is to be achieved, they cannot express these things like singing potted palms. For that is not the way *we* express them. Not only can we walk and talk at the same time, we do. We speak, gesture, move, in one fluid motion; and expression is not just one of these things: it is all of them at once. If opera is to portray human expression at all convincingly, then, the opera singer, one would think, must not just stand and deliver.

But that is easier said than sung. Consider, by way of example, one small portion of what Rinaldo has to sing, pretty much as a matter of course, throughout the opera that bears his name (Example 8). The fact is that music of this complex and florid kind cannot be sung adequately except by planting oneself pretty much in one place and giving forth. The aria of the *opera seria*—which is to say, essentially, the *opera seria* itself—is, at least under one of its possible descriptions, a concerto for the

EXAMPLE 8
George Frideric Handel, *Rinaldo*, Act I, Scene IX

voice. And concertos for the voice can no more be rendered properly by strolling and gesticulating performers than can concertos for the violin.

The conclusion to be drawn from this is that certain aspects of a singer's delivery are, in the nature of the case, bad acting and good singing; and, in these specific respects only, never the twain shall meet. Certain artifacts of performance are implied by the essential nature of *opera seria* and are, therefore, essential to its being. Within certain limits, of course, there are, among singers capable of performing in Handelian *opera seria*, good actors or actresses and bad. But certain features of a singer's performance will always be at odds with good acting; and the critic of Farinelli, quoted above, has espied one of them.

It might, I suppose, be argued that this of itself damns the *opera seria* as an impossible form of drama; for if the nature of a work of dramatic art is such as to preclude its being acted convincingly—indeed, forces the performers into absurdity in that department—then it cannot, one might think, be counted a viable aesthetic entity. But this carries things too far. Every form of drama, after all, has conventions that are, when scrutinized from the point of view of verisimilitude, "absurd," and they are so common and well known that there is no need to name them. Further, the artifact of operatic performance we are now considering is not peculiar to the *opera seria*: it is universal to all opera of a complex musical kind. One can no more sing "Martern aller Arten" or "Come scoglio," the *Preislied* or the *Liebestod*, while doing stage business than one can an aria in a Handel opera; and directors who don't know this always come a cropper musically. If this argument damns anything, therefore, it damns *all* serious opera, if not perhaps the entire musical stage. But right now we are not defending the entire operatic corpus, merely one special case, the *opera seria*, which, it is claimed, is *more* absurd than the "enlightened" varieties of the genre, and on that account fatally flawed. At least in this respect, however, it is on all fours with the rest. It may have a fatal flaw elsewhere in its character, but if standing still when you sing were revelatory of such a flaw, *Figaro* and *Otello* would have it too; and it is more than at this point in the argument we need grant. In this particular regard, if *Figaro* will fly, so will *Rinaldo*. We must turn elsewhere for really threatening criticism.

o 5 o   We have considered, so far, only criticism of *opera seria* performance. Where that criticism has been aimed at ephemeral and therefore reformable lapses in taste, it has, of course, in no way cast doubt on the works themselves; and even where an essential point has been touched—namely, the compromise that must be made with good acting in the interest of good singing—we have seen that *opera seria* is no worse off in this regard than other operatic forms that are considered more dramatically valid. The time has come now to look at critical claims not about performance, which are easily dealt with, but about the genre in its essential nature, which are not. As prelude to that, we must sketch in at least a silhouette of the beast we are tracking. I will rely here on the descriptive powers of (by anyone's standards) the ranking expert, Winton Dean:

> If we open the score of a Handel opera, or any Italian opera of the period, we are confronted with a long string of arias for solo voice introduced and separated by secco recitative, that is, recitative accompanied only by a bass part, figured or unfigured, which was filled out by the continuo harpsichord player. The recitative would seem to enshrine the maximum of action in the minimum of music. In the arias the reverse obtains: one character after another holds forth about the situation in which he finds himself and immediately leaves the stage. There are occasional short ariosos, nearly always at the beginning of a scene, that are not followed by an exit; but the vast majority of the arias are in da capo form—a first part in the tonic key, a second part often on the same thematic material but shorter and in a contrasted key or mode, and a repeat of the first part that is not written out in the score. At rare moments of tension the recitative is accompanied by the orchestra—usually, though not invariably, the strings and continuo. These accompanied recitatives offered the composer his most obvious opportunity to express emotional conflict. . . .
>
> Duets are introduced sparingly, and for the most part confined to set pieces, also in da capo form, in which a pair of lovers welcome or bewail their destiny. Ensembles of more than two voices are very rare, and most operas have no chorus in the modern sense. The one occasion when the audience could rely on hearing all or most of the voices singing came at the end of the opera, when a brief concerted piece in dance rhythms and simple block harmony brought down the curtain on a conventional happy end. This was called a coro or chorus, but was sung by the soloists. There is an overture in several movements, with little apparent relation to what follows in the opera, and a few short instrumental pieces here and there to represent such events as battles or ceremonial functions.[13]

A Handel opera, then, is a vast, flat plane of secco recitative and da capo aria, bordered on one side by an overture, at the other by a somewhat perfunctory "chorus." Occasionally—very occasionally—there is a perturbation, a bump in this uniform texture: arioso, accompanied recitative, instrumental interlude, duet, dramatic ensemble.

There is no question but that the "bumps" are what the contemporary ear finds most congenial, most operatically viable, most musically familiar. Of the accompanied recitatives, Dean says: "they are the easiest things for a modern audience to accept as genuinely dramatic, especially since the method of treating them changed little throughout the eighteenth century and continued well into the nineteenth."[14] The other breaks in the continuous march of secco recitative and da capo aria, particularly the more dramatic of the duets and larger ensembles, as well as any violations of strict da capo aria form, are also bound to strike a modern audience as genuinely dramatic, if only (but not only) because we tend to associate drama with sudden or unexpected change in any uniform progression of events, musical or other—a point which I will return to somewhat later on. It is therefore all too tempting to try to defend Handelian *opera seria* against its detractors by making the bumps into mountains and isolated peaks into ranges: for these are the congenial elements. So tempting is it that even a commentator as careful as Dean, who insists that understanding Handel's opera "means accepting it on its own terms . . . ,"[15] seems to me to exaggerate sometimes the breaks in continuity by piling up examples, a process which tends to make us forget how infrequent, in any one opera, these departures from orthodoxy are—another point to which we will return.

But the truth is that if the basic formula of overture, secco recitative, da capo aria, chorus is not viable opera, the bumps, as brilliant and fascinating as they are, cannot make it so. Only accepting this unadorned formula, no warts at all, can really constitute accepting Handelian *opera seria* "on its own terms."

∘ 6 ∘   There is little point in defending the closing choruses of Handel's operas. They are musically trivial. But my own view is that if you can get as far as the chorus without giving up on Handel, the *opera seria* has won its case, and you can be excused for being on your way home before the chorus begins. After all, these choruses are no more perfunctory (say) than the choral perorations of *Die Entführung* or *Die Zauberflöte*; and no one complains about those.

The overture, however, is another matter, or at least it has traditionally been felt to be. For although eighteenth-century voices were frequently raised against the trumped-up "happy ending" of the *opera seria* libretto, seldom if ever (I can't think of a case, although I dare say there must be some) was the music in which this happy ending is celebrated—that is to say, the final "coro"—criticized; musically, which is to say, dramatically *qua* music, it apparently satisfied, if dramatically *qua* literature it did not. But the overture never enjoyed that critical immunity; and although Benedetto Marcello, in *Il teatro alla moda* (c. 1720), objected only to the musical laziness and incompetence of opera composers that was evidenced in their "avoiding fugues, suspensions, *soggetti*, etc., as antiquities entirely excluded from modern practice,"[16] later contemporaries were not so much exercised over the musical as over the dramatic faults of these compositions: in particular, as Dean puts it, their lack of "apparent relation to what follows in the opera. . . ."

Francesco Algarotti, one of the best-known critics of the opera in the eighteenth century, had reference to the Italian (fast-slow-fast) rather than the French (slow-fast-dance) overture of the Handelian *opera seria* when he wrote the following excoriation of the beast (in 1755); but he must surely have been aware of the older form, and of the artistic practice which it at least seemed to enshrine, for the present criticism might equally well be thought to apply to it.

Among the errors observable in the present system of music, the most obvious, and that which first strikes the ears at the very beginning of an opera, is the hackneyed manner of composing overtures, which are always made to consist of two allegros with one grave and to be as noisy as possible. Thus are they void of variation and so jog on much alike. Yet what a wide difference ought to be perceived between that, for example, which precedes the death of Dido and that which is prefixed to the nuptials of Demetrius and Cleonice. The main drift of an overture should be to announce, in a certain manner, the business of the drama and consequently prepare the audience to receive those affecting impressions that are to result from the whole of the performance, so that from hence a leading view and presaging notions of it may be conceived, as is of an oration from the exordium. But our present composers look upon an overture as an article quite detached and absolutely different from the poet's drama.[17]

This, or criticism much like it, was, of course, later echoed by Gluck and answered in practice in the overture to *Alceste*: "I have felt that the overture ought to apprise the spectators of the nature of the action that is to be represented and form, so to speak, its argument. . . ."[18]

There are two basic strategies to answering such criticism: denying the general principle on which it is based, or denying that the object of criticism fails to satisfy the principle. The principle, stated in as general terms as possible, is that the overture should, so to speak, form part of the drama itself; should *begin* the drama, not just in the nominal sense of being the first movement of an opera but in the real sense of being the first musico-dramatic "event" of the drama-made-music that an opera is construed (at least here) to be. And one might, alternatively, defend the Handelian overture by claiming that, appearances to the contrary notwithstanding, it does fulfill that role; or that that is not the only aesthetically valid role for an overture to perform, that, in fact, Handel's overtures perform an entirely different but nonetheless rational function and, understood on their own terms, perform this function as well as (say) the overtures to *Alceste* and *Don Giovanni* perform their very different ones. (These alternatives are very familiar ones in all art-critical discourse.)

I intend to utilize both strategies, and I hope to get away with it. I read somewhere that in law a logically contradictory defense is permissible; that, in fact, the great trial lawyer Earl Rogers once defended a client against a murder charge on the grounds that the defendant was in another city at the time and hence could not have done the alleged murder, and anyway it was self-defense. If this is true of the law, I will not go so far as to say that the law is an ass; but I will be presumptuous enough to insist that even in talking about music, where nonsense seems to be the rule rather than the exception, we think more of the law of contradiction than this. And I will hasten to assure the skeptical reader that in employing both of the above strategies, I will not deny the deed and plead self-defense in the same breath.

The overtures to Handel's operas are all of them of the French overture kind. That means that each opens with a slow, stately, dignified homophonic section, invariably in dotted or double-dotted rhythm, followed by a fast, informal, but clearly recognizable fugue, which comes to a close with a return to a truncated version of the slow introductory section, or with a similar slow section with no thematic relation to the first, or simply with a slow measure or two of cadence. There then follows a dance movement: usually a minuet or gigue but occasionally, when the business of the first scene suggests it, a march or, rarer still, a chorus, as in *Giulio Cesare*, where what starts out as the customary (and expected) minuet turns into a choral greeting to the conquerer.

The charge that Handel's overtures are all the same is largely true; there can be no real doubt about it. And except for the very rare case in which, as in *Giulio Cesare*, the last movement of the overture is joined to the text and action of the play, they are as completely interchangeable as industrial parts. The question is: Does the "charge" amount to anything? Does anything musically, dramatically, aesthetically, or in any other relevant way follow from it of an odious nature?

Algarotti complained that overtures generally "are . . . void of variation and so jog on much alike"; and I suppose, within certain limits, that is true not only of the Italian overtures of which he spoke but of Handel's French overtures as well. What is supposed to follow from that? That they therefore must be inappropriate, presumably. Of course, that depends on a lot of things.

To stay at an abstract level, for a moment, consider the case of an overture in the French manner, composed by composer X for opera Y, and then, in the rush of work, used over again next season for opera Z. Perhaps it was inappropriate for Z because Z's "argument" is very different from Y's. But it would be a very unlucky or unskillful composer indeed who managed to write the universally inappropriate overture—inappropriate for *every* occasion. It would, one might think, even require a special kind of devilish genius to achieve that. So the fact that Handel may have written the same opera overture forty times has for all pratical purposes, if it has any implications at all, merely the implication that sometimes he hit it right and sometimes he didn't. French overtures must, after all, be appropriate for *something*.

Suppose now we try to look a little deeper into the charge of sameness. Algarotti is worried over the fact that all Italian overtures "are always made to consist of two allegros and one grave. . . ." Without laboring the point, I think it will be readily granted me that Algarotti is saying something here about the relation of "form" to "content." How, he is asking, can overtures, all of the same form, be appropriate to the content of so many different operas from "the death of Dido" to "the nuptials of Demetrius and Cleonice"? And since Handelian overtures are equally instantiatiations of the same form over and over again, the objection will apply, *pari passu*, to them as well.

But it needs only to state this objection to perceive immediately its utter bankruptcy. We might just as well conclude that the overtures to *Le Nozze di Figaro*, *Idomeneo*, and *Fidelio* cannot all be appropriate to their respective operas, since they are all instances of the same "form"—that is, "sonata" form. Surely it is not the form of the French overture itself that is at fault if Handel's overtures are, indeed, to a man, inappropriate to the operas they introduce, any more than it is the form of Gluck's overture to *Orfeo ed Euridice*—also in at least rudimentary sonata form—that makes it singularly inappropriate for his first great "reform" opera.

The analogy that was so popular in the eighteenth century, and before, between music and rhetoric does plenty of mischief here. Algarotti compares the detested all-purpose overture (as he sees it) with an overblown oratorical flourish. "If some [composers], however, employ it [i.e. the operatic overture] as an exordium, it is of a kindred complection to those of certain writers, who, with big and pompous words, repeatedly display before us the loftiness of the subject and the lowness of their genius; which preluding would suit any other subject as well and might as judiciously be prefixed for an exordium to one oration as another."[19]

What is it that makes an exordium appropriate to many orations? Clearly, it must be excessive vagueness. For if I am at all specific about what I am about to say, I cannot use the same exordium for my House Divided speech as for my Cooper Union address. But it is very doubtful that I can transfer the notion of "excessive vagueness" to music at all, because vagueness is a semantical notion, and music is a "syntax" without a semantics, a grammar without a meaning. The fact is that the overture to *Don Giovanni* (say) would have made an excellent overture to a *Faust* if Mozart had written one—not because it is "vague," for that concept simply fails to apply to music (except if the music is said to "represent" or "express" vagueness, as the overture to Haydn's *Creation* represents "chaos," although it is not chaotic). It is certainly a criticism of an exordium that it can introduce many different speeches, because to be appropriate to everything it would have to say nothing. As music, however, says nothing anyway, it is hardly a criticism of an overture that it is appropriate to more than one opera.

Notice, by the way, that the use of thematic material from the opera in the overture (as in the case of *Don Giovanni* or *Così fan tutte*) does not obviate what has been said above about vagueness. The overture to *Don Giovanni* is not "less vague" than the overture to *Figaro* by virtue of the former's using in its slow introduction thematic material from the penultimate scene, and the latter's being musically unrelated to its opera. It is even doubtful that it is "more appropriate" in any clear sense. And whether or not Mozart had used themes from the *Don Giovanni* overture in his (alas) uncomposed *Faust*, it still would be just the right overture, I think, for such a work.

The Gluck-Algarotti camp has, perhaps, one more string to its bow. For, after all, it is not merely some vague sort of "appropriateness" being insisted upon, but something very specific, not unlike the kind of exordium that really does not tell the audience in summary what the speech is going to be about. As Algarotti puts it, "an overture should . . . announce . . . the business of the drama . . . so that from hence a leading view and presaging notions of it may be conceived, as is of an oration from the exordium." In Gluck's more pithy words, "the overture ought to . . . form, so to speak, [the opera's] argument. . . ."

But now, I dare say, if we are going to take these claims seriously, we are off somewhere in the vicinity of Cloud-Cuckoo Land. For the fact is that it is not in music's power to give the "argument" or state the "business" of a first-grade reader, let alone of *Don Giovanni* or *Alceste*.[20] What more can I tell from the overture to *Don Giovanni* about what is going to happen in the rest of the opera than I can tell about Handel's *Rodelinda* or *Partenope* from theirs? Given the musical conventions that surround opera overtures, I can, I suppose, in listening to Mozart's overture, reasonably surmise that some somber things are going to happen (slow introduction), and some exuberant things as well (allegro); but I can pretty much surmise, at about the same level of uninformative generality, that some somber things (slow introduction) and some lively dramatic things (fast fugal section) are going to transpire in *Rinaldo* by listening to the ubiquitous French overture with which it begins. Let's face it: an opera overture, even at its best, is about as useful in foretelling the operatic future as an oracle who tells you "Che sarà sarà."

At this point, perhaps, my reader—at least my musical reader—may begin to grow impatient with what may seem a bag of "philosopher's tricks." Granted, these arguments don't *prove* that Handel's overtures are not appropriate introductions; all you have to do is listen to them, and your ears will tell you what arguments cannot.

This is a reasonable challenge. Indeed, the only ultimate test of whether music is good is listening. Unfortunately, however, as Winton Dean warns, the only ultimate test of whether a Handel opera is good is to see and listen; and that goes for the constituent parts thereof, including overtures. Operas—Handel's no less than anyone else's—are composed with full theatrical performance as the goal. But since the operas of Handel are only rarely performed, few of us have ever seen and heard even one in its proper setting. All we can do, always with a grain of salt, is to surmise as best we can, from phonograph records and scores, whether or not these much-maligned overtures are adequate, although we have plenty of experience of such oratorio overtures as those to *Messiah* and *Judas Maccabaeus*, both of which are quite distinctive and, it seems to me, peculiarly appropriate to the works they introduce: the stately, melancholy solemnity of the first in sharp contrast to the dramatic, "warlike" quality of the second (in its fugal section).

Perhaps we are not in a completely advantageous position, then, to make a fair assessment; but others have been. So far we have heard only unfriendly witnesses. Let us now give ear to a sympathetic one, Johann Joachim Quantz, who wrote in his celebrated treatise on playing the flute:

> An overture, played before an opera, requires a magnificent beginning, full of gravity, a brilliant, well-elaborated principal section, and a good combination of different instruments, such as flutes, oboes, or horns. Its origin is due to the French. Lully has provided excellent models. German composers, however, among them Handel and Telemann, have far surpassed him in this.[21]

Quantz, by the way, no less than Algarotti or Gluck, is committed to the precept that overture must be relevant to opera; and for that reason he is not altogether pleased with the custom (to which Handel is no exception) that the French overture end with a dance: "it stands to reason . . . that a sinfonia [i.e. overture] should have some connection with the content of its opera or at least with the first scene of it and not, as frequently occurs, conclude invariably with a gay minuet."[22] In justice, however, to both Handel's musical and Quantz's critical subtlety, it should be pointed out that Quantz only objects to the universality of *gay* minuets, and Handel's are much better described as stately and majestic: in some cases, as, for example, the gigue in the overture to *Partenope*, even somber and stately. Nor should this seem surprising, or a lame defense: it is merely another of the many cases in the history of art where a convention, boring and recalcitrant in the hands of the merely talented, is put to real expressive use by genius.

Here, I think, is the key to the appropriateness of the Handelian opera overture. An overture, Quantz tells us, should be "full of gravity"—that is to say, serious—and "brilliant." And all of Handel's surely fulfill these requirements, right down to the concluding minuets, marches, and gigues. But how can seriousness and brilliance always be in keeping? Very simply, because the Handelian *opera seria* is itself always serious and brilliant, whatever else it may be.[23] If Handel wrote the same overture forty times, it is because it worked. The *opera seria* was remarkably long-lived and stable, as musical (particularly operatic) genres go. And Handel was a musical pragmatist supreme. Long after his audiences sent him the unmistakable message that they had had enough, he doggedly pursued the operatic muse because, musically, it worked: it worked as an artistic enterprise if not as an economic one. He continued to write French overtures, one assumes, for the same reason.

Perhaps the fact that Handel failed to make any innovations in the form of the overture itself (although he found a number of ingenious and imaginative ways of joining it to the first scene of its opera) makes him unoriginal (at least in that regard). But it is easy, in such matters, as Monroe Beardsley has pointed out,[24] to confuse criticism of the artist with criticism of the art work, and to take "originality" for a relevant art-critical category when arguably it might not be. If Handel wrote the same overture forty times, it implies nothing about the goodness or badness of any one of them. As a matter of fact, they are all fine instrumental compositions, some of them great ones; and there does not seem to be one inappropriate to the opera it begins. If they are basically all the same, then I would prefer not to hear twelve of them at a sitting. But an opera, after all, has only one overture; and twelve of Rossini's all in a row might be equally palling.

The *opera seria* is a stately, brilliant, sometimes violent and dramatic, always emotionally charged stage work. Every one of Handel's overtures, aside from being the composition of a master of harmony, counterpoint, orchestration, and instrumental form, reflects and embodies all of these expressive properties. Can these works, then, possessing just the expressive properties that, as exordia, they are supposed to possess, fail to be superb examples of the operatic overture, as envisaged by Algarotti, and Gluck, and you? I think I will rest my case for the *dramatic* virtues of the Handelian overture with that. But I promised something more.

o 7 o   I promised, it will be recalled, not only to give the conventional defense (which I have done) of the Handel overture as fulfilling the familiar requirements of "appropriateness to the argument," but to question that requirement itself, at least to the extent of denying its universality. Could there not be another kind of overture, with another but no less worthy kind of task to perform? And mightn't the Handelian one be of that kind?

There is, to be sure, a pitfall to be avoided in defenses like these: we must not counter with a task unworthy of a worthy art work to perform, or trivial, or not germane to its evaluation *qua* art work. To do so would be to damn just the thing we are trying to save. A flippant answer to the question of why Hamlet delayed so long in killing his uncle is that if he hadn't the play would not have lasted long enough. To be sure, the answer is correct; but it is not an answer that casts light on the aesthetic nature of Shakespeare's play or on the reason for its greatness. In a similar and equally trivial vein is the retort that the purpose of Handel's overtures was to fill up the time during which latecomers were arriving with some sort of musical diversion. Again, it is the truth: that surely is (lamentably) a task opera overtures perform. But it is not an aesthetic task—and that is what we seek.

Like many others, I remember with great fondness the proscenium arch of the old Metropolitan Opera House: Baroque curlicues out of which peeked ornate plaques with the names of the giants enshrined thereupon: Mozart, Verdi, Beethoven, Wagner, Gluck, Meyerbeer, Handel. (Handel, I think, got as far as the arch, but never as far as the boards.) The proscenium arch is, like the picture frame, a kind of artistic no man's land. It separates fiction from reality; but it partakes a little bit of both, and hence is not exactly either. The picture frame is part of the art work, and it isn't. Outside of it is the world, inside of it the "world of the work." But what is *it*? Inside or outside? Like all borders it is both within and beyond itself: both in and out of the worlds it abuts. So it is with the proscenium arch. The picture frame and the proscenium arch perform, then, the same function: to stand between physical space and fictional space, between art and the world. But the works that they frame are in one very important respect radically different: the works that the proscenium arch frames, be they operas or plays, are temporal works,

instantiated in performances, and their performances have a beginning
and an end in time.

Operas, then, require more than a spatial frame: they require a temporal frame as well. They need, if the aesthetic of the proscenium arch
is to be adopted, a boundary that says: Here physical space ends and
fictional space begins. They need, too, a boundary in time that says: Here
"real" events end and fictional events begin. This, I would suggest, is the
function performed by the Toccata which Monteverdi placed at the head
of *Orfeo*, and by similar instrumental flourishes that prelude other of the
first generation of operatic works. And that is why it is so aesthetically
wrong-headed to try to find, as Donington does, thematic connections
between the Toccata and *Orfeo* proper. That is a different aesthetic altogether.

Imagine objecting that the proscenium arch bears no thematic, dramatic, or scenic relation to the operas which it frames. Perhaps a proscenium reformer might suggest that there be a different one for each scene
or, more modestly, at least a different one for each opera: for example,
a proscenium arch with iron bars as a motif for *Fidelio*. There is nothing
inherently absurd in the suggestion. What would be absurd would be to
think that one was still applying the aesthetic of the proscenium arch. For
to have the bars of Don Florestan's dungeon continue onto the frame
would be to make the frame part of the scenery: part, that is, of the fictional space that is the world of that work. It would cease to occupy that
shadowy world of half-reality, half-illusion, that picture frames and proscenium arches inhabit, and would be swallowed up completely by the
illusion. Indeed, if one wanted to remain committed to the aesthetic of
the proscenium under these conditions, one would have to frame the
frame, at the cost of falling into a regress *in infinitum* of prosceniums for
prosceniums for prosceniums. . . . We might call this the Seurat fallacy,
because the French pointillist provided "frames" of his own devising for
some of his pictures, onto which the dots of the canvas have migrated,
thus, in essence, making the frame part of the painting—which is to say,
really dispensing with the frame aesthetic entirely. The amusing thing is
that framers are not so easily outwitted, and we now find Seurats with
their own dotted "frames" framed again by the same gilt ones that frame
Rembrandts.

When Algarotti, Gluck, et al. made their pleas for overture "reform,"
whatever might be the truth of their allegations against French and
Italian overtures of the period, what they were essentially doing was recommending the rejection of the overture-as-frame aesthetic, in favor of
the overture actually becoming part of the opera: part of the first scene,
or at least part of the opera's general mood and character. They were the

Seurats of the opera's temporal "frame." What such an overture aesthetic accomplishes is just what is accomplished by Seurat's dotted frames, theatre-in-the-round, or Elizabethan theatres: a blurring of the distinction between appearance and reality, the work and the world, fact and fiction, which now tend to shade off into one another. The "contour lines" are gone. This is not, contrary to what they thought, a better aesthetic; it is, however, a different one.

Is it too much to suggest, then, that Handel was working in the seam, both historically and aesthetically, *between* these two aesthetics of the overture; that some of his overtures are temporal picture frames, some of them opera-parts in Gluck's and Algarotti's sense, and some, perhaps, even both at the same time? The *opera seria*, after all, like the eighteenth-century English novel, is a highly conventional, stylized, and self-conscious artistic production, where framing is not at all out of place, as it would be, for example, in *verismo* opera or the realistic novel of the nineteenth century. Some Handel overtures are optimally appreciated as "parts of the argument," but some, rather, as the proscenium of events, saying: Here real history is in abeyance and fictional history begins. And it would be no more rational, aesthetically, to object that such overtures have nothing to do with the events of the opera than it would be to object that the proscenium of the old Met had nothing to do with the plot of *Fidelio*. Iron bars do not a proscenium make; indeed, they are its logical undoing.

Here, then, is my second defense of the Handelian overture; and before my reader has the opportunity of complaining that at this rate I will never even get through the first act in finite time, I will move on to other matters. With regard to overtures, the defense now rests.

o 8 o   The secco recitative—that is to say, the rapid parlando accompanied only by the figured bass line and improvised keyboard accompaniment—that evolved as the bearer of the narrative conversation in *opera seria* was a particularly hard pill for the English to swallow. For one thing, it was, of course, delivered in rapid-fire Italian. And more than one English critic, longing, quite understandably, for a native musical stage, lamented the spectacle of an audience in the theatre like foreigners in their own country.

But there was more to it than that: there was the question of rationality; of whether it made dramatic sense, or was too great a sacrifice of verisimilitude, for characters to *converse*, frequently expressing the most humdrum sentiments, in music. Somehow the arias did not raise such a difficulty in this particular respect. For it seemed easier to rationalize the singing of such lofty and emotionally charged words as the da capo arias invariably consisted of than the often prosaic exchanges of the secco recitative. As John Brown put it, in his somewhat cranky book called *Dissertation on the Rise, Union, and Power . . . of Poetry and Music* (1763), "To hear Kings, Warriours, Statesmen, Philosophers, Patriarchs, Saints, and Martyrs, holding long Conversations with each other in musical Recitative, is a Circumstance so totally out of Nature, that the Imagination immediately revolts, and rejects the Representation as absurd and incredible."[25]

Brown's scruples may seem to the sophisticated opera-goer somewhat childish and naive, perhaps appropriate to an age and a country where Italian opera was novel and unfamiliar, but beneath the notice of the enlightened. I am inclined to believe otherwise. The aversion of many to opera as an art-form, now and then, can be understood as an unwillingness, born of scruples about "realism," to accept wholeheartedly the operatic convention of an entirely sung drama. Antique aversion that it is, one can but answer it, I think, with the equally antique answer of, among others, Jean-Jacques Rousseau, who observed of the exalted personages that populate the dramas of Zeno and Metastasio—"Cyrus, Caesar, Cato himself . . .": "We easily suppose, that sentiments so different from ours, ought to be also expressed in another tone."[26] Someone who cannot accept a singing Caesar is not likely to be able to accept, either, a Richard III who speaks in verse (or, for that matter, an ancient Roman who speaks in French). This is a familiar but, I think, altogether convincing *reductio* of the claim that opera is irrational or foolish because real people don't converse in music. If there is another answer, I don't know what it is; and the regularity with which this one resurfaces in every generation must say something to its convincingness, if not to its validity, as to our natural reluctance to try to find some other, while this one satisfies. What Rousseau said in the eighteenth century seems quite at home in the twentieth, witness this splendid evocation of it in Isaiah Berlin's characterization of Sir Winston Churchill's prose: "The texture and the tension are those of a tragic opera, where the very artificiality of the medium, both in the recitative and in the arias, serves to eliminate the irrelevant dead level of normal existence and to set off in high relief the deeds and sufferings of the characters."[27] If Sir Isaiah was not thinking specifically of Handel's *opera seria* when he wrote these words, it is true serendipity; for none could better suit the subject, or answer the cranky Dr. Brown.

The real objection of substance to secco recitative seems to be not dramatic but musical in nature. It is simply that secco recitative is utterly devoid of all musical interest or value. It is music's limiting case, and not to be endured in a full operatic dose.

There is a kernel of truth here; but it can become an objection to secco recitative only by being inflated into a monstrous falsehood. The kernel of truth is this: secco recitative, by itself, does not fulfill enough of the pure musical parameters to sustain interest as a separate, autonomous musical entity. This, of course, is something of an exaggeration, for the purpose of making a point. There are secco recitatives in Handel's operas and oratorios, and elsewhere, that achieve a high level of musical beauty and dramatic intensity. And the secco recitative of Bach's cantatas is another animal entirely—a musical art-form of the first water. But when all of the necessary qualifications are made, it still remains true that, for the most part, by itself secco recitative is not music. That is why, obviously, a concert of secco recitative would be unendurable. But to be "minimal music" is just the very point of the thing. Were it more than that, it could not perform its very special function.

A comparison with the *stile rappresentativo* puts into bold relief just what the secco recitative is and what it does. The *stile rappresentativo*, as we have seen, is an attempt to represent speech in music; and that means to be music in the fullest sense. Secco recitative, whatever its historical connection may (or may not) be with the *stile rappresentativo*, has a different aesthetic entirely. It is not intended to be, nor is it, music in the fullest sense; it is music denuded of flesh: if you will, a skeleton of keys. All that is required of it musically is that it does not cease to be *tone*, does not, in other words, fall into speaking; and, of course, does not commit any "grammatical" errors of harmony, melody, or counterpoint. It must stay as close to speaking as it can without becoming speech.

Secco recitative is the connective tissue between the organs of real music: that is to say, the da capo arias (and whatever other concerted pieces the opera may contain). This tissue, of course, seldom has musical value by itself; but to conclude from that that it has no musical value at all would be like concluding that organs on a dissecting table have no value because they cannot function *there*. That is the monstrous falsehood that the kernel of truth becomes.

The mistake, I think, is very much like that of assuming the smallest bearer of meaning in a language is the single word rather than the sentence. It is tempting to think of the secco recitative and da capo aria as the basic, self-contained atoms of musical "meaning" out of which the *opera seria* is made. That is not the case: indeed, not only is it not the case with the secco recitative, it is not even the case with the aria. The basic unit of "meaning" in the *opera seria*—its sentence, if you will—is the da capo aria *and* the secco recitative that connects it with the previous aria (or concerted piece). The secco recitative and the aria which it introduces are one indissoluble whole. It is more obvious, perhaps, that the recitative cannot survive dismemberment from the aria than that the aria cannot survive dismemberment from the recitative, because the aria can, of course, be performed by itself. It does embody the full panoply of musical parameters. The heart will continue to beat when severed from the rest of the body, but the beat will not be strong and full; nor will the da capo aria, though a complete, self-contained musical entity, retain its entire musical integrity when parted from the secco recitative which precedes it. This is most apparent, of course, in the cases where Handel, for dramatic purposes, either makes the last line of the recitative the first line of the aria, as in "Dove sei?" in *Rodelinda* (Example 9), or where, although the recitative comes to a full close, Handel dispenses with any instrumental introduction to the aria and plunges, *subito*, into the middle of things, as in "Vado al campo" in *Sosarme* (Example 10). (The even more severe case is where, as in Cleopatra's "V'adoro pupille" in *Giulio Cesare*, the course of the aria is interrupted by a secco recitative and then continues.)

These anomalies, of course, are the very clear cases in which the da capo aria loses its musical integrity when severed from recitative. "Vado al campo" begins too abruptly, without its preceding *recitativo*, for it to work musically by itself (much like Mozart's "Non so più," which always cuts a rather poor figure as a concert aria). And "Dove sei?" really has no clearly defined beginning at all when it stands alone, its front end naked and forlorn, like a single bookend facing the wrong way. But it is much more important to see that even in its normal form, with full instrumental ritornello at its head and foot, the Handelian da capo aria does not constitute a complete, self-contained musical (or dramatic) unit. For it is meant to be a musical and emotional katharsis, a tremendous release of musical energy and tension; and a katharsis or release of tension cannot initiate itself, like the *causa sui*: it must be the consequence of something, and that something is the secco recitative.

We are now in a position, I think, to see just what the musical function and value of the secco recitative is. In a word, it is the musical tension-builder, the energy-accelerator that provides the occasion for the tension release, the explosive burst of energy, or the slow but intense burn of the ensuing, expected, and awaited instrumental introduction to the da capo aria. If, while listening to the secco recitative, you find yourself getting a little impatient for the aria, that is not because the recitative is a defective artistic device; on the contrary, it is just because it is doing extraordinarily well the very job it is supposed to do, like a musical Leyden jar, storing by slow degrees the material without which we cannot have the lightning-bolt to follow.

I want to emphasize that this is principally a *musical* task, not a dramatic

EXAMPLE 9
Handel, *Rodelinda*, Act I, Scene VI

EXAMPLE 10

Handel, *Sosarme*, Act II, Scene XI

one (to the extent that the two can be separated in a discussion of the opera). To be sure, what the characters say in musical conversation is necessary if we are to understand what the situation is in which one of them will sing of his or her love or despair, resolve or capitulation. But, as Burney long ago observed, even if it were our own language being sung, and sung by the best possible declaimer of it, we would probably not get the gist ("What do we understand when English is singing on our Stage without a book?").[28] And I dare say this is as true of Verdi or Mozart as of Handel. (How many of us could tell what was happening in *La Forza del Destino* or *Figaro*, even when sung in English, with no previous knowledge of the story and no libretto in hand?) As a narrator of the story, the secco recitative is both useless and dispensable: useless because we can't understand it, and dispensable because if we are going to appreciate the *opera seria* at all as anything but the *completest concert*, we must follow the "book" or do our homework.

But this admission must not lead us into thinking that the secco recitative is dispensable altogether. Paradoxically, this borderline musical form that has frequently been excoriated as music and defended as a necessary dramatic evil is, quite to the contrary, dramatically otiose and musically essential. I have said in general what its vital function as music is: to create the musical tension necessary for the kathartic release of the da capo aria. Something more specific must be said, however, if that is not to be what a lot of music talk ends up being finally, so much critical patter or noise, expressively moving and quite devoid of meaning.

I choose, almost at random, Act I, Scenes II and III, of *Rodelinda*. The situation (as usual) is complicated; and since we are interested here only in the musical function of the recitative, I will not waste the considerable time necessary to apprise the reader of it. Suffice it to say, Grimoaldo and Garibaldo spend Scene II discussing (entirely in secco recitative) how Grimoaldo can win Rodelinda (whom he presently loves) and jilt Eduige (who presently loves him). In Scene III, Eduige enters, complaining of Grimoaldo's neglect (he formerly courted her), in answer to which he sings this splendid aria of rage and rejection:

> Io già t'amai, ritrosa
> sdegnasti esser mia sposa,
> sempre dicesti nò.
> Or ch'io son Rè, non voglio
> compagno nel mio soglio,
> aver chi mi sprezzò,
> nò nò.

(When I loved you, you wilfully scorned to be my wife; you always said "no." Now that I am king I do not want as consort one who spurned me.)[29]

Without giving a complete harmonic analysis of the secco recitative—36 measures of it—which precedes the aria, it is appropriate to point out that it wanders in its course through at least the following keys: C major, F major, D minor, B-flat minor, E-flat major, F minor, C major (again),

D minor (again), G major, E minor, C major (for a third time), E major,
A major, D major, G major (again), C major (fourth time), and finally a
full close—the only one in the 36 measures—in F major. The aria that
follows is in B flat, which makes F its dominant, and it the natural next
step. There is, it must be emphasized, no harmonic or melodic resting
place in the recitative, this being achieved, in a familiar way, by usually
having the third of the chord in the bass, thus making any given key that
is arrived at obviously active and transitory. All of this, by the way—at
least ten different key areas in 36 measures—to get from the previous
aria, in G minor, to the present one, in its relative major: a step that could
have been taken directly, without any musical transition at all! Obviously,
there is method here: and it is, in a word, the creation of musical ambiguity, in order to keep the listener in doubt about where the music is
(since all of the chords are active) or where it is going (since each of the
chords has more than one "syntactically" possible destination). In other
words, the secco recitative, because it is harmonically and melodically
protean, musically formless and ill-defined, is a breeding ground for
musical tension: the building up (but not the fulfilling) of doubt and
expectation. Secco recitative, as Leonard Meyer might characterize it,
"tremble[s] on the brink of chaos";[30] the listener thus

> has a general feeling as to what the final goal of the series is, but he is
> uncertain as to how the present process will get him there and what
> detours and obstacles will be encountered en route. As it is only at the
> point of "reversal," the point at which the process is broken and
> another mode of continuation takes its place, that the listener finally is
> able to envisage his goal with any degree of security. It is thus the point
> of reversal of process which constitutes the climax and turning point
> of the passage, the point at which doubt and anxiety are replaced by
> more certain anticipation.[31]

Of course I have appropriated from Meyer passages that were meant to
characterize something else entirely, not secco recitative and da capo aria.
But for our purposes, the point of "reversal"—where musical doubt and
anxiety are resolved, musical energy released, musical katharsis
achieved—is the point where the instrumental ritornello of the awaited
and expected da capo aria finally burgeons from the secco recitative
(Example 11).

These, then, are the nuts and bolts of the secco recitative; to dispense
with it is to render the da capo aria far less effective as a musical form.
Granted, the recitative cannot fly alone, and the aria to a degree can—at
least it can limp. But as I hope I have shown, the basic building blocks of
the *opera seria* are not recitative and aria but recitative-and-aria. One can,

EXAMPLE 11
Handel, *Rodelinda*, Act I, Scene III

of course, commit all sorts of offenses, of varying degrees, in performing music: one can have a scherzo without the symphony, or an aria without its recitative or with it severely cut. But a scherzo is a part, not a whole; and so too is the da capo aria, in spite of its perfect musical form. And to the extent that secco recitative is essential to the optimal functioning of the da capo aria, it is by no means musically worthless or superfluous: on the contrary, it lies next to the very heart of the *opera seria*. The heart is the da capo aria; and to that we must, finally, turn for a long look. Without it, the *opera seria* is nothing.

∘ 9 ∘   The da capo aria is the crux of cruxes. Much scorn and vilification were heaped upon it in its own time and have been ever since. Yet it seems to me to be, at least as Handel practiced it, one of the most perfect musical forms ever to have evolved: an ideal solution to the problem of opera that called it forth.

Let me begin the formidable task of defending that seemingly hopeless claim by taking just a brief look at what the da capo aria is, in the form in which it most frequently appears in Handel's operas. I cannot, I should warn, examine it in every guise in which it was seen. I cannot pursue all of its varieties; and I will characterize it in a way that for many purposes—though not for mine—may be excessively vague.

Let us first outline form, dimensions, and key relationships. More or less at random, I will take "Molto voglio" from *Rinaldo* as a model, pretty much typical of its kind in everything but its orchestration (it has an elaborate oboe obbligato). It is in three sections: it begins with a 33-measure section in C major, which comes to a full close on the tonic; a second section follows, of 9 measures, beginning in the relative minor (although the first few notes are ambiguous between C and A minor) and closing in the dominant of that key (i.e. E minor); at this point the instruction "da capo" appears, indicating that the entire first section is to be repeated (no doubt with some embellishments by the singer, and perhaps with some by the oboist as well). The length of the sections is in the proportion of somewhat more than three to one, which is about average for the lot. And in part because of this disparity in length, the musical character of the sections is quite distinct (of which more anon).

The opening section is introduced by an elaborate 8-measure instrumental ritornello, which both sets the emotional tone of the piece and presents the thematic material to be developed. At the ninth measure the voice then enters, with the instrumental ritornello replying to it in concerto-like exchanges between solo and tutti. The thematic material is fragmented (as, in consequence, is the text) and worked out in the familiar manner of Baroque *Fortspinnung*. There are three solo entries of varying lengths, separated by instrumental tuttis, and a repetition of the opening as a coda, reduced now to 6 measures. The impression is one of a musical mosaic: lyrical, to be sure, but at the same time, within small dimensions, structured of various parts, and thematically developed and worked upon.

In sharp and purposeful contrast, the second section is without instrumental ritornelli and presents, in its 9 measures, one long, unbroken, and sinuous melodic line, with no obvious thematic relation to the previous section. Its character is decidedly lyrical, without real development. It is accompanied only by the continuo instruments. In all of this the second section of "Molto voglio" is more or less representative. The details of orchestration vary, some second sections are more elaborate and concerto-like, and some do have thematic relation to the first section; but by and large this aria is paradigmatic.

Because the second sections of the da capo arias are considerably shorter than the first, frequently minimally orchestrated, and without much "development," they have gotten the thoroughly undeserved reputation of being musically perfunctory and of comparatively low quality. At least with regard to Handel's second sections, nothing could be more mistaken or musically obtuse. What the second sections require of the listener is a change of musical perspective. While one listens primarily for structure, development, and counterpoint in the first sections, one listens for a pure and splendidly extended melodic line in the second. And if one does that, Handel's second sections will display stirring melodic beauty. When that beauty fails, it is not because second sections are congenitally poor in musical quality, but simply because Homer nods.

The point of the second sections, then, is to provide not merely key contrast; but musical contrast in general. If we think of the da capo aria as, within its small dimensions, a concerto for voice, the second section is its "singing" middle movement.

A complete Handelian da capo aria, with the repetition of its first section tastefully ornamented by the singer (and solo instrumentalists, if there are any), is a perfect musical form. And except for the traditional (and groundless) disparagement of the second sections, probably no one has ever doubted that; but it bears repeating, and elaboration, for present purposes. The da capo aria is a perfect embodiment of the eighteenth-century aesthetic ideal of pure beauty, as expressed (among other places) in Hutcheson's formula *uniformity amidst variety*. The tripartite form itself exhibits that, with the second section providing the "variety," and the return—intact or, where "dal segno" rather than "da capo" is the instruction, more or less intact—of the first section providing the "uniformity." But the first section alone is a model of *uniformity amidst variety* as well, with the recurrent ritornello as the unifying principle, the changes rung on the thematic material as the varying one.

If we recall now the bifurcation of music aesthetics in the early eighteenth century, which it was one of our concerns to outline in the previous chapter, we can see that that branch providing philosophical justification for the pure musical parameters found full practical realization in the da capo aria. If early-eighteenth-century philosophy, albeit indirectly and deviously, pushed the opera composer to cultivate fully musical dramatic forms, the da capo aria seems to me to be (in retrospect, to be sure) a predictable result. Whatever might be criticized in it as a dramatic "representation" (and we shall get to that shortly), there is nothing that can be faulted as pure music: in that it is the perfect realization of the Enlightenment musical ideal.

But of course it is as a dramatic vehicle that the da capo aria was criticized in its own time (and ours), on the grounds (roughly) that verisimilitude was sacrificed to pure musical form. Before we get to these very formidable criticisms, we must first examine the relation of these works to their texts. We will then be in a position to evaluate them as dramatic music, and to pass reasoned judgment on their detractors.

o 10 o   "The total number of arias in Handel's operas and Italian cantatas, including many still unpublished, must amount to something like two thousand, more than three times the number of Schubert's songs."[32] Given the variability of human nature, such a number must contain, even allowing for the strictures of the *opera seria* conventions, a considerable variety of texts. Nevertheless, for my own particular purposes, two basic kinds can be distinguished, the first breaking down into two sub-classes. The second, although figuring prominently in Handel's operas, will not concern me here; for if I can defend the first and most characteristic kind of aria against its detractors, I think I will have done enough to secure the Handelian *opera seria* as a dramatic representation.

The first class of aria texts I shall call "emotive soliloquies." These are texts in which a character tells us how he or she feels about things at this particular point in the drama. They are introspective revelations; and each expresses some dominant or leading emotion which, of course, gives Handel a cue for his musical invention. These emotive soliloquies, I have said, are of two kinds: those where the leading or dominant emotion is actually named, as "resolve" and "hope" are in "Molto voglio":

> Molto voglio, molto spero
> Nulla devo dubitar. . . .
>
> (Much I resolve, and more I hope
> Doubt is below my soul. . . .);[33]

and those where, although the leading or dominant emotion is not named, it is obvious enough from the circumstances in which the character is placed and from the words that are uttered. (There are other ways, after all, of expressing grief in words besides saying "I am grieving.") "Io già t'amai," quoted earlier, will do as an example of the latter kind, where "defiance" and "scorn" are not mentioned but are surely expressed (both the singer's and his former lover's).

The other class of aria texts, which I mention only to put aside, comprises what I would call "rhetorical soliloquies." These are comments—usually, but not necessarily always, more "cerebral" than emotional—about the situation in which the character finds him- or herself, built around some elaborate metaphorical figure or simile. Often the metaphor or simile gives Handel at least part of his musical inspiration—a horn obbligato and hunting calls, for example, in *Giulio Cesare*, where Caesar compares himself to a hunter, "l'astuto caccitor." (Images of snakes and serpents, which are frequent, invariably call forth sinuous musical lines.)

Now it should be pointed out that the class of emotive soliloquies and the class of rhetorical soliloquies are not mutually exclusive: one can, after all, use rhetorical figures to talk about emotions. Where a rhetorical soliloquy is, at the same time, an emotive one, what I shall have to say about the da capo aria will apply to it *pari passu*. Where not, not. But I will put rhetorical soliloquies of the purely "cerebral" kind aside, for present purposes; for it is the emotive soliloquies that are the real machinery of the *opera seria*. As Dean aptly and accurately puts it, the librettist's "task is to evolve a sequence of strong aria situations for each character in turn, and they must be sufficiently varied to evoke arias in as many different moods as possible—vengeful, despairing, amorous, reflective, pathetic, and so on."[34] The composer's dramatic task, then, is to "represent" in music these emotional outbursts. The *opera seria* is basically a drama of emotions; and its verisimilitude, if it has any, must therefore lie in the composer's ability to make the da capo aria a believable vehicle of emotive "expression." How did Handel accomplish this?

The instrumental ritornello, whether (as is usually the case) it forms the introduction to the first section or (less frequently) delays its entrance until after the first vocal phrase, is obviously intended to be a kind of emotive icon. Whatever the leading emotion of the text, the ritornello will reflect it, and so, by consequence, will the vocal line, for which the ritornello more or less provides the musical material. Sometimes the way in which the thematic material is expressive of the leading motive is very obvious, as in the classic "rage" aria, where the "darkness" of the passion is reflected in minor key and "somber" theme, its violence by busy, violently active musical figuration (Example 12).

> La turba adulatrice
> da me ritiri'l piè;
> basta che l'ira ultrice
> rimanga sol con me:
> vo' vendicarmi.

Regnante vilipeso,
gl'oltraggi soffrirò?
Padre dal figlio offeso,
l'orgoglio no sapro
punir coll'armi?

(Troublesome flattery be gone; vindictive anger need only remain with me; I shall be revenged. Shall I, despised ruler, suffer these outrages? Father by the son offended, shall I not know how to punish with arms?)[35]

EXAMPLE 12
Handel, *Sosarme*, Act I, Scene VIII

Or, again, in the conventional expression of grief, halting pace, minor key, touches of chromaticism, with the familiar "drooping" melodic line—all, in the present instance, reinforced by a rich woodwind coloring that favors the "mournful" accents of the double reeds (Example 13).

> Ah! crudel, Il pianto mio
> Deh! ti mova per pietà!
> O infedel al mio desio
> Proverai la crudeltà.
>
> (Cruel charmer that I love thee,
> Fain would move thee with my pain;
> 'Tis with grief that cold I prove thee
> Lov'd so truly, love again.)[36]

Sometimes, to be sure, the musical realization of emotions may not be quite so obvious and easy to divine, as in the figure Handel chooses to "express" hope and resolve in "Molto voglio" (Example 14). But even here it does not require *much* craft to see what Handel is up to, as long as we start out with the assumption that although we might, without the help of a text, recognize a melody as expressive of joy or melancholy, or recognize a melody as inappropriate for hope and resolve, it requires a text to help us see that (and how) a melody might be hopeful or resolute. Surely, though, we are able to see that Handel's tune in "Molto voglio," with its vigorous thrust and jaunty, confident mien, can be described as "hopeful" and "resolute"—certainly not halting or tentative—or at least "appropriate" rather than "inappropriate" to the expression of those emotions or states of mind.

Nor is it without significance that all of the arias we have so far examined "express" emotions that are contained both in Descartes' and Mattheson's catalogues and, indeed, comply fully with the latter's instructions for their realization in musical terms, in so far as these instructions are specific enough to be followed. "Hope is an elevation of the soul or spirits . . . ," Mattheson tells us; and although he omits to say just how this might be represented in music, it is not too much to surmise that that is because he thought it obvious rather than difficult. If hope is an elevation, a "going up," of the animal spirits, what more natural way to represent them and it than to begin with an upward leap of a fifth, as Handel does, and, where possible, to write an upward-moving scalewise line, combined with an upward leap, as again Handel does not fail to do (in the oboe solo of measures 5 and 6). I do not suggest for a moment that Handel composed with *Der vollkommene Capellmeister* at his elbow (although "Molto voglio" is remarkably consistent with that hypothesis).

There was no need for that. For one thing, Mattheson's book was as much a reflection and rationalization of already existing musical practice as it was a set of prescriptions for it. For another, its contents, and the contents of other books like it, were pretty much common property by this time, having filtered down and become part of what Leonard Meyer likes to call "intellectual scuttlebutt." In other words, one needn't have read, or even heard of *Der vollkommene Capellmeister* to know what it said about musical "expression" and a great many other things, any more than one would have to have read the *Principia* to have heard about gravity.

The upshot of all of this is that the principal thematic material of the Handelian da capo arias—that is, those that are of the emotive soliloquy kind—is pretty much always a recognizable representation of the leading emotion: that is to say, a representation of its phenomenology and behavioral manifestations as those were understood, in the Cartesian tradition,

EXAMPLE 13
Handel, *Rinaldo*, Act II, Scene VIII

through the instrumentality of the "vital spirits." In short, as representations of the Cartesian emotions, the first sections of Handel's da capo arias are, from the point of view of emotive similitude, entirely satisfactory. Where they are not, which is seldom, it is a failure not of the genre but of the composer.

The reason why a modern audience may sometimes fail to perceive this emotive verisimilitude is that both our theoretical understanding and our common understanding of the emotions diverge in important respects from the Cartesian. Aside from the obvious fact that the "vital spirits" have joined phlogiston and the ether in the museum of failed scientific curiosities, we tend to think of the emotions as far more messy and ill-defined than did Descartes and his followers; and hence we tend, I would think, to find Handel's representations of emotions somewhat staid, stiff, and conventional: therefore not responsive to the emotions they are sup-

EXAMPLE 14
Handel, *Rinaldo*, Act I, Scene V

posed to reflect. For just as the Cartesian emotions are (as I denominated them in the previous chapter) "set pieces," so Handel's evocations of them are musical "set pieces," self-contained, hard-edged, and each complete in itself: emotions carved in marble.

But that is just the point. All artistic verisimilitude is relative to some theory, whether formal or informal, explicit or implicit, of the way the world is. And unless we wait for the final theory and the last work of art, we will always have to make the conceptual leap into other people's views of the world to appreciate their artistic representations of it. This is to ask no more of an audience at *Radamisto* than of an audience at *Hamlet* or the *Oresteia* (with regard to the last it is probably asking less). Given the implicit theory under which Handel labored, his musical representations of the emotions are perfect. He represented the world of feeling as a Cartesian would have known it, as Shakespeare represented that of the Elizabethans; and to the extent that the Cartesian view differs from our own, we must become imbued with it in order to appreciate the perfection with which Handel succeeded in representing the emotive life in music.

Whether this is too much to ask of an opera audience I will inquire in the next chapter. Certainly it would not have had to be asked at all of the audiences of Handel's day, for they shared (implicitly or explicitly) his Cartesian views. What, then, could they have objected to in the da capo aria on grounds of lack of verisimilitude? For object they did, on just those grounds. To that vexed question I now will turn, with, I hope, an answer to their objections—too late, alas, for them, but not for us.

◦ 11 ◦   What contemporary auditors of the da capo aria objected to was not the lack of verisimilitude of the first or second sections *per se*: it was the form as a whole—in other words, the return to the first section after the second had been completed. "People don't behave that way" was essentially what they were saying: they don't repeat, verbatim, what they said just a moment before; or, if you prefer to conceive of the da capo aria, when the character is alone, as thought made audible (as Orson Welles and Sir Laurence Olivier apparently conceived of Shakespearean soliloquy in their films), people don't think that way either. And to that extent, anyway, the da capo aria is a false, inaccurate representation of nature. As Algarotti puts it: "Words are to be treated in no other manner but according as the passion dictates; and when the sense of an air is finished, the first part of it ought never to be sung over again, which is one of our modern innovations and quite repugnant to the natural process of our speech and passions, that are not accustomed to thus turn about and recoil upon themselves."[37] This was a familiar refrain; and Gluck echoed it in the Dedication to *Alceste*, where he expressed his reluctance, as in the da capo aria, "to finish the aria where its sense may perhaps not end for the convenience of the singer who wishes to show that he can capriciously vary a passage in a number of guises. . . ." Furthermore, Gluck objected not only to the repetition of the first section of the aria, but to the very structural principle—that is, the ritornello itself—on which the first section was based, a principle that would require the composer "to arrest an actor in the greatest heat of dialogue in order to wait for a tiresome ritornello. . . ."[38]

Such charges did not remain unchallenged in Gluck's time; and what Gluck's contemporaries had to say in defense of "florid" dramatic song is not without interest and some merit. Jean François de Laharpe, an admirer of Gluck as well as a frequent critic of him, defended the aria more or less as a convention that must be accepted, like speaking poetry in a play.

> I find these objections [of Gluck's] completely illusory. To begin with, if one is to admit the song [into opera], then one must admit it at its most beautiful and it is no more natural to sing badly than to sing well. All the arts are founded on conventions, on certain basic factors. When I go to the Opéra, it is to hear music. I am not ignorant of the fact that Alceste did not bid farewell to Admetos by singing an aria, but as Alceste is on the stage to sing, if her grief and her love are communicated to me in a very melodious aria, I will enjoy her song and at the same time become interested in her misfortune. For I have come for that, just as, when I go to see Zaïre [a tragedy of Voltaire's] at the Comédie Française, I expect to weep over the unhappiness of love and to hear charming verses.[39]

There is something in the nature of a "slippery slope" argument here. On the one hand, we want to agree fully with Laharpe that the appreciation of any art must begin with the accepting of conventions, the appreciation of opera with the accepting of the convention that people will "speak" in music. Further, once this convention is accepted—and if it is not, opera, of course, cannot ever get a foothold—it certainly seems to follow that we will have good reason to want the best music possible in our operas, which is to say, music with all of the formal, structural, harmonic, and contrapuntal artifice music was capable of mustering in the high Baroque: in a word, the da capo aria.

But once on the slippery slope, it is difficult to get off before the slide to the bottom. For if you allow that accepting the operatic convention of speaking in song entails accepting also the unconstrained premise of the best—which is to say the richest—music possible, you will inevitably end up not with drama-made-music but with the completest concert, which is opera's limiting case as a dramatic form. Gluck saw this quite clearly when he replied to Laharpe: ". . . I would perhaps venture to try to prove to him that the delightful melody which he admires and which I also admire in the beautiful Italian arias, that those symmetrical forms, those periodic repetitions which give the arias a piquant and pleasant effect, that all these are incompatible with the expression and force needed to depict great inner emotions while at the same time lending truth, speed and unity to the dramatic action. . . ."[40] It was not that, as a pure musician, Gluck did not love the complex and convoluted beauty of the large da capo aria; on the contrary, he "also admire[d] . . . the beautiful Italian arias, . . . those symmetrical forms, those periodic repetitions which give the arias a piquant and pleasant effect. . . ." But as a dramatic composer, he saw that some constraint must be put on the musical parameters in the interest of dramatic and emotive verisimilitude, or "mere" music would be the result.

A more fruitful direction, to this end, than Laharpe's was at least hinted at by another contemporary critic of Gluck, Antoine Fabre, who wrote to the composer:

> How is it possible, Monsieur, to argue that passion is constantly unbalanced and without repose? It is well known that great movements must not be confined by measure, cadence, etc., and that there must be the recitative obbligato [i.e. accompanied recitative] in which you so excel; but when Nature, tired of effort, reverts to one sole interest, to one feeling which is the amalgam of the crowd of emotions to which one has been subject, it is this one feeling which remains in all its force and to which Nature returns and is reduced despite herself.[41]

There is here a strategy that is clear, and a content that is somewhat opaque. The strategy, which I consider the right one, is to re-examine the premise, offered without argument by both Gluck and Algarotti, that the "form" of the emotive life, as of human behavior, is at odds with the form of the da capo aria. The content, that is to say, the conclusion Fabre reaches about emotions and behavior as a result of this strategy of re-examination, is not as easy to make out; and as I had come to my own conclusions in this regard independently of the passage quoted above, and prior to reading it, I may well be reading into it what conclusions I already reached. But as I am more interested in arguing for my conclusions than in interpreting Fabre, I shall not worry over much about trifles. In any case, what excites my interest is Fabre's use of the words "revert" and "return." Nature, Fabre says, "reverts to one sole interest, to one feeling . . ."; and, again, "it is this one feeling which remains . . . and to which Nature returns and is reduced despite herself." The suggestion here, I think, is one of compulsion, of *obsession*: we are forced, sometimes, to feel the way we do, or to think about something, whether we will or no.

Now musically, Fabre and I are fishing, I think, in different waters. Gluck had, it should be noted, objected not only to the da capo aria but, at least at times, to aria *per se*—to "florid song"—on the grounds that emotions, which music is supposed to representationally reflect, are fleeting and flitting, one giving way to another, not to return, whereas aria makes this emotive train—quite unnaturally, it is claimed—stand still and dwell, for the length of the aria, on one single emotion or mood. Gluck proposed to reflect this train of fleeting emotions, which he thought characterizes the true emotive life, with the nervous flow of accompanied recitative, or "recitative obbligato," as it was then frequently called. Fabre countered by observing that although we may indeed experience the ebb and flow of emotions, and that that ebb and flow is indeed accurately represented by accompanied recitative, not by aria, there is sometimes at least one emotion that is dominant, and to this the mind will tend to "revert," to "return"; and it is just this dominant emotion on which the aria can realistically dwell.

But could we not apply this observation to the external and internal structure of the da capo aria itself? In the first section of the aria, a character, possessed of some emotion—hope, grief, anger, or what-have-you—expresses it to a collocutor, or perhaps in soliloquy. In the second section, some tangential but relevant detour of thought or emotion is explored, only to return obsessively to the leading emotion again in the repeat of the first section. Unrealistic, says Algarotti: "quite repugnant to the natural process of our speech and passions, that are not accustomed to thus turn about and recoil upon themselves." Quite to the contrary, I say, it is the most natural thing in the world both in thought and in speech: a well-known psychological phenomenon. It is typically obsessive behavior. When possessed by an overpowering emotion or thought, our minds, no matter how we try to prevent it, return inexorably to the emotions that consume us; and this is as true of our speech as of our thought. Have you ever talked to someone in the throes of grief or the first flush of love? You can lead the conversation where you will—always it will return, "recoil," to the object of grief or love: the death of the husband, the mistress' eyebrow. The da capo aria, in the return of the first section, is the perfect musical representation of obsessive emotion: of the *idée fixe*. And so too is the internal structure of the first section itself. What better musical representation of the obsessively recurring emotion than the obsessively recurring ritornello theme? Only if the theme were ill suited to the emotion would the ritornello principle be ill suited to this psychological phenomenon. In Handel, however, that is hardly a worry. Indeed, it is just the leading emotion of the text that dictates, in almost every case, the emotional tone and musical structure of the ritornello's thematic material. Berlioz found a way to represent this phenomenon musically, in his *Symphonie fantastique*, in the recurrent *idée fixe* theme, and has been praised for his psychological insight. The *opera seria* composers devised the same method a century and a half before, and were damned as psychologically obtuse.

In both the ritornello and the da capo, then, the Handelian aria is a perfect musical representation of the thought and speech, the emotion and expression of the character obsessed. But, it will surely be objected to this claim, emotive obsession may very well be one character's dominant trait; and the da capo aria would surely be the ideal representation of that character's inner and external emotive life. However, all the characters in *opera seria* sing da capo arias: surely it can't be the ideal representation of them all? The answer to that question is "Yes it can."

That is just the genius of the *opera seria*: the perfect adaptation of its music to its text, its text to its music. Indeed, the *opera seria* libretto presents us with a complete stable of obsessed personages; and that is precisely why the composer can present us, without the least sacrifice of verisimilitude on the one hand or of perfect musical form on the other, with an unending string of da capo arias. Now Handel wrote in excess of forty Italian operas; and, needless to say, in order to fully support my claim that they are populated for the most part by obsessive characters, I would have to go into exhaustive length, examining each in detail. That neither I nor my readers could endure. But failing that, I can, I think, give some more specific idea and justify what I have in mind by adducing an example which, I urge, can be multiplied without much trouble forty times over.

Consider, then, the main characters of *Ariodante*. Prince Ariodante, the hero, is in love with Princess Ginevra, who reciprocates his affection. She is also courted (for political as well as amorous motives) by the villain of the piece, Polinessa. Her father, the King of Scotland, fully approves the union of Ariodante and Ginevra; and Polinessa plots to get her instead.

Of these four, Polinessa remains absolutely steady to his text throughout the whole opera: the complete villain who will stop at nothing (including murder, of course) to gain his ends. He is, in short, the totally single-minded bad guy; and nothing more need be said to prove his obsessive, unrelieved wickedness.

Each of the other three undergoes a violent change of character in the second act, due to Polinessa's successful plot to make Ariodante and the King falsely believe that Ginevra is "unchaste." (The details of his scheme need not detain us.) The King completely rejects his daughter following the "discovery," swinging manically from doting father to "You are no daughter of mine." Ginevra, in true operatic tradition, simply goes mad. And Ariodante swings, in an equally manic change, from obsessively devoted lover to attempted suicide. So the point is that even where the characters of a Handelian opera undergo a transformation, it is never a psychologically moderate one but a "conversion" from one obsession to another. To see this one need only reflect on what more "normal" people might do in similar circumstances. Most parents do not disown their erring children but undergo more reasonable changes in attitude. Jilted young ladies get somewhat depressed but seldom go mad. And suicide, although not an unknown reaction to a lover's unfaithfulness, is not a very common one either: one need only compare Figaro's behavior to Adriodante's to see that. Thus, like moral, religious, and ideological fanatics, the characters of *opera seria*—emotional fanatics, if you will— either remain obsessively faithful to the last or, where they change, change to an equally obsessive fanaticism at (usually) the opposite pole. And this the da capo aria, that most obsessive, fanatic of musical forms, forever returning to its original complaint, perfectly reflects: perfectly transforms into drama-made-music.

Like two living organisms, in perfect symbiotic relation, mutually beneficial to one another, the *opera seria* libretto and the da capo aria perform their reciprocal functions, to the end of constituting the first successful and, if we have ears to hear it, one of the most perfect translations of drama into pure musical form, conceding no advantage to either. That the da capo aria is a perfect musical form no one has ever doubted. That it is also a perfect representation of human emotion, in thought and in expression, is equally true, just so long as the emotion is Cartesian, and the character obsessed. The librettist, whether he knew it or not, assured the composer of both; and the composer, whether he knew it or not, fell naturally into line. When the stars were propitious, as they sometimes were for Handel, a genuine operatic masterpiece was the result.

◦ 12 ◦ I have argued, in this chapter and the last, that Handel's *opera seria* is a perfect embodiment of the bifurcated musical aesthetics of the early eighteenth century: a theory that, for the first time, provided the opera in particular, and vocal music in general, with a philosophical foundation both for musical representation and for the pure musical parameters. That the Handelian *opera seria* was successfully propelled in the direction of pure music has never been denied; it was in that respect the completest concert. That it was also propelled, to some extent, in the direction of dramatic verisimilitude has, I suppose, been more or less grudgingly recognized by a few "enthusiasts"; but that it was propelled far enough to account it a dramatic and representational—and *operatic*— success has been denied by almost everyone. And even where, as in the case of Winton Dean, to whom we owe so many sympathetic insights, the defense has been wholehearted, it seems to me, at times, to a certain extent self-conscious: running scared.

But the defense I have tried to give of Handelian *opera seria* as real drama-made-music—Cartesian, and peculiarly devoted to the emotively obsessed rather than to the emotively healthy—is certain to be met with some degree of skepticism. With a friend like me, perhaps, Handel doesn't need any enemies. Can an art-form as direct and open, as over-stated and emotively straightforward, as opera is commonly thought to be really survive, if such a cerebral defense as the one I have offered is the best one can do? If Descartes and Leibniz, Hutcheson and Mattheson are required reading for *Orlando* and *Rodelinda*, can they really be oper-atic masterpieces? Or are they merely exercises for the mind of the musical zealot?

What perhaps suggests itself here is that my defense of Handel's opera *itself* is in need of a defense. I accept that assessment, and will try to give such a "meta-defense" in the following chapter, while also trying to show what, in the more traditional defense, I find questionable.

CHAPTER VIII

Listening with the ear of theory

o 1 o We know better than to think that music is the "international language." Taken literally, it cannot be true if only because music is not a language at all. But I doubt that such an assertion was ever meant to be taken literally in the first place. Rather, it was supposed to convey something about the purported immediacy of music to the "uneducated senses." To appreciate *Faust* or *The Magic Mountain*, you have to read German and know a whole lot about philosophy, politics, religion, history, and so many other things. To appreciate Beethoven's *Eroica*, however, all you have to do is to be born, not be tone-deaf (if there is such a thing), and have the price of admission. (You can even be born in China.) That is what it means for music to be an "international language" and *Faust* or *The Magic Mountain* a laboriously acquired national taste.

We know better, however, than to think, even in this metaphorical sense, that music is an "international language." We know, for example, that a person of exquisite musical sensibilities, born and raised in South India, will evince little or no interest in or appreciation of the *Eroica* if it is his or her first encounter with Western music; and we know the reverse to be true as well: that the finely trained Western ear will find the Indian raga a pleasant and exotic jangle for about five minutes, and then unutterably boring.

Not only is music not "international," it is not even "national": witness the fact that many highly trained musical people find Bach unintelligible, while they listen with pleasure and understanding to the complex polyphony, intricate rhythmic structure, and variation techniques of jazz while their equally musical counterparts dote on the intricate canonic writing of the *Goldberg Variations* and find jazz a buzzing, blooming confusion.

The only lesson to be learnt from this is that music no more appeals directly to the uneducated senses than does literature to the uneducated mind. To appreciate even a folk song or a Strauss waltz, let alone the *Goldberg Variations* or a Josquin motet, we have to know a whole lot of things, as we do if we are to appreciate *Faust* or *The Magic Mountain*. And to appreciate them *fully* requires not merely what I shall call subliminal knowing, but knowing in the full-blooded conscious sense as well, as I must know about politics in Germany prior to the First World War to fully appreciate *The Magic Mountain*, or philosophy in Germany in the late eighteenth century to fully appreciate *Faust*.

What I referred to as subliminal knowing, in music, is the kind of awareness that the musical baptism of simple immersion in a culture produces. By being born in the United States, and living a life there, a person will, without necessarily being aware of it, acquire certain inner expectations that constitute what we would call a familiarity with the musical culture of the place: in this place, the harmonic major-minor system, key structure, and melody built on the equal-tempered whole- and half-step. Likewise, the person born in South India will, equally unawares, internalize the monophonic and microtonal musical style that permeates his or her life. Appreciation begins with some sort of built-in system of tonal expectations, "hypotheses" about what will come next, and so on; and these expectations and hypotheses, and the tones they will apply to, will, of course, be vastly different if they were brought into being (not necessarily awareness, remember) by the music of the West or the music of South India.

Such subliminal knowing is, of course, a necessary condition for musical appreciation in any musical culture whatever. No music anywhere, in this sense of "music" and of "know," appeals to the uneducated ear. Only sounds do that. (Infants and dogs can be fascinated with sounds but not with music.) But it is hardly a sufficient condition for a full and rich musical appreciation, at least where the musical culture in question is of the complexity of Western or South Indian, or any other comparable kind.

Two refinements in musical knowledge, both involving a full-blooded, conscious sense of "know," lead to a richer and deeper musical experience. To begin with, what I have called subliminal knowledge may, in varying degrees, be brought to consciousness. I then can put some vague sense of "something funny has happened, and now things are straightened out" under some such description as "a deceptive cadence to a six-chord postponed the expected full close in the tonic," and so forth. But even where a solid course in theory and harmony has brought most of this subliminal knowledge to consciousness and put it under commonly accepted descriptions, there will be a good deal lacking (to take but one kind of example) in one's appreciation of so complex a work as the *Goldberg Variations*. For one needs here something to make the work coherent. One can, of course, just listen to the splendid musical sounds; but that will quickly pall, and it will be hard not to be basically dissatisfied, musically, without some guiding principle as well to bind one's attention and to make sense of the work. In this case, of course, it would be knowledge of what a canon is, what its varieties are, and how that musical form, in some of its varieties, is instantiated by various crucial movements of the work. I cannot see how a rich experience of the *Goldberg Variations* is possible without that: without, that is, full conscious knowledge of what canonic writing is, and what constraints it put Bach under when he undertook to write basically canonic variations.

With these distinctions in the background, let us return again to the subject of Handel's *opera seria*.

○ 2 ○   Generally, we approach puzzlement with, or outright rejection of, the larger musical forms in two ways. The less radical procedure is the reduction of the unfamiliar to the familiar, by use of comparisons. "You don't like X, but you do like Y; but notice how like Y X really is, in respects 1, 2, and 3. Perhaps you missed that. If, however, you liked Y for having 1, 2, and 3, now that you see them in X surely you will begin to like X as well." (You may substitute "understand," "appreciate," "value" for "like," and follow the procedure through for those as well.) There is, of course, nothing wrong with this way of doing things, and just as long as you can find a Y that is sufficiently familiar, and sufficiently like X in relevant respects, the fact that there is something incomplete about the strategy will not trouble you—any more than being told that "horse" means "equine quadruped" need trouble you on account of the fact that it doesn't also tell you what "equine" and "quadruped" mean, just as long as *you* know what they mean.

Not surprisingly, the name most frequently invoked by Dean, in his discussion of Handel's operas, is Mozart's. Indeed, he avers that

> The music of no other dramatic composer comes closer to Mozart in its detached but penetrating insight into human nature, its capacity to make a profound statement in a frivolous or comic situation, and its peculiar mixture of irony and pathos, solemnity and grace, tragedy and serenity. These things can be found from time to time in Handel's oratorios; in the operas, where he is concerned not with nations or spiritual concepts but with the emotions and sufferings of individuals, they are his central preoccupation.[1]

I shall discuss in another place whether, in fact, it is possible at all for any operatic music to provide insights into human nature or make profound (or any other kind of) statements about anything. What I merely wish to bring out here is the strategy that Dean is employing to defend the Handelian *opera seria*; and that, clearly, is the strategy of rendering the unfamiliar familiar by comparison. "You know and love Mozart's operas, don't you? And you don't care for Handel's. But look: you love Mozart's operas for their insights into human nature, and for their profound statements, etc. Handel's have those too; no dramatic composer comes closer to Mozart in these respects than Handel. So now you can know and love Handel's operas also; they are really just another version of the old, familiar, and loved Mozart pattern."

Another way of doing the same kind of thing for Handel's operas is to concentrate on what I called in the last chapter the "bumps": those perturbations in the uniform texture of secco recitative and da capo aria that has given Handel the reputation for being "undramatic" and just plain boring when taken in the full, uncut operatic dose. These "bumps" include orchestrally accompanied recitative; arioso and aria without da capo; da capo arias that deviate from the normal form, either by being interrupted (by recitative) or by blending into the recitative; instrumental interludes (usually, but not always, "battle" pieces); choruses; duets of the da capo aria kind; and, most interesting (but most unusual), "dramatic ensembles" for two or more voices.

Why should our calling attention to the bumps be a defense of Handel's operas? Because, to begin with, they are familiar ingredients of later operas. Further, they are the kinds of things we associate with "dramatic" music. We tend to think of the "dramatic" as the sudden change. (The meeting ended "dramatically"—i.e. suddenly—when the Fredonian delegation walked out. The Second World War ended "dramatically"—i.e. suddenly—with the dropping of the atom bombs.) Rapid alternation of musical forms in an opera, or even rapid alterations of musical style, texture, mood, structure, or harmony in a purely instrumental composition, inevitably invite the epithet "dramatic." And since the dramatic is the familiar thing and the thing we like in opera (if we like opera at all), calling attention to this "dramatic" aspect of Handel's operas is thought to make them more accessible, more familiar, more likable to an audience that dotes on the "dramatic" operas of Mozart and Verdi. And to a certain extent, of course, this is true.

But the more compelling truth is that the attempt to defend Handel's operas by the reduction to the familiar is an exercise in futility, at least at the surface level we are examining; it must fail because so much more *separates* Handel's operatic practice from Mozart's, or Verdi's, or Weber's, or any other "modern," familiar, and accepted one that invites comparison, than joins it with any of those that the ammunition just isn't there. And Dean, although he does employ this defense (at least implicitly) throughout his book, recognizes full well the gap that separates Handel from the "regular operatic repertory," a gap that "may require a conscious act of adjustment even from an intelligent audience before it can tune to the right wave-length."[2] My own view is that it not only "may require a conscious act of adjustment . . ." but that it must.

There is a view abroad in philosophical circles that represents criticism of the arts as solely directed toward what is unique in any given art work.[3] I do not subscribe to that view and certainly do not wish to be seen as arguing from it in insisting that little can be gained in defense of Handelian opera by pointing out its similarities to Mozart, or Verdi, or anyone else. Where such similarities do exist, it is the duty of a responsible critic to point them out, nor is doing so unhelpful; on the contrary, it enriches knowledge and enhances appreciation.

With regard to Handel's operas, however, the reduction to familiarity has severe limitations as a defense strategy. To emphasize the bumps is only to court frustration. Their occurrence in any given opera is so infrequent that if they are the measure of the opera's success as a work of art it cannot fail to seem poor indeed, in comparison (say) to Mozart or Verdi (or even to lesser musical figures than Handel himself). Mere frequency, of course, is not a measure of aesthetic import; and, indeed, as Dean has quite wisely pointed out, the very infrequency with which the bumps occur to agitate the surface of a Handel opera makes them larger than life, the effect far exceeding what one might expect from their modest dimensions.

> The point here is an axiom of aesthetics. The more restricted a convention within which an artist works, the greater the scope for achieving the maximum effect with the minimum means, always provided he has the stature to command his materials. One of the most potent weapons in the armory of any composer is the ability, with the help of a formula or convention, to lead his audience to expect one thing and then surprise them by doing something different. . . . The restrictions of a closed form become, in the hands of a master, the gateway to freedom.
>
> Just as Beethoven or Haydn or Mozart uses the sonata form to arouse, prolong or disappoint expectation, Handel uses the da capo aria and the other opera seria conventions.[4]

Even allowing, however, that the effect of the bumps is out of all proportion to their modest dimensions and infrequent occurrence, a defense of Handel's operatic corpus based on them alone is bound to fail. Not only is there too little there; but calling attention unduly to this aspect of the works falsifies their essential nature. When a dramatic ensemble or "broken" da capo aria occurs, it is pennies from heaven. The fact nevertheless remains that the real wealth of the Handelian *opera seria* is in the nearly unbroken texture of secco recitative and da capo aria in its normal form. A responsible defense of the genre with any hope of success must address itself primarily to that.

o 3 o   That the reduction to the familiar, even when successful, is incomplete as a defense can readily be seen. For it will only work if what it reduces the problematic to is itself unproblematical. Just as it does no good to tell someone that "horse" means "equine quadruped" if he or she does not know what "equine" or "quadruped" means, so, similarly, it serves little purpose to show that Handel's operas are really much like Mozart's and Verdi's if those are also problematical works for those to whom this news is imparted. The reduction to the familiar is, at best, an enthymeme in danger of falling into an infinite regress. In any event, it really tells us nothing, of itself, about what the aesthetic nature of the work it "reduces" really is, only that it is like some others which themselves will be in need of explanation if we are ever to get at the heart of the matter. What alternative does this leave us?

What is left, when the reduction to the familiar fails, is to start from scratch: to get to the bottom of things by providing the work, or, as in this case, the body of works, with an accounting that makes them hang together as functioning aesthetic entities in their own right. If no such accounting is possible, the works must be fatally flawed. It is this kind of accounting that I have tried to give Handel's operas in the preceding pages.

I said that I would offer a defense of my defense—an accounting of my accounting—and I want to get to that now. Let me begin by reverting to the distinction made earlier between subliminal and conscious knowing. Certainly, my defense of the Handelian *opera seria* requires that a considerable amount of seemingly extraneous knowledge about the philosophical and psychological background of the genre be acquired, and applied by the listener: knowledge not of the subliminal kind that any acculturated music-lover could be expected to have, or even the subliminal made conscious in the form of music theory, which the trained amateur might possess, but, rather, knowledge of a distinctly non-musical kind, and some esoteric knowledge at that. But let me remind the reader, to start with, of a point made already about such knowledge, namely, that it is required for any rich and full experience of any complex musical work. In this the *opera seria* does not differ from other kinds of music and should not somehow be thought musically deficient because of it. No music speaks to the untutored ear, and no complex music speaks deeply to the ear that has not been trained accordingly.

To be sure, the *Goldberg Variations* requires for its appreciation only what might be thought of as purely musical knowledge: what a canon is, what various forms it takes, what a French overture is, fugue, chaconne, and so forth; but that of course is because it is itself a work of pure, textless, programless music. It is only to be expected that an operatic work, with a text and a plot, characters, and dramatic situations, requires not only that kind of knowledge but knowledge of non-musical kinds as well. Where questions of dramatic verisimilitude arise and where dramatic verisimilitude (or lack thereof) will be an evaluative criterion, I must surely know something about *what* is being represented as well as *how* to either appreciate or judge. And what is represented (except in unusual cases) is not music but the world as the librettist, the composer, and (at least some of) their contemporaries construe it. I appreciate or judge verisimilitude, then, in no other way than by knowing at least something of this world of theirs.

All art requires theory—not just for its creation but for its appreciation. It may require theory even, so to say, to enfranchise it as art in the first place;[5] and certainly theory with which to see its individual instances as (if they are) coherent, functioning aesthetic entities. It is the latter kind of theory that I have tried to provide for Handelian *opera seria*, in making it out to be the perfect embodiment of the Cartesian world of emotions. Listening to a Handel opera with the ear of theory makes it, at least, a coherent experience; and to the extent that coherent is a valued feature of art, it places the opera in the realm of valuable musical objects.

There is no doubt, of course, that the kind of theory I have proposed makes heavy demands upon a listener, as does Handelian opera in the light of this theory. Art works, of course, vary in the degree of difficulty they present; and certainly Handel's writing for the stage makes severer demands upon us, both musically and "theoretically," because of its remoteness from our world, than (say) Puccini or Leoncavallo (to neither of whom do I intend any disrespect in the comparison). Whether it requires too much is a question that only experience can answer; and since it is almost impossible at the present time to hear and to see an opera of Handel's in anything like the way he meant it to be performed, that experience is not yet available. Is it too much to expect that the musical rewards will be well worth the considerable effort of understanding required? Certainly complex and sophisticated art of the kind the Handelian *opera seria* exemplifies does not yield up its rewards easily.

There is this to consider: the *opera seria* was one of the longest-lived of all musical forms; and considering that in the age in which it flourished music in general, and opera in particular, were considered completely ephemeral phenomena, no more permanent than fashions in clothes, its longevity is all the more remarkable. When Mozart set *La clemenza di Tito*, the genre was well over one hundred years old: truly the DC-3 of operatic forms. Surely it must have provided considerable satisfaction to the people of those times for it to have lasted so long. Were those audiences completely degenerate in their musical taste? Or was there something in the *opera seria* deeply satisfying, not just musically but as drama-made-music as well? Perhaps they knew something we don't, and perhaps it would be worth finding out. But to do that we must put ourselves into their world; and that is no easy task. It is the task, however, that every art work of the past sets us—the *opera seria* no more than some, although perhaps considerably more than most.

◦ 4 ◦   One concluding note about *realism*. I have suggested that this must be considered a relative notion at least in the sense that whether X is a "realistic" representation of Y is relative to a theory or theories—informal perhaps—as to what the nature of Y is. In that sense of "realism," the Unicorn Tapestry may be construed as "realistic" in so far as it accurately embodies the beliefs about unicorns of those who fashioned it, whether or not (I presume not) unicorns are instantiated in the world as I construe it (with my informal theory or theories). And in that sense of "realism," I have argued that the Handelian *opera seria*—in particular, its most important feature, the da capo aria—is a realistic musical representation of the world of obsessive, Cartesian emotions. And to appreciate *that* realism is to go a long way toward appreciating Handel's operas as (at least the best of them) perfect realizations of the ideal of drama-made-music: perfect solutions to the problem of opera.

But if realism is *an* evaluative category of opera, as I believe that it is, there is always a further question to ask, namely: How closely does the world that the opera projects resemble my world as I construe it? (which is another sense of "realism"). And if the answer forthcoming is that it is very remote indeed, that certainly might give me reason to reject it as lacking "realism" in that particular respect, and hence not so valuable, *in that respect*, as some other operatic "world projections" might be.[6] That the projected world of *opera seria*, with its eternally overwrought heroes and heroines venting their pre-fabricated emotions in perfectly formed musical set pieces, is very remote indeed from your world and mine hardly requires stating. That there are operatic worlds less remote may be granted as readily, although the very nature of sung drama seems to guarantee to them all a high degree of remoteness as compared (say) to the realistic novel or naturalistic theatre. In this sense of "realism," then, *opera seria*'s lack of realism might well be a stumbling block.

One thing can, I think, be said straightaway. To be fixated primarily on how closely the world of the work does or does not reflect the world as one takes it to be is to function at a relatively low level of artistic appreciation, and it will not get one very far with any kind of opera: neither Mozart nor Verdi, neither Weber nor Wagner. The world of *Così fan tutte* or *Il Trovatore* is hardly less remote from your world and mine than is the world of *Rodelinda* or *Giulio Cesare*.

Indeed, if one considers for a moment what the mission of opera is, to translate drama into pure, self-sufficient musical form, one is compelled to realize how truly remote from the world of everyday affairs the world of an opera, *seria* or no, must be. It must so abstract from the normal course of human affairs to achieve human drama in musical form that one can scarcely expect it to still speak the language of "realistic drama." (My life, after all, does not proceed in sonata form.) Once one makes the big step from the world of "the world" to the world of an opera, whether it is the world of *Figaro*, or *Fidelio*, or *Tosca*, the world of *opera seria* is hardly much farther away. Whatever Handelian *opera seria* may lack in its reflection of your world and mine it more than makes up for by the perfection with which it reflects its own world of Cartesian emotions—a world that is musical to a degree that even the world of *Figaro* is not.

It is, needless to say, a very heavy question as to just why we find the translation of drama into pure musical form aesthetically rewarding, when the price we must pay is the remoteness of the resulting projected world from ours. Can we learn something from that projected world of drama-made-music about our own world (or worlds)? If not, does that make the experience valueless, at least "intellectually" (as Addison and Johnson seem to have thought)? Or if it has value, where does that value lie?

I intend to say at least something helpful to this question (or rather this nest of questions) later on. But at least it can be pointed out here that there are many other questions, and also questions of a similar nature, that arise with regard to all forms of art and, *a fortiori*, all forms of music. I presume that if it is mysterious what the value, epistemic or any other, is of experiencing the world of Handelian *opera seria*, with its remoteness from the world of twentieth-century America, it is all the more mysterious what the value, epistemic or any other, is of experiencing the world of Beethoven's string quartets, with its utter remoteness from *any* world (but the world of musical sound itself), at least as the musical "purists" would have it. That aesthetic experience itself raises serious philosophical problems few would deny today; and it should not be forgotten that music far less "problematic" and far more universally accepted than Handel's operas raises philosophical problems at least as heavy as they do.

o 5 o   I would be unhappy indeed if, *per impossibile*, my eloquence in behalf of Handel's operas produced in one of my readers a musical sensibility so "refined" as to prefer the austere perfection of *Rodelinda* to the sprawling, volatile world of *Don Giovanni* or *Otello*. That would be an aesthetic, I am almost tempted to say a moral, monstrosity. But a musical sensibility that has taken in not only *Don Giovanni* and *Otello* but *Rodelinda* as well seems to me to be the richer for it, and a sensibility that cannot seems to me seriously flawed. I think the time has passed when we can dismiss Handelian *opera seria* either as the irrational entertainment or the completest concert. It is drama-made-music, possessed of a lean and spare and cold beauty uniquely its own; and its absence in the repertory leaves a gaping wound. The first successful solution to the "problem of opera" deserves a hearing: if not for itself, then at least for a proper understanding and appreciation of the solutions that followed.

CHAPTER IX

Expanding universe

o 1 o I argued in the three preceding chapters that there is a palpable congruity between the Handelian *opera seria*, as a "psychological drama," and the reigning psychology of that time, which I took to be the Cartesian. I begin now to make a similar argument for Mozart's *opera buffa* and what I take to be the counterpart of Cartesian psychology in the second half of the eighteenth century, namely "associationism."

The psychological universe of Descartes is a closed, "finite," "Aristotelian" one. Its repertoire is basically innate: "hard-wired," as we now say in computer jargon. There are derivative emotions as well as basic ones; and Descartes gives at least lip service to the view that, in principle, the universe of derivative emotions might be infinite. But our overall impression, the impression that prevailed in practice, is one of static, preformed dispositions to respond, very much hard-edged and denumerable. And this was the view that Handelian *opera seria*, and even the instrumental forms of the high Baroque, so faithfully reflected.

The psychological universe we are about to enter is, I shall argue, in sharp contrast to the Cartesian one in crucial respects: where the Cartesian emotions are innate, those of the associationist school are acquired; where the Cartesian are hard-edged and discrete, the associationist are blurred and continuous; where the Cartesian are finite and fixed, the associationist are infinite and proliferating; where the Cartesian suggest a static, stable emotive life, the associationist suggest a fluid, evanescent one, of rapid and perhaps violent change. (I underscore the word "suggest.")

What late-seventeenth- and eighteenth-century British philosophy erected into a psychological theory of the association of ideas had existed, and still does exist, as an item of "folk psychology." As part of the ordinary way we explain certain internal, psychological events, it provides the following kind of familiar, retrodictive account. I am opening to Part I of Hobbes's *Leviathan*, and all of a sudden, I know not how or why, an image of 116th Street and Broadway pops into my stream of consciousness. The reason this happened, I conclude subsequently, is that I was examined on Hobbes as a first-year graduate student at Columbia University, which is located there; and I "associate" that location with that event, and that event with that text. Of course I could not have predicted that that image would have popped into my head upon opening that text, because I associate so many other things with it as well; and any of those might have popped into my head instead. But after the fact I can understand, through the train of associations rehearsed above, why it was what did pop in, and not just any old thing at all.

The association of ideas had already reached theoretical proportions by the middle of the seventeenth century, with Hobbes as a major exponent. It was, on Hobbes's view, the explanation for one of the two "Trayne[s] of Thoughts, or Mentall Discourse . . .": "The first is *Unguided, without Designe*, and inconstant; Wherein there is no Passionate Thought, to govern and direct those that follow, to it self, as the end and scope of some desire, or other passion. . . ." But "The second is more constant; as being *regulated* by some desire, and designe."[1] The second is rational thought, directed to some purpose; the first the aimless background noise of our stream of consciousness, the engine idling.

It is this apparently random stream of consciousness, "In which case the thoughts are said to wander, and seem impertinent one to another, as in a Dream," that the association of ideas is seen by Hobbes to direct, apparent randomness to the contrary notwithstanding. He writes, providing his own example:

And yet in this wild ranging of the mind, a man may ofttimes perceive the way of it, and the dependence of one thought upon another. For in a Discourse of our present civill warre, what could seem more impertinent, than to ask (as one did) what was the value of a Roman Penny? Yet the Cohaerence to me was manifest enough. For the Thought of the warre, introduced the Thought of the delivering up the King to his Enemies; The Thought of that, brought in the Thought of the delivering up of Christ; and that again the Thought of the 30 pence which was the price of that treason; and thence easily followed that malicious question; and all this in a moment of time; for Thought is quick.[2]

The doctrine of association went through two stages in the seventeenth and eighteenth centuries: what might be called a negative and a positive one. In its early, negative phase, it was employed to explain the ways in which human responses differed from some expected innate one. Locke, for example, who was sometimes credited in the eighteenth century with introducing the associationist idea into British philosophy, uses it to explain, among other things, why something that is innately pleasant and therefore should be universally so might nevertheless be unpleasant to some individual. Thus:

a great part of those [antipathies] which are counted natural, would have been known to be from unheeded, though perhaps early, impressions, or wanton fancies at first, which would have been acknowledged the original of them, if they had been warily observed. A grown person surfeiting with honey no sooner hears the name of it, but his fancy immediately carries sickness and qualms to his stomach, and he cannot bear the very idea of it; other ideas of dislike, and sickness, and vomiting, presently accompany it, and he is disturbed; but he knows from whence to date his weakness, and can tell how he got this indisposition. Had this happened to him by an over-dose of honey when a child, all the same effects would have followed; but the cause would have been mistaken, and the antipathy counted natural.[3]

∘ 2 ∘   Where the turn from negative to positive was made is not altogether clear; it was, in any case, a change in emphasis, rather than an absolute discontinuity. But the thinker whose name was most closely connected with the doctrine in its full-blown and positive phase, David Hartley, claimed that he himself was chiefly indebted, on this regard, to John Gay (cousin of the poet). Concerning the lineage of associationism, Hartley wrote, in 1748:

> About eighteen years ago I was informed, that the Rev. Mr. Gay, then living, asserted the possibility of deducing all our intellectual pleasures and pains from association. This put me upon considering the power of association. Mr. Gay published his sentiments on this matter, about the same time, in a Dissertation on the fundamental Principle of Virtue, prefixed to Mr. Archdeacon Law's Translation of Archbishop King's Origin of Evil.[4]

Gay's dissertation, *Concerning the Fundamental Principle of Virtue or Morality*, was prefixed to the first edition (1731) of Edmund Law's translation of William King's *Essay on the Origin of Evil* (*De origine mali*, 1702–1704). In it he proposed that Francis Hutcheson's idea of an innate moral sense, which approves of virtue, and an innate love of public good, which motivates us to pursue it even where virtue and its pursuit are seen by us to be contrary to our own private interest, may not be innate "senses" or "instincts" at all but, rather, acquired dispositions to approbation and action, based, in the end, on self-love and association. Indeed—and this is most important for our purposes here—he sees the moral "affections" as simply special cases of affections as a class, all of which are seen to be acquired tendencies to feel and behave, not innate and hard-wired as in the Cartesian tradition. As he puts it, "our approbation of morality, and

all affections whatsoever, are finally resolved into reason pointing out private happiness, and are conversant only about things apprehended to be
means tending to this end; and that whenever this end is not perceived,
they are to be accounted for from the *association of ideas*, and may properly enough be called habits."[5]

Gay is concerned, in his dissertation, primarily with questions of moral
epistemology and psychology; and these questions do not concern us.
Fortunately, however, he uses, for illustrative purposes, examples of
ordinary emotions and their etiology which are instructive in the present
context. His account of the emotion of envy is particularly so and
deserves close attention.

"Envy is generally defined," Gay says, "to be that pain which arises in
the mind from observing the prosperity of others: not all others indefi-
nitely, but only of some particular persons."[6] What is of immediate
interest, to begin with, is that the emotion is defined in terms not of its
particular subjective quale but of its object, "the prosperity of others."
That is to say, aside from being "painful," envy has no other identifying
introspective marks, but is determined to be envy rather than some other
painful emotion by what it is directed toward, i.e. the successes of other
people. Indeed, if Gay were to follow this line of reasoning about emotions rigorously, it would turn out that, subjectively speaking, the only
thing you can say about any emotion is either that it is painful or that it
is pleasant. Beyond that, what makes any emotion what it is and not
another thing is what it is "about"—what the object is, and what the
nature is of the connection between emotion and object. And if envy, or
any other emotion, does have any particular introspective phenomenology in addition to pleasantness or pain, it must have it simply by
having the objects it has, and being connected with them in the way or
ways that it is.

How, then, does the emotion of envy arise? Gay's answer deserves to
be quoted in its entirety.

> Now the examining who those particular persons whom we are apt to
> envy are, will lead us to the true origin of this passion. And if a man
> will be at pains to consult his mind, or to look into the world, he'll find
> that these particular persons are always such as upon some account or
> other he has had a rivalship with. For when two or more are competi-
> tors for the same thing, the success of the one must necessarily tend to
> the detriment of the other, or others: hence the success of my rival
> and misery or pain are join'd together in my mind; and this connec-
> tion or association remaining in my mind, even after the rivalship
> ceases, makes me always affected with pain whenever I hear of his

success, though in affairs which have no manner of relation to the rivalship. . . .[7]

Envy, then, is acquired by the association of ideas in this wise. A and B, let us say, are competing for the same job. It will give A pleasure if he gets the job and pain if B gets it and A does not—the pain, of course, being caused not by B's getting the job but by the consequence of that, i.e. A's not getting it. (Likewise, *pari passu*, for B.) B gets the job, causing A the pain of disappointment, denial, rejection, and so forth. The seeds of envy are now sown in A's breast. And when A subsequently hears that B has won a trophy in a bowling match he feels the psychological pain called "envy," by "association" with his previous experience. B's success in their rivalship for the contested job caused A pain. From then on, whenever A witnesses or hears of B's being successful at anything, even though they are not rivals now at all, there will be associated in A's mind with thoughts of B's success traces of that pain A was caused when, in their rivalship, B got the job that A was seeking. A may, indeed, be quite unaware of why this is so and may no longer remember the rivalship— but it is the cause: "envy" is the name for the particular psychological pain that that particular kind of association results in.

We can take this as the model for the way any emotion is formed. All are acquired, none is pre-formed: "these approbations and affections are not innate or implanted in us by way of instinct, but are all acquired, being fairly deducible from supposing only sensible and rational creatures dependent on each other for their happiness. . . ."[8] The only innate materials are the propensity to feel pleasures and pains of self-love: emotions are made, by association, from that; and where the appropriate associations are not formed, the appropriate connections never made to the appropriate objects, the emotion will never arise, will literally never exist. A person who has never been disappointed in rivalship is incapable of feeling the emotion called "envy," in as strong a sense of "incapable" as that in which a blind person is incapable of sensing colors, or a deaf person sounds.

It is worth a moment's reflection on Gay's account, to assess some of its implications and remark on its departure from the Cartesian scheme. I have already drawn attention to the fact that in contrast to the apparent innateness of the Cartesian passions of the soul, emotions, as Gay sees them, are all of them acquired by the association of ideas. This manner of acquisition suggests a number of other things about the emotions, enumerated at the beginning of this chapter, that put them in sharp contrast to the Cartesian ones; and although Gay does not make them explicit, they appear to me to be a very palpable part of the psychology which he at least adumbrates. We are now in a position to begin to see how these suggested consequences seem to follow from the associationist doctrine.

Gay's view of the emotions suggests, to begin with, that the emotions are not hard-edged and discrete, like the Cartesian passions of the soul, but are, rather, fuzzy and blurred. This is because of two things: first, the emotions are distinguished not by some unique, hard-wired introspective quality that each possesses, but by their objects; and, second, each individual who acquires a given emotion will acquire it in a different way, which is to say, by different experiences with (consequently) different objects. So that even if envy, for example, is always acquired through rivalship of some kind, your rivalry and mine will be different experiences; and as these experiences with their consequent objects are what "define" the emotion, my feeling of envy and your feeling of it will be different from each other's, and from every one else's. Indeed, there will be as many "shades" of envy as there are individuals who have had or will have the emotion; and envy itself, as a class of emotions, will not mark itself off from those other classes of emotions, acquired in a similar way, in any but a vague and continuous manner.

Second, Gay's associationist psychology suggests that the emotions are not finite and fixed like the Cartesian but, rather, infinite and proliferating. This is because while an individual lives the association of ideas never ceases. Thus an emotion is not acquired once and for all, in a fixed, unchanging state, but alters with time as more associations accrue, like patina on bronze. Nor are we stocked at birth with a finite collection of emotive responses, or even a finite collection of acquisitional possibilities. The association of ideas is a process whereby emotions are continually acquired as well as continually altered (and indeed it is a nice question which is which). This process has no fixed boundaries, and no fixed termination point other than the end of consciousness itself.

Finally, Gay's association of ideas suggests an emotional life susceptible of rapid change, whereas the Cartesian psychology suggests, in contrast, a more sluggish course of the inner life, with emotions as resting places rather than transitory stages to be traversed. Perhaps one might compare Descartes' passions of the soul to a digital system where each state is discrete and must last for a certain protracted period before the next can be attained, and so on. (Think of first gear, second gear, etc. of an automobile with a clutch, or a digital clock with the minute as the smallest temporal measure.) The association of ideas, on the other hand, might better be compared to an analogue system, where change is constant and on a continuum, but with this proviso: the association of ideas can make for gradual shading of emotions into one another, as the Cartesian system cannot; but it also can make for sudden and distant quantum jumps to emotions of the most disparate kinds, just because associations can be made to connect even the most widely separated and contrasted ideas. (Think of Hobbes's value of the Roman penny.)

o 3 o   If Gay, and others at the time, might be said to have been at least attracted to the association of ideas as a possible alternative to various kinds of innate senses, instincts, and the like, and as a ruling principle of emotive psychology, David Hartley, it is fair to say, was positively obsessed with the doctrine—a slave, a disciple; no man was ever more in thrall to a theory than was Hartley to what he called the doctrines of *vibrations* and *association*. And it was Hartley's compendious work *Observations on Man, His Frame, His Duty, and His Expectations* (1748) that, more than any other, made the association of ideas the psychological and philosophical nostrum that it became in the second half of the eighteenth century, and beyond. In order to appreciate the full sweep and influence of the associationist creed, we must examine, at least briefly, Hartley's prototypical version of it.

What Hartley essentially did, besides offer an associationist account of just about every mental function imaginable in the eighteenth century, was to give the association of ideas a machinery: a mechanical model, the "doctrine of vibrations," which he got from suggestions of Newton's, as he had the "doctrine of association" from Locke and Gay. The mechanical model and its source gave Hartley's version all the credentials it needed in an age and country that saw the mechanical model of the world as the way to go, and Newton as its transcendent architect.

In Queries 23 and 24 of the *Opticks*, Newton made the following conjectures about human perception and bodily motion:

> *Query* 23. Is not Vision performed chiefly by the vibrations of this Medium [i.e. the ether], excited in the bottom of the Eye by the Rays of Light, and propagated through the solid, pellucid and uniform Capillamenta of the optick Nerves into the place of Sensation? And is not Hearing perform'd by the Vibrations either of this or some Medium, excited in the auditory Nerves by the Tremours of Air, and propagated through the solid, pellucid and uniform Capellimenta of those Nerves into the place of Sensation? And so of the other Senses?

> *Query* 24. Is not Animal Motion perform'd by the Vibrations of this Medium, excited in the Brain by the power of the Will, and propagated from thence through the solid, pellucid and uniform Capillamenta of the Nerves into the Muscles, for contracting and dilating them? . . .[9]

What Hartley did with Newton's conjectures was to expand them into a complete model for human sensation, perception, consciousness (including the emotions), and bodily motions, both voluntary and involuntary. As a model it is not very different in its main outlines from Descartes' *esprits animaux*. What is very different about it, for our purposes, is what it models as a theory of emotions. For whereas the *esprits animaux* provided the mechanism for a discrete, digital system of emotional states, Hartley's vibrations of the ether—or, as Newton conceded, perhaps some other pliable medium—modeled the flexible and fluid emotional flux of the association of ideas. Until Hartley, the associationist "laws" had remained without a physical basis; the attitude towards them seems to have been more or less "hypotheses non fingo." Hartley provided the hypothesis by appropriating Newton's grand hypothesis of the ether.

It would be tedious and pointless to pursue relentlessly the intricacies of Hartley's theory in all of their mind-deadening detail: over six hundred pages in the sixth edition. But I do wish to convey some of the flavor of Hartley's highly influential views, as well as a fair idea of their content; and to do that at least some of the detail is required. One cannot, after all, have a taste without a bite.

According to Hartley, we may assume that some subtle medium—call it the ether—is diffused throughout the brain and nerves. It is in constant vibratory motion, and has been since before birth. "These vibrations are motions backwards and forwards of the small particles; of the same kind with the oscillations of pendulums, and the tremblings of the particles of sounding bodies."[10] Sensations, perceptions, bodily motions, and all changes in our conscious states are to be understood as resulting from perturbations of this continually vibrating medium, whose effects reach to and from all of the senses, the brain, and the muscles of the human frame.

That the Newtonian conjecture of a vibrating ether suffused through the human body should bear on the psychological laws of association Hartley anticipated would raise some eyebrows, as one was a materialist hypothesis and the other a mentalistic one. But he urged that if mind and body were related, so too might a set of psychological laws be reduced to a set of mechanical ones. "One may expect, that *vibrations* should infer *association* as their effect, and *association* point to *vibrations* as its cause."[11] Whether Hartley was dualist, some sort of epiphenomenalist, or a materialist monist with regard to the philosophy of mind is not easy to make out, but that is not an interpretational problem that need detain us here. Rather, we should press on to the doctrine of association, and Hartley's psychology of the affective life.

Let us begin by stating Hartley's formulation of the law of association.

It goes like this: "*Any Sensations A, B, C, &c. by being associated with one another a sufficient Number of Times, get such a Power over Ideas a, b, c, &c. that any one of the Sensations A, when impressed alone, shall be able to excite in the Mind, b, c, &c. the Ideas of the rest.*"[12]

To understand this statement we must first distinguish between what Hartley calls "sensations" and what he calls "ideas." Hartley writes in the Introduction to the *Observations* (following Hume, I imagine) that "*Sensations* are those internal feelings of the mind, which arise from the impressions made by external objects upon the several parts of our bodies." The remainder of "those internal feelings of the mind" are called "ideas"; and "The ideas which resemble sensations are called *ideas of sensation*: all the rest may therefore be called *intellectual ideas*." The argument of Hartley's book is empiricist throughout; and so "It will appear in the course of these observations, that the *ideas of sensation* are the elements of which all the rest are compounded."[13]

Imagine, now, that I experience a simple sensation: a visual sensation of redness, let us say. This takes place when external motions of the ether—i.e. light—cause my optic nerve to vibrate in a certain way, and those vibrations, propagating themselves through a complicated neural network, cause vibrations of a similar kind in my brain. When the light ceases to perturb my optic nerve, it will, of course, cease to vibrate in the "red mode" (as I will call it); and my brain, likewise, will cease so to vibrate. In other words, my sensation of redness will cease when I stop seeing red. But—and this is crucial to Hartley's system—the process will not cease immediately. Just as a pendulum (which is his model) will continue to swing for a while after I have stopped imparting motion to it with my finger, the ether in my nerves and brain will continue for a while to vibrate in the red mode, after the red light goes off, before gradually "winding down." In other words, as a general rule, sensations will endure for a short period of time subsequent to the cessation of stimulation to the external senses. After-images are an example of this.

The formation of ideas of sensation is simply a function of this tendency of sensations to endure. In a manner of speaking, then, an idea of sensation is simply a fairly permanent after-image. Thus, "it seems reasonable to expect, that, if a single sensation can leave a perceptible effect, trace, or vestige, for a short time, a sufficient repetition of a sensation may leave a perceptible effect of the same kind, but of a more permanent nature, i.e. an idea, which shall recur occasionally, at long distances of time, from the impression of the corresponding sensation, and *vice versa*."[14]

Now, Hartley believed that the substance of the brain is in a continual state of motion and that this motion begins before birth. He called the prenatal motion *natural vibrations*. Given Hartley's notation, *N* for *natural vibrations*, *A, B, C* . . . for *sensations*, and *a, b, c* . . . for *ideas of sensations*, here is how Hartley conceived of the acquiring of ideas, beginning at birth:

> let us suppose the first object [of perception] to impress the vibrations *A*, and then to be removed. It is evident from the nature of vibratory motions, that the medullary substance will not, immediately upon the removal of this object, return to its natural state *N*, but will remain for a short space of time, in the preternatural state *A*, and pass gradually from *A* to *N*. Suppose the same object to be impressed again and again, for a sufficient number of times, and it seems to follow that the medullary substance will be longer in passing from *A* to *N*, after the second impression than after the first, after the third impression than second, &c. till, at last, it will not return to its natural state of vibration *N* at all, but remain in the preternatural state *A*, after the vibrations have fallen to a diminutive pitch, their kind and state, or chief seat, and their line of directions, continuing the same. This state may therefore be fitly denoted by *a*, and, being now in the place of the natural state *N*, it will be kept up by the heat of the medullary substance, and the pulsation of its arteries. . . . And this will much facilitate and accelerate the transition of the state *N* into *a*; since we are to suppose a predisposition to the state *A*, or *a*.[15]

With this basic mechanism in hand, for getting from *N* to *A* to *a*, we can now see how, on Hartley's view, the association of ideas takes place "physiologically."

> If *A* and *B* be vibrations impressed successively, then will the latter part of *A*, *viz.* that part which . . . remains, after the impression of the object ceases, be modified and altered by *B*, at the same time that it will a little modify and alter it, till at last it be quite overpowered by it, and end in it. It follows therefore, by a like method of reasoning, that the successive impression of *A* and *B*, sufficiently repeated, will so alter the medullary substance, as that when *A* is impressed alone, its latter part shall not be such as the sole impression of *A* requires, but lean towards *B*, and end in *b* at last. . . . And as *B*, by being followed by *C*, may at last raise *c*; so *b*, when raised by *A* in the method here proposed, may be also sufficient to raise *c*; inasmuch as the miniature *c* being a feeble motion, not stronger, perhaps, than the natural vibrations *N*, requires only to have its kind, place, and line of direction, determined by association, the heat and arterial pulsation conveying to it the requisite

degree of strength. And thus *A* impressed alone will raise *b, c,* &c. in successive associations, as well as in synchronous ones. . . .[16]

The various permutations and combinations of association that the above scheme gives rise to are dilated upon at excruciating length by Hartley. Happily, there is no need for us to follow him in this exercise. But with this minimal mechanism in hand, we can press on to the relevant subject of the emotions and witness its application there.

∘ 4 ∘   Considering the importance we feel justified in placing upon the emotions, and the importance placed upon the subject in the second half of the eighteenth century, Hartley's account of "The Affections in General" is remarkably brief (in the edition cited, four pages out of 604) and quite unilluminating. Indeed, one must pretty much work it out for oneself, with little help from the author. But we must not be misled by the paucity of Hartley's remarks. Sometimes small things make very loud noises.

"Of Affections in General" consists of twelve claims about them, whose purpose it is *To explain the Origin and Nature of the Passions in general.*"[17] In working through those of these claims that seem relevant to us, and expatiating on them one by one, we should get a fair idea of Hartley's emotive psychology.

"First, That our passions or affections can be no more than aggregates of simple ideas united by association." This must be so, Hartley thinks, because passions or affections "are excited by objects, and by the incidents of life." But our knowledge of and attitude toward the objects and incidents of life can only be acquired by experience, which is to say, "these . . . can have no power over us, but what they derive from association. . . ."[18]

"Secondly, Since therefore the passions are states of considerable pleasure or pain, they must be aggregates of the ideas, or traces of the sensible pleasures and pains, which ideas make up by their number, and mutual influence upon one another, for the faintness and transitory nature of each taken singly."[19] There is an important point to be extracted here. Passions, Hartley remarks, are frequently characterized by their strength; and this consists simply in the high degree to which they are either pleasurable or painful. But no single idea can be as strong as even the weakest passion in respect of pleasure or pain (at least so Hartley thinks); so each passion or affection, to achieve the level of pleasure or pain that it does, must achieve it by the summation of a whole chain of individual pleasurable or painful ideas. The important point to notice is this. Each person's passion or affection will be distinctively his or hers, even if it is the "same" passion, called by the same name, "love," let us say. For since love is an aggregate of associations, and my individual experience will have produced a different aggregate from yours, my "love" will be a markedly different emotion from yours, though called by the same general name. (We have already drawn this implication from Gay's account.) To quote Hartley in another, but directly related context, "the differences which are found in different persons in this respect, are sufficiently analogous to the differences of their situations in life, and of the consequent associations found in them."[20]

"Fourthly, As all the passions arise thus from pleasure and pain, their first and most general distribution may be into the two classes of love and hatred, i.e. we may term all those affections of the pleasurable kind, which objects and incidents raise in us, love, and those of the painful kind, hatred."[21] The thought behind this classification of all of the emotions into merely two, love and hate, can perhaps be instructively got at by looking at what relevant meanings the *Oxford English Dictionary* gives to the term "affect" or "affection." They are: "The way in which one is affected or disposed"; and, specifically, "Feeling, desire, or appetite." Affections or passions are either pleasurable or painful. If the former, they express pro attitudes; if the latter, anti ones. In other words, affections are preferences and aversions; and, loosely speaking, what we prefer we "love," and what we don't we "hate." Passions and affections are simply "likes" and "dislikes"; and if we know how, in any one case, a human being, by association, develops a like or a dislike, we will have a model for how our whole emotive repertoire is acquired. To this end, here, then, is how, on Hartley's view, we acquire the passion of anger.

> The appearance, idea, approach, actual attack, &c. of any thing from which a child has received harm, must raise in his mind, by the law of association, a miniature trace of that harm. The same harm often arises from different causes, and different harms from the same cause: these harms and causes have an affinity with each other: and thus they are variously mixed and connected together, so as that a general confused idea of harm, with the uneasy state of the nervous system, and the consequent activity of the parts, are raised up in young children upon certain appearances and circumstances. By degrees the denial of gratifications, and many intellectual aggregates, with all the signs and tokens of these, raise up a like uneasiness in the manner before explained. And thus it happens, that when any harm has been received, any gratification denied, or other mental uneasiness occasioned, a long train of associated remainders of painful impressions

enhance the displeasure, and continue it much beyond its natural period. Thus is the nascent state of the passion of anger, in which it is nearly allied to fear, being the continuance of the same internal feelings, quickened on one hand, by the actual, painful, or uneasy impression, but moderated on the other by the absence of the apprehension of future danger.[22]

The above explanation of how anger is acquired can serve as a model, as I have said, for all of the emotions: what Hartley calls "the five grateful passions, love, desire, hope, joy, and pleasing recollection," and "the five ungrateful ones, hatred, aversion, fear, grief, and displeasing recollection." "And the whole ten," Hartley concludes, "taken together, comprehend, as appears to me, all the general passions of human nature."[23]

That Hartley believes there are only ten "general passions" should not be taken to imply that his psychological universe is even less spacious than Descartes'. For it is clear that these hardly exhaust even the emotions that we do have names for, like anger or jealousy, neither of which appears on Hartley's list of ten. And, of course, at an even higher level of abstraction, Hartley pares the emotions down to but two, as we have seen: love and hate. Thus, what is important here is not how many names are adduced, but how the individuation among emotions is made: how the many are generated from the few, which Descartes, no less than Hartley, recognized as at least an aspect of emotive psychology. And the answer, I think, is that on Descartes' view the emotions that "fit" between any two are a finite number, the steps discrete, whereas Hartley's associationism suggests that the number is numberless, the "steps" continuous. The model for Cartesian psychology in this regard would be (say) the number of whole numbers between one and one hundred, whereas for Hartley's it would be the number of fractions between one and two. For as we have already remarked, the fact that Hartleyan emotions are acquired by the association of ideas, rather than hard-wired like Descartes' passions of the soul, assures that there will be endless gradations and variations even for a named emotion like jealousy or anger, since in each individual case there will be different associated ideas. Hartley's emotional universe, then, for all of its mechanical paraphernalia so like the Cartesian *esprits animaux*, presents a phenomenal world of far different mien: boundless where the other is confined, vague where the other is precise, fluid where the other is congealed. That is the world which, as I shall hope to show, another music as accurately reflects as the Baroque opera did the world of Descartes. But more exploration is yet to be done before this new psychological world is adequately surveyed. For, like the Cartesian psychology, the association of ideas profoundly influenced thinking about the arts in general, music in particular. It was a guiding aesthetic principle of the second half of the eighteenth century, as Descartes' *Passions of the Soul* had been of the first; and we must look at that aspect of associationism, at least briefly, before we can go on to the specific case of Mozartian opera.

o 5 o   The history of the association of ideas as an aesthetic principle recapitulates its history as a purely psychological one in the respect that it too has an early negative phase and a later positive one. This is not at all surprising, since the young discipline of aesthetics, like seventeenth- and eighteenth-century theories of the emotions, passed through an "innatist" period into an "empiricist" one (and this is true of moral psychology as well).

A logical place to begin is with Hutcheson, who, it will be recalled, thought of the perception of beauty as being accomplished through a "sense of beauty," closely analogous to the five external senses and, therefore, unquestionably innate. But if we all have this innate sense of beauty as a natural gift, part of our hardware, why do we disagree sometimes about whether something is beautiful or not, or about whether one thing is more (or less) beautiful than another? We do not have similar disagreements about the color red. What, in short, is the cause of aesthetic diversity, on the innatist's view? It is, *in part*, according to Hutcheson, due to the association of ideas—only in part, I emphasize; but it is the only part that need concern us here.[24]

Hutcheson thinks of the association of ideas as perverting our natural tendencies to respond to beautiful things. It happens in two ways.

The first way is this. Let us suppose that two people, call them A and B, are looking at the same physical object: a peculiarly formed piece of driftwood, rather like a club, with a knob at one end. A thinks it is beautiful and B does not. On Hutcheson's view, if A really is experiencing the idea of beauty and B is not (and if some other conditions obtain which I do not have time to go into), they cannot be perceiving the "same" object; because if they were there would be no disagreement about its beauty. But just because they are both looking at the same physical object it does not mean that they are both perceiving the same "phenomenological object," that is, that both are being stimulated to have the same sensations; and it is the aggregate of sensations, the "phenomenological object," that they are availing themselves of in passing their respective and opposing judgments. They are, in effect, making judgments about different "objects," and hence not really disagreeing, not really contradicting one another. How does this come about?

Let us suppose that B, when he was a boy, had a particularly cruel Latin teacher who used to beat him when he got things wrong, with the knob end of just such a stick as this one that he and A are looking at. Because of the association he has with sticks like it the knob seems larger to him than it does to A; for to B as a child it must have seemed immense indeed, due to the immense pain that it caused. But in that case, B's phenomenological object has different proportions from A's—a larger knob in proportion to the length; and that in turn might mean that A's phenomenological object possesses *uniformity amidst variety* and B's does not. Then, since it is *uniformity amidst variety* that causes the idea of beauty to arise in the observer, small wonder that it is aroused in A though not in B—all because of the poisonous influence of association.

The second way is more obvious and direct. "The *association of ideas* . . . ," Hutcheson says, "is one great cause of the apparent diversity of fancies in the sense of beauty, . . . and often makes men have an aversion to objects of beauty, and a liking to others void of it, but under different conceptions than those of beauty or deformity."[25] Here is how that happens. Let us now imagine that A and B are looking at the facade of the house in which A was born and raised. B thinks it quite an aesthetically indifferent one, while A describes it as beautiful. Now, A has had a particularly happy childhood in that house, and it arouses many pleasant associations in him when he looks at it. He associates security with it, and familial affection, both very pleasant ideas. Not so B, who is seeing it for the first time. B reacts to its total lack of *uniformity amidst variety* by declaring it aesthetically indifferent. A, on the other hand, *confuses* the pleasures he is experiencing in its contemplation with the pleasure that *uniformity amidst variety* would have aroused in him if the facade had possessed the property, and he declares it beautiful. Again, the association of ideas has poisoned the well of beauty: not, this time, by making two phenomenal objects, one with and one without *uniformity amidst variety*, but by making the same phenomenal object produce pleasure for one person, none for another, "but under different conceptions than those of beauty or deformity." So the association of ideas performs a negative function in each case—but by rather different means.

○ 6 ○   The positive phase of the association of ideas, as an aesthetic principle, probably began even before Hartley; for it was a concomitant of the associationist principle in ethics, which, as we have seen, was already in its positive phase in Gay. But Hartley is the proper place for us to begin, as we are interested here in the aesthetics of the late eighteenth century, and not in its dim origins.

It is natural enough that Hartley should apply the doctrine of association both to the moral and to the aesthetic. For in the tradition which he apparently followed, of Hutcheson and Hume, moral and aesthetic judgments were taken to be a species of expression of likes and dislikes, preferences and aversions, and thus, on their view as well as Hartley's, species of passions or affections: "calm passions," or "sentiments," as Hume preferred. In explaining aesthetic predilections and aversions, Hartley was merely extending his associationist account "Of the Affections in General" to another special case: another kind of emotion.

The appreciation of art works Hartley places under the head of "The Pleasures and Pains of Imagination," getting his cue, of course, for that classification from Addison's famous *Spectator* series "On the Pleasures of the Imagination." As such, they are part of a sixfold division of "Intellectual Pleasures and Pains," the other five being the pleasures and pains of "Ambition," "Self-interest," "Sympathy," "Theopathy," and, finally, "The Pleasures and Pains of the Moral Sense." The pleasures and pains of the imagination are themselves divided into seven kinds: those derived from useful artifacts, those derived from the sciences, those derived from nature, those derived from beauty or deformity of person, those derived from wit and humor, the pains which arise from "gross absurdity, inconsistency or deformity," and—our concern here—those pleasures and pains derived from what Hartley calls "the liberal arts of music, painting, and poetry."

Let us look, for obvious reasons, at the "liberal art" of music. As might be expected, considering the state of theorizing about the subject in the seventeenth and eighteenth centuries, Hartley places more importance upon what he takes to be innately pleasing in music than the general tenor of associationist psychology would countenance anyplace else. The "natural" pleasantness of "consonance" and painfulness of "dissonance," so exactly marked out by the Pythagorean proportions, still exerted a powerful influence on the philosophical mind. Thus Hartley writes:

> Now in respect of music, it is to be observed, that the simple sounds of all uniform sonorous bodies, and particularly the single notes of the several musical instruments, also all the concords, or notes whose vibrations bear to each other the simple ratios 1 to 2, 2 to 3, 3 to 4, &c. sounded together, or near to each other, may be considered as originally pleasant to the ear. Discords are originally unpleasant, and therefore, as in other like cases, may be made use of to heighten our pleasures, by being properly and sparingly introduced so as to make a strong contrast.[26]

These inherently pleasant (or unpleasant) materials—to which we must add, Hartley says, "the uniformity and variety observable in all good music"—are the materials upon which association will subsequently work, and which comprise "the chief pleasures affecting children and young persons, upon their being first accustomed to hear music."

The association of ideas seems to work on music at two basic levels, for Hartley: the "syntactic" level of the pure musical parameters, and the "semantic" level of extramusical accessions. At the "syntactic" level, "By degrees the discords become less and less harsh to the ear, and at last even pleasant, at least by their association with the concords, that go before or follow them; so that more, and also more harsh discords, are perpetually required to give a relish, and help the sweetness of the concords from cloying." But music fulfills two very palpable functions as well, beyond its purely musical parameters (if "functions" is the proper term to use): it is a setting for words, and a setting for ceremony, celebration, worship, both public and private. And these musical functions produce further and, in many cases, specifically expressive and semantic musical associations.

> Particular kinds of air and harmony are associated with particular words, affections, and passions, and so are made to express these. . . . Music in general is connected with gaiety, public rejoicings, the amorous pleasures, riches, high rank, &c. or with battles, sorrow, death, religious contemplations . . . till by these and such like ways, the judgments and tastes of different persons, in respect of music, become as different as we find them in fact.[27]

Two points to notice here: first, the idiosyncratic nature of associations—their dependence on the variegated experiences of unique individuals, and their proneness to proliferate, in any given individual, in so many different ways—leads directly to the conclusion, as it had in the general case of passions, that musical "passions"—i.e. musical preferences and aversions—are different wherever they are found, and not uniform in individuals or cross-culturally. And as it is on these preferences and aversions that any standard of musical taste would be erected, their completely fortuitous nature guarantees that there will be no standard at all. Hartley, as we have seen, draws this conclusion himself. What is interesting is that he is quite untroubled by it, whereas in the case of poetry he is careful to moderate this relativism, although, so far as I can see, with no real rational support, as the two cases seem equally bad *or* equally good. For the reason Hartley gives, that "since mankind have a general resemblance to each other, both in their internal make and external circumstances, there will be some general agreements about these things common to all mankind,"[28] seems equally applicable or inapplicable to both. Why he is comfortable with relativism in musical but not in literary taste is not far to seek. Music, at the mid eighteenth century, had not unequivocally achieved the status in the art world where it could claim to have produced enduring masterpieces of the kind that literature could claim from Homer to Milton;[29] and thus it was much easier to dismiss musical taste, like fashions or foods, with *de gustibus non disputandum est*.

Second, and far more germane to our discussion, it is to be noted that Hartley has provided here an association explanation of musical expressiveness quite different from that provided by the *Affektenlehre*, which built its psychological foundations upon the Cartesian *esprits animaux*. To this most important development we must now turn our full attention.

o 7 o   Hartley's hints about musical "expression," fragmentary though they are, are worth reverting to for a moment. It is usual to think of the composer as appropriately setting a "sad" text, let us say, or providing music for a "happy" occasion, by providing, respectively, "sad" and "happy" music. This would mean, of course, that the sadness or happiness of the music is prior to the association it is to have with the sad text or happy occasion. Hartley turns this idea on its head, claiming that music becomes sad by being associated with sad texts or happy by being associated with happy occasions. Whether this is an entirely plausible view I will not undertake to examine here. That it is an intriguing view seems evident; and its application of the association of ideas to the explanation of expressiveness in music points out a new direction which others were quick to follow.

One such follower of the associationist line was Charles Avison, whose *Essay on Musical Expression* (1752) seems to have enjoyed a certain popularity in its author's time. Avison, "Organist in Newcastle," as the title page of his book describes him, was certainly no philosopher or theoretician and was able to provide little in the way of a nuts-and-bolts account of how expression might actually be accomplished through the association of ideas. But he did plump wholeheartedly for the notion, and provided a concise statement of it that would be instructive to look at.

By musical "expression" Avison makes it clear he means the supposed power of music to arouse emotions in us. Here is his account, pretty much in its entirety, of how that is imagined to take place.

> The force of sound in alarming the passions is prodigious. Thus, the noise of thunder, the shouts of war, the uproar of an enraged ocean, strike us with terror: so again, there are certain sounds natural to joy, others to grief or despondency, others to tenderness and love; and by hearing *these*, we naturally sympathize with those who either *enjoy* or

suffer. Thus music, either by imitating these various sounds in due subordination to the laws of *air* and *harmony*, or by any other method of association, bringing the objects of our passions before us (especially when those objects are determined, and made as it were visibly and intimately present to the imagination by the help of words) does naturally raise a variety of passions in the human breast, similar to the sounds which are expressed: and thus, by the musician's art, we are often carried into the fury of a battle or a tempest, we are by turns elated with joy, or sunk in pleasing sorrow, rouzed to courage, or quelled by grateful terrors, melted into pity, tenderness, and love, or transported to the regions of bliss, in an extacy of divine praise.[30]

I spoke in an earlier chapter of the difficulties of theories like Avison's that equate musical "expression" with the arousal of emotion, and, in particular, of Avison's rather lame and unconvincing attempt to deal with the problem of "painful" emotions by limiting the arousal of emotions, in an altogether *ad hoc* way, to "the *sociable and happy* passions. . . ."[31] I shall not renew that discussion here, except to point out that there is no pressing need for the associationist account of musical expression to be committed to the arousal of emotions, any more than there was for the *Affektenlehre*. That music might suggest to us, by association, certain emotional states does not imply that those emotional states need be aroused. I can, after all, think about fear without becoming afraid.

Of greater importance to us, at this point, is to understand the implications of this view of musical expressiveness that the musical forms and styles of its period might reflect. The *modus operandi* of Avison's account is this. By exciting a chain of associations in the listener's mind (how, besides by "imitation," Avison does not say), music can bring to his or her consciousness some "object" the presence of which would ordinarily arouse some specific emotion; and the thought of it does likewise. The implications of musical associationism, a spinoff of associationism in general, are that the emotions any given musical work can be expressive of are numerous, highly individual, and, at times, marked by sudden, violent, and extreme contrast as well as, at other times, by imperceptible shadings into one another. They have analogous counterparts in human emotive life in general and arise from the same source: the individual experiences by which associations are acquired. Whether Avison was even dimly aware of these implications or problems seems doubtful. What he was aware of, perhaps, is that he did not have much in the way of an explanatory elaboration of the theory he was appealing to, which is why, I suspect, he concluded, in one place, "After all that has been, or can be said, the energy and grace of *musical expression* is of too delicate a

nature to be fixed by words: it is a matter of taste, rather than of reasoning, and is, therefore, much better understood by example than by
precept."[32] It would be well for us, therefore, to turn to a more ripe and
filled-out version of this doctrine of musical expressiveness, to have
before us all the materials that we will need, and in sufficient detail.

o 8 o   In the period of which I am speaking, philosophers and theoreticians of the arts, with increasing frequency, appealed to the association of ideas to explain the expressive properties of music, as of the other
arts. Thus, Alexander Gerard, for example, in his *Essay on Taste* of 1759
remarks, much in the manner of Avison, that "by the natural fitness of
sound for accomplishing an imitation of, or association with, their objects
and natural expressions, it infuses in the breast passions correspondent.
. . ."[33] But in my view the most elaborate and convincing form that the
association of ideas took, in the British Enlightenment, as an aesthetic
theory, was in Archibald Alison's *Essays on Taste* (1790). A consideration
of the theory of musical expression there presented will conclude the
present chapter.

Alison presents a thorough and systematic account of what we would
today call "aesthetics," including discussion of all of the major arts as well
as of natural beauty (which the eighteenth century took far more seriously as a subject of philosophical inquiry than contemporary thought
would allow). This is not the place to deal with Alison's general theory;
to the extent that it is possible, I shall confine myself to the musical part
alone.[34]

The basic associationist premise of Alison's conception of musical
expression is that "matter in itself is unfitted to produce any kind of emotion."[35] That means that nothing in the material world is capable of producing any emotion in us (including the "emotions" of beauty and sublimity) naturally, but only as the result of some acquired association. And
since sounds, whether natural or musical, are merely a perturbation of
the material medium, the associationist premise applies to them as well.
In other words, no sound at all, natural or musical, can produce any
emotion in us, including the "emotions" of beauty and sublimity, except
by acquired association. Alison is, indeed, forced to admit, on the usual
"arithmetic" grounds, one supposes, that some combinations of sounds
are naturally pleasant and others not. "By a peculiar law of our nature,
there are certain sounds of which the union is agreeable, and others of
which the union is disagreeable"; and music, "as an art intended to produce pleasure . . . ," must be subservient to that law, "which cannot be
violated without pain."[36] But that is a small matter to Alison; for all of

the expressive qualities of music, as well as its beauty and sublimity, are the result of association. Obeying the natural "law" of musical combinations can produce pleasing music; but only the law of association can go beyond that to produce expressive, beautiful, and sublime music, which is to say, all music worthy of sophisticated attention.

There are, according to Alison, three sources of musical expression: what he calls "the nature of the key, and the nature of the progress" of a musical composition,[37] and what he calls "accidental associations," the other two being denominated "permanent."[38] We must now go on to unpack these notions, bearing in mind (particularly with regard to the first, "the nature of the key") Alison's admonition "that I speak upon an art of which I have no theoretical knowledge, and of which I can judge only from the effect that it produces on myself."[39]

What Alison understood by "key" is not altogether clear (nor does it seem it was altogether clear to Alison what musicians mean by it). He certainly meant something more than what *we* ordinarily mean when we talk about the key of E flat in normal discussion, judging by the expressive powers he ascribed to keys, which go beyond even what the most liberal believers in the expressivity of keys would allow as sane. We can best get an idea of this by quoting the crucial passage on the expressiveness of keys in full. Alison writes:

> The key or fundamental tone of every composition, from its relation to the tones of the human voice, is naturally expressive to us of those qualities or affections of mind which are signified by such sounds. . . . The relation of such tones in music to the expression of the qualities of mind is indeed so strong, that all musicians understand what keys or tones are fitted for the expression of those affections, which it is within the reach of music to express. It is also observable, that they who are most unacquainted with music, are yet able immediately to say, what is the affection which any particular key is fitted to express.[40]

What first strikes the eye and puzzles the mind is the renewal of the old analogy between music and the expressive tones of the human voice and, along with it, the altogether mystifying claim that the analogy is between voice and "keys," as if just being in D major can sound like the voice under the influence of one emotion, while just being in E major can sound like it under another, quite independent of the nature of the music itself. It is that initial and stupefying claim that immediately suggests we must read "key" here in a wider sense than the musician is wont to do.

Alison, then, is saying that, by the law of the association of ideas, something in music called 'key" suggests the tones of the human voice in the expression of the various emotions, and that that, in turn, again by association, suggests the emotions themselves. The renewal of the voice analogy theory, in the new context of associationism, is a quite comprehensible development; for the associative law was able to supply a viable psychological mechanism that the voice analogy lacked in its first incarnation, where a rather vague appeal to "sympathy" was about all one could expect. So much, then, is clear. But what sense can we make of the troublesome notion of "keys"?

That composers have tended to associate certain keys with certain moods—C minor, G minor, and D minor with *Angst, Sturm und Drang* (*vide* Haydn and Mozart), E major with calm, noble tranquility (*vide* Handel), and so on—cannot be denied, although its net worth for musical expressiveness has been hotly denied as well as vigorously asserted. This aspect of the expressivity of keys *per se* was clearly known to Alison and is reflected in the above passage. But there must be more to it than that if Alison's more ambitious claims are to be credited, particularly as regards the suggested isomorphism between "keys" and the tones of the passionate human voice, which has "structure" as well as "quality." What more, then, can Allison mean by "key"? There are, I think, at least three further things that he seems to have had in mind.

First, Alison must surely have been thinking, in his discussion, of the distinction between major and minor (for which "mode" would be the more appropriate term, although "key" is quite commonly used). And that the structure of major and minor scales, as well as the distinctive major and minor third, might suggest distinctively different accents of the passionate human voice is neither outlandishly absurd nor infrequently asserted. The connection between the major mode and happy emotions and between the minor and dark ones was, needless to say, already a commonplace long before Alison's time.

Second, it seems very likely that Alison thought of different "keys" as implying different pitch-ranges: i.e. low, middle, high, etc. Again, if that is part of what he means by "key," his claim that different "keys" are analogous to different emotionally charged vocal expressions becomes quite comprehensible; for we use quite different parts of our vocal range to express different emotions and moods, and musical lines can (and do) reflect that. (It is no accident that the Queen of the Night expresses her hysterical rage in the highest tessitura of the soprano voice.) Furthermore, there is a direct relation of voice range to key, in this sense (which might also be in the back of Alison's mind): if I write an aria for soprano (say) in G major, it will, other things being equal, lie in a higher part of her range than if I write it in E major, and hence might suggest a "brighter" emotional tone.

Finally, and certainly most remote from what musicians think of as having to do with "key," I think Alison must have been referring here to the general intervallic structure of musical lines: that is, whether they go up or down, in scales or in leaps, chromatically or diatonically. It may be difficult to see how a writer could use the word "key" to refer to something as distant from the concept as that; but I think the inference is inescapable. Furthermore, the word "tone" slips into the discussion in a way that suggests just this sort of thing, where Alison says that "The relation of such tones in music to the expression of the qualities of mind is indeed so strong, that all musicians understand what keys or what tones are fitted for the expression of those affections. . . ." Now, if there is a transition from talking about "keys" to talking about "tones"—which is to say, simply "notes" or "sounds"—it is not altogether outlandish to interpret Alison, at least in the sentence just quoted, to be talking about, among other things, the analogy there might be assumed to be between the way "tones" or "notes" or "sounds" are related, intervallically, to one another and the way the "tones" of the speaking voice might be when under the influence of this, or that, or the other emotion. Again, it is a common claim in the seventeenth and eighteenth centuries (as we have previously seen), and not such a foolish one either.

So much, then, for the first source of expressive associations. What of the second, that is to say, "the nature of the progress" of the musical composition? Here Alison's meaning is clearer and less problematical. He is talking of tempo and pace; and I suspect rhythm is at the back of his mind as well.

> In all ages, quick time, or a rapid succession of sounds, has been appropriated to the expression of mirth and gaiety: slow time, or a slow succession of sounds, to the expression of melancholy or sadness. All the passions or affections, therefore, which partake of either of these ingredients, may be generally expressed by such circumstances in the composition, and the different degrees of such movements may, in the same manner, express such affections as partake of any intermediate nature between these extremes.[41]

The association of tempo, pace, and rhythm with these same parameters of tone in human utterance is, of course, part of the traditional speech theory of musical expression that Alison was dressing up in associationist garb. But he added to it an ingenious and insightful touch of his own. He suggested that the pace of music models not only the pace of expressive speech but the pace of thought as well under the influence of one emotion or another. For, Alison remarks, "It is observable . . . that different passions have an influence upon the progress of our thoughts, and that they operate very sensibly either in accelerating or retarding this progress"; and so, he concludes, "The progress of musical sounds, therefore, may very naturally express to us the nature or character of particular passions . . . from the analogy between such progress of sounds, and the progress of thought. . . ."[42]

The third of Alison's sources of musical expressiveness, the "accidental associations," comes, seemingly, as an incidental afterthought; but it would be a mistake to underestimate the importance Alison placed on it: for better or for worse, it was taken quite seriously by him, as by his predecessors. Alison writes:

> In the preceeding observations, I have considered only permanent associations we have with musical compositions, or the expressions which are every where felt both in the tone and the time of such successions of sound, from their analogy to the character and progress of sound in the human voice. With music, however, we have often many accidental associations, both individual and national; and the influence of such associations upon our opinions of the beauty or sublimity of music might be shown from many considerations. On the one hand, from the dependence of the beauty of music upon the tempo or habitual dispositions of our minds—from the different effect which is produced by the same composition, according to the associations we happen to connect with it—and from the tendency which all national music has to render those who are accustomed to it insensible to the beauty of any foreign music, from the association of particular sentiments with peculiar characters or modes of composition: And, on the other hand, from the influence of individual or national associations, in increasing the sublimity or beauty of music, both by increasing its natural expressions, and by rendering these expressions more definite and precise.[43]

Permanent expressive associations are, we have seen, those that accrue to music in virtue of its affinities with modes of human expression, which themselves Allison takes to be permanent and universal. Musically expressive associations are permanent, then, to the extent that human emotive expression is. Accidental associations, on the other hand, are neither permanent nor universal, as they rely upon what accrues to one as an individual or, on a broader canvas, as the member of a group: nation, culture, class, generation, and so forth. The accidental associations are just those, one would think, that pose a problem for the kind of view Alison is espousing: just those that one would like to find a reason, not too *ad hoc* for respectability, for excluding from serious consideration as not bona fide properties of musical works. But that is not how Alison,

Hartley, et al. saw it. They, on the contrary, thought of these associations in an absolutely positive manner: as contributing to the expressive character of musical works and (in consequence) to their artistic excellence, their beauty and sublimity. Be that as it may, it is not our purpose here to pass judgment on the validity of their theory: rather, it is to study its implications for the operatic forms that flourished under its influence. And the implication of Alison's placing some of music's expressive powers in "accidental associations" is, clearly, to widen, beyond anything the *Affektenlehre* could (or would) countenance, the variety of emotions any single musical composition might be *correctly* said to express. For, what he said of the natural beauty of sounds was equally true, on his view, of the musical ones as well, to wit: "Every man, therefore, has some peculiar emotion associated with such sounds, or some quality of which they are considered as the signs or expressions."[44]

We now have in hand Alison's basic account of musical expressiveness. But before we leave off consideration of it, and press on to our conclusion, three further points might usefully be made, beyond what we have already observed about it. All might be thought to come under the head "signs of the times."

First, it is worthy of note, although not of great importance to our argument, that our modern word "emotion," in something like its contemporary meaning, has now apparently become current for what the seventeenth and early eighteenth centuries called "passions" and "affections." These words are, to be sure, still in evidence in Alison's text; but "emotion" predominates. When, why, and how that word came into use has, so far as I know, not been studied. It would make, I think, an interesting and valuable contribution to the history of ideas.

Second, and perhaps more significantly for us, the word "expressive" has come to predominate over the words "express" and "expression" in Alison's text. This may or may not be fraught with meaning; but "expressive" is the word favored today by philosophers who want to emphasize that emotive properties of art works are properties of the works themselves, not either "expressions" of the emotions of their makers or dispositions to arouse emotions in those who perceive them.[45] This is not to say that Alison has gone all of the way in this direction; he has not, and still seems committed to some version of the "arousal" theory of musical expression. But one can, nevertheless, read on for pages at a time where the word "expressive" bears the brunt of the argument, and the text is quite amenable to a contemporary interpretation in which music rather possesses emotive qualities than arouses or "expresses" them.

Third, and most significant as a "sign of the times," Alison is committed to the view that music is beautiful or sublime—that is to say,

musically excellent—solely in virtue of its possessing expressive properties to a high degree. In other words, the whole weight of musical value
is to be placed on emotions: "the beauty [and sublimity] of musical composition . . . is altogether to be ascribed to the qualities of which it is
expressive to us . . . ," Alison says.[46] And again:

> The terms plaintive, tender, cheerful, gay, elevating, solemn, &c. are
> not only constantly applied to every kind of music that is either sublime
> or beautiful; but it is in fact by such terms only that men ever charac-
> terize the compositions from which they receive such emotions [i.e. the
> emotions of sublimity and beauty]. If any man were asked what was it
> that rendered such an air so beautiful, he would immediately answer,
> because it was plaintive, solemn, cheerful, &c. but he never would
> think of describing its peculiar nature as a composition of sounds.[47]

The reason I call this particular view of Alison's a sign of the times is
that it follows hard by a whole bevy of artistic movements in various
countries—*Sturm und Drang, Empfindsamkeit*, "sensibility"—in which music
was certainly a prime mover, and in which emotion was elevated to a
position of heretofore unparalleled importance. And surely Alison's
musical aesthetics must reflect these movements, sometimes seen, perhaps mistakenly, as proto-Romantic. The Baroque aestheticians of music
were content to place musical expressiveness alongside of the purely
formal and "syntactic" parameters as a fully equal partner: this was the
"bifurcated" theory of which we spoke in Chapter V. But in the second
half of the eighteenth century, expression, clearly, had gained the upper
hand, to the extent even, as in Alison's case, of crowding out the "pure"
musical parameters altogether. Alison was, no doubt, writing in a state of
almost complete innocence as regards these technical aspects, so much at
the vital center of the connoisseur's interest. Ignorance, however, can
lead anywhere; and that it led Alison to the enshrinement of emotive
expression, in 1790, is no accident: it is the *Zeitgeist* at work.

o 9 o   It is time to step back and take stock. At the risk of being
repetitive, we must review what we have concluded in this chapter, even
though we have previewed it at the outset and drawn attention to it at
various stopping places along the way. It is important not only to have
seen where we were going but, now, to see where we have been.

I tried to show, in a previous chapter, how the Cartesian psychology
provided, for the Baroque, both a particular "world" of passions for
music to represent and a particular psychological mechanism for music
to make use of to that end. In the present chapter I have tried to do the

very same thing for the period in the eighteenth century that, for want of a better description, I will simply call post-Baroque (since it comprises, after all, a number of musical styles). My candidate for that role, in the post-Baroque period, was the doctrine of the association of ideas, pioneered and brought to maturation by the British, both as a theory of psychology and as a philosophy of art.

As a theory of the human emotions, the association of ideas presented a picture of the emotive life in sharp contrast, I have argued, to that of Descartes' *Passions of the Soul*. Let me summarize that argument briefly. The Cartesian view suggests very strongly that the emotions are innate responses; that they are a discrete, denumerable repertoire; that emotions do not "shade" into one another but are quite distinct, nameable entities; that they are "impersonal," in the sense of being alike in all individuals; that the transition from one emotion to another is rather a ponderous affair in which an emotion must live out its natural life and reach a psychological cadence before another can be entered upon; and that, by consequence, the Cartesian emotive life is sluggish rather than nervous, static rather than quixotic. In almost every way, the associationist psychology suggests a very different emotive life: emotive responses on this view are completely acquired rather than innate; they are not a discrete, finite collection, but an almost unlimited array of subjective shades and hues; they bleed into one another imperceptibly; they are highly personal and idiosyncratic because of the way they are acquired, no emotion being quite the same in any of its instantiations; they can quickly succeed one another, by virtue of the quickness of the association of ideas, having no preordained duration or natural history; and, by consequence, the emotive life, as orchestrated by the association of ideas, is nervous rather than sluggish, quixotic rather than static.

As these two views present two contrasting subjective worlds for music to represent (if that is its office), they present two contrasting mechanisms for the way in which music is imagined to acquire its expressive properties. On the Cartesian view—which is the basis for the *Affektenlehre*—music is to model the structure of the *esprits animaux*, whether the ultimate goal is merely representation, or whether it is the further one of arousal. But in either the representation or the arousal version, the nature of the Cartesian psychology, as outlined above, must be reflected in the expressive properties of the music, since the music models the *esprits animaux*, and they the emotions as the Cartesian understood them. Similarly, the associationist mechanism for musical expressivity assures that the expressive properties of music will reflect the image of the human emotive life that the association of ideas projects. For as music acquires its ability to suggest emotions to the listener by just that process whereby the listener acquires emotive responses to anything in his or her environment—that is to say, by association—it will have just those characteristics that the emotive life itself is thought to have, on the associationist view, whether it is conceived as an emotive stimulus or an emotive icon.

Notice, however, that it is completely immaterial, for my argument, that both of these theories are false theories of psychology, and immaterial whether either is even close to being a true theory of musical expressiveness (although I happen to think one of them is). What is important is that each of them suggests to the composer what it is possible for music to do, and to be, as an art of expression. I am arguing that there are things one would think of doing to make music expressive only if one were in thrall to the Cartesian psychology and aesthetics; and, likewise, very different things one would think of doing only if in thrall to associationism as a psychological theory, or at least in thrall to beliefs about emotions that are its consequences. We have already seen what results Cartesianism had for music in the Handelian *opera seria*. We have next to see what results associationism had (so I shall argue) for Mozart's *opere buffe*.

CHAPTER X

Form, feeling, finale

∘ 1 ∘ No one disputes that the da capo aria is the essential and altogether pervasive musical form of the Handelian *opera seria*. Granting that (as anyone must), I have argued that this much-maligned operatic convention is, contrary to received opinion both then and now, of remarkable dramatic integrity, given what was taken for psychological reality in its day. That reality I supposed to be the staid and steady Cartesian emotions; and it was just these emotive features of repose and durability, I argued, that the da capo aria perfectly expressed in music—its uncontested musical virtues being, in the proper context, representational virtues as well.

Further, it will not, I think, be a matter of dispute among musicologists that the da capo principle is dominant not only in the vocal music of the Baroque period but in its instrumental forms as well. The large number of solo concerto, concerto grosso, and trio sonata movements with clearly demarcated "second section" and the instruction "da capo" or "dal segno" at the close clearly attests to that. And even where the formal trappings of rigid da capo form are absent, the da capo principle of clearly discernible sections and a near-"verbatim" repetition is palpable. Would it be mistaken to suggest that even here, in the realm of "pure" instrumental music, psychological realism prevails?

It was, after all, already a common way of thinking in the high Baroque that music, be it vocal or instrumental, is, among other things, a sequence of expressive properties. And whether you tend to think of these as dispositional properties—that is, dispositions to arouse emotions in listeners—or whether you tend rather to think of them as perceptible qualities of the music—that is, the redness of the apple—your conception of what particular sequences of expressive properties are musically permissible must be mediated by psychology: that is, by what your conception of an emotion is. This is more obvious, of course, in the case of the person who thinks of musical expression in terms of arousal. For, clearly, if music is to literally move the listener to grief or love, it is a hostage to the human capacity to feel those emotions; and that capacity, in the age of the da capo, was taken to be as Descartes envisioned it in *The Passions of the Soul*. But even where the emotions are perceived as properties of the music, it is natural to think of possible sequences of them in music as limited by what would be possible sequences of them in the actual life of a human being experiencing them: a reflection in music of a possible segment of a conscious life. So here again, what is possible as a musical sequence of expressive properties is a function of what is a possible sequence of emotions in the human experience: that being determined, in the present instance, by the Cartesian view.

The da capo principle is, of course, both musically and emotionally, a principle of contrast: at least, the possibility of contrast is always there. From the point of view of musical contrast, there will frequently be in the second section a change in musical texture (from thick to thin), a change in key and (frequently) in mode as well, possibly a change in harmonic or contrapuntal character, and, almost certainly, a change in thematic material; for even when the structure is monothematic, the thematic material will be sufficiently varied in the second section to be "different" as well as "the same." From the expressive point of view, needless to say, there is almost invariably a change in mood, as those musical changes enumerated above must inevitably bring with them expressive changes as well.

From the expressive point of view, then, the da capo can be seen as a sequence of emotions or moods, whether we are talking about a vocal composition—da capo aria or chorus—or an instrumental movement in da capo form. And in most cases it will be a sequence of different, perhaps diametrically opposed, emotions or moods: a leading emotion in the first section, a secondary emotion in the second section, and a return to the leading emotion in the da capo.

That this expressive sequence as embodied in the da capo form perfectly reflects the Cartesian conception of how such a sequence of emotions would occur in a human being's conscious experience bears repeating and, perhaps, some elaboration here, in light of our discussion in the previous chapter. Let us recall that a Cartesian emotion is something of a "set piece." Because of their discrete, self-contained, and unblending character, one tends to think of these subjective states as having separate lives of their own, each with a distinctive pace and a kind of pre-ordained routine that, once started, must be run through from beginning to end, coming to something like a full close before the *esprits animaux* can reverse their field and initiate another emotive performance. But it is just such an expressive sequence that the da capo principle realizes in musical terms: the fully developed first section embodying expressive musical material that works itself out in some more or less elaborate process, closing fully at what will be, the second time around, the final cadence of the movement; the sometimes less developed, but nonetheless complete, second section, expressive of some contrasting emotion or mood, again working itself out in a coherent, self-contained way and also coming to a full close; finally, the return of the first section in its entirety, with its particular expressive mood, running the same inevitable course to its same inevitable and reposeful conclusion.

Consider, by way of example, a well-known movement from Handel's *Water Music*, beginning with an exuberantly cheerful and buoyant theme (Example 15), worked out in concerto grosso style, and coming to a full close in the tonic (Example 16). A contrasting section in the relative minor (the "trio" section of what is essentially a dance movement, a hornpipe), with a gentler and more contemplative theme, more sparingly orchestrated (trumpets and horns are silent) (Example 17), then goes through its paces, to reach a full and quiet close (strings alone) in its tonic key (Example 18). Then, of course, the first section is literally repeated, with the movement ending at the full close of the first section.

This is but one instance; but it could be multiplied a thousandfold in the instrumental compositions of Bach, Handel, and the lesser practitioners of the period. (Every dance movement with a "trio" exemplifies it.) From the strictly musical point of view, it is simply a perfect formal structure, with the two sections providing variety in their contrasting keys, modes, thematic material, dynamics (by virtue, at least, of the reduction of orchestral forces in the second section), and so on, the return of the first section providing the necessary unifying principle. But read as an expressive tableau, it is the perfect embodiment of a short emotional autobiography, as told by a disciple of Descartes' *Passions of the Soul*. It is a simple story, to be sure: the passage from some kind of exuberant cheerfulness to a more contemplative, calm emotion, tinged perhaps with melancholy, and then a return of the former mood. Simple or not, it proceeds in the stately Cartesian manner. Notice the complete separateness of the two emotions that the musical form implies. Although there is emotive contrast here, one state of mind giving way to another of quite opposite subjective tone, there is not the slightest hint either of one emotion blending gradually into another, as where joy might, almost imperceptibly, become tinged with sorrow, or of one emotion giving way abruptly to another without the first having, so to say, "quite finished," in a kind of manic-depressive swing—both of which cases are allowed for in the associationist school but are quite incompatible with the Cartesian. The contrast here is hard-edged and discontinuous, as a manic-depressive swing would be, but it is not *abrupt*. The first emotion runs its course and comes to a completely rounded-off close before the second emotion is allowed to begin its career; and it, in turn, does likewise before the return of the first.

EXAMPLE 15
Handel, *Water Music*

EXAMPLE 16

EXAMPLE 17

EXAMPLE 18

We have, then, in the period of Handelian *opera seria* the following situation: a musical technique, the da capo, that is the predominant form in instrumental music as well as in opera and a psychological theory, the Cartesian, that is the undisputed psychology of the time, and which the predominant instrumental and operatic forms both reflect—the latter being the da capo aria, the former the da capo concerto grosso movement, read as an emotive "tableau" (which is to say nothing more daring than as an expressive sequence of musical sounds). Can we find a similar set of musical and psychological circumstances in the period of Mozart's great operas? I think that we can.

o 2 o   That sonata form is the overwhelmingly predominant instrumental "principle" (as many like to call it) is such an obvious fact of late-eighteenth-century musical life as to require no further argument or elaboration. So the first term of our sought-for equation, a reigning instrumental technique, is immediately established.

That the dramatic ensemble and ensemble-finale are to Mozart's *opera buffa* what the da capo aria is to Handel's *opera seria*—the predominant and characteristic musico-dramatic operator, the very essence of the thing—may be somewhat more newsworthy but not, I think open to very much controversy. In any case, it will be assumed here without very much argument, but at least with the support of Charles Rosen, whose views on the Mozartian finale will be a prominent topic for discussion in the present chapter. Rosen writes, in *The Classical Style*:

> The importance of the Mozart finale within the operas as a whole cannot be placed too high: they gather together the disparate threads of both the drama and the musical form and give them a continuity that the opera had never before known. The arias, beautiful as they are, serve in part only as a preparation for the finale of the act, which is the set piece of the occasion.[1]

If sonata form is dominant in late-eighteenth-century instrumental music, and the ensemble-finale the *modus operandi* of Mozart's mature comic operas, our musical parallel with Handel and the *opera seria* can only be extended further by establishing that the ensemble-finale is indeed in something like sonata form. In a rigid and pedantic sense this may not be true. But in any understanding of "sonata form" that is really faithful to the enormous variety and flexibility of what Haydn, Mozart, and Beethoven actually wrote, Mozart's ensembles are bona fide examples of it. To quote Rosen again, "In fact, no description of sonata form can be given that will fit the Haydn quartets but not the majority of forms in a Mozart opera."[2] What is, no doubt, most troublesome in conceiving of Mozart's dramatic ensembles in sonata form is the apparent incompatibility of the recapitulation with dramatic verisimilitude; for whereas the sonata recapitulation demands a repetition (albeit not literal as in the da capo aria), the dramatic situation frequently has changed at the point where the recapitulation must occur, thus rendering the musical material of the exposition dramatically and expressively inappropriate. Rarely will the more literal kind of recapitulation be appropriate, as it is, perhaps, in the first trio of *The Marriage of Figaro*, where, one commentator suggests,

> The supreme joke of this terzetto is the employment of a sonata-form recapitulation for a situation which is no longer identical with that of the exposition. In the beginning the Count's anger is aroused by a malicious remark of Basilio's about Cherubino. Basilio apologizes by calling the basis for his remark a personal suspicion rather than a factual observation. In the development section, Cherubino's unauthorized presence in the room is discovered. This dramatic change justifies a renewed outburst of the Count's anger in the recapitulation. In the due course of the sonata form, Basilio repeats his apologetic remark, which now—Cherubino fully visible to everybody—sounds like the most wicked irony.[3]

Nevertheless, Rosen insists, quite rightly, I think, that "The sense of form in the finales is very similar to that in the symphonies and chamber music; the dramatic exigencies of eighteenth-century comedy and musical style have no difficulty walking in step."[1] It is only a rigid textbook notion of sonata form that can blind us to the fact of a recapitulation in the cases where it does not (as it does in the first trio of *Figaro*) thematically "follow the rules" (which, of course, come after the "form"). For Rosen (again), "the harmonic structure and the proportions outweigh the letter of melodic pattern . . ."; and so

> When the dramatic situation will not lend itself easily to a symmetrical resolution and recapitulation, the sonata aesthetic still remains valid in Mozart's operas. Its use is only superficially more complex: there is the same need of resolution, the same sense of proportion.[5]

We shall have occasion, a little bit later, to study one of Mozart's ensembles in detail; but for now I will take it as established that the sonata form, or at least the "sonata principle," is what musically motivates them all. And this extends our parallel with Handel and the *opera seria* one step further. Da capo is to the concerto grosso (and other instrumental forms in the Baroque) what sonata form is to instrumental music in general in the Classical era; da capo aria is to Handelian *opera seria* what ensemble-finale is to Mozartian *opera buffa*—that is to say, the single most important motivating principle. That we have already established. Now we can add: sonata form is to dramatic ensemble in Mozart's operas what (obviously) da capo form is to the aria in Handel's operas; the operative musical principle. This brings us at last to the main argument of the present chapter.

○ 3 ○   Behind the da capo aria, and the instrumental forms animated by the da capo principle, stand the Cartesian emotions as reality to representation. If the skeptical reader has found that hard to swallow, there is a bigger lump to come. For I now want to argue that behind Classical sonata style, both as an instrumental form and as an animating principle of Mozart's dramatic ensembles, stands another psychological reality: the busy emotive hurly-burly of the association of ideas. It is not necessary to claim that the mechanical workings of Hartley's associationism were everywhere acknowledged, or even heard of—that probably is not the case. For whether the theory of association profoundly changed ordinary people's understanding of emotions and the nature of the emotive life, or whether some profound change in the way ordinary people construed emotions and the nature of the emotive life led to associationism as a scientific model of their new "folk psychology," the picture that associationism projected was, with or without the theory, widely accepted. Thus, to take but one example, whether or not Forkel, the influential German music theorist and J. S. Bach's first biographer, had any knowledge whatsoever of British psychology, he could still, in 1777, express the central notion and leading implication of the associationist creed, that "not a single person's emotions exactly coincide with those of another . . . ," and this in conjunction with the highly significant claim that "music is a language of the passions and emotions. . . ."[6]

That instrumental music in the Classical era was considered, as Forkel put it, a language of the passions and emotions is far more easy to make out than that it was so considered in the Baroque. It is a notorious question of interpretation in Baroque music aesthetics whether, when an author does not make it explicit, he is talking only about vocal music as bearing identifiable emotive qualities, or whether instrumental music is intended as well. Frequently it is left unspecified, and although there is no evidence that all writers during this period believed music could not be emotively expressive without the help of a text, there is certain evidence that some thought so: it was not an uncommon view.

But the stature that instrumental music had gained by the 1770s put it beyond doubt, if nothing else did, that it was to be the equal, at least, of vocal music in expressive power. And if the brief passage from Forkel does not make the point, the aesthetical writings of another influential German writer, Johann Georg Sulzer, do. The influence of Sulzer's *Allgemeine Theorie der schönen Künste* (1771) on the culture and times in which Mozart plied his trade make it of obvious relevance here. If it was not read by composers (and, of course, I do not suggest that it was), it nevertheless was much a part of the intellectual background noise surrounding them. We would do well to give it a look, if only a brief one.

What is immediately evident in Sulzer is the paramount importance that "expression" has taken on in all the arts. It has become their very essense.

> Emotions play such a significant role in the fine arts that their place in aesthetic theory merits special and fairly detailed consideration. It is the artist's immediate purpose to excite or to temper emotions; to illustrate their true nature and expression; and to demonstrate their various good and evil effects as vividly as possible.[7]

That Sulzer's concept of what an emotion is is no longer Cartesian, but is far more like the associationists', can also be seen straightaway. Thus, Sulzer writes:

> Our feelings are not engaged by images that are wholly clear. Anything that is designed to move the heart and awaken our sensibility must at the same time offer a great deal to the imagination. . . .
>
> The imagination, then, must make the greatest contribution to emotion, for when a strong emotion is felt it is the imagination that gives birth to *the great mass of simultaneously associated images.*[8]

When it is remarked that, in many ways, Sulzer was rather a philosophical conservative than a radical, the presence of the "new" psychology in his thought is all the more indicative of its wide acceptance not only in Britain but on the Continent as well.

For Sulzer, as for Alison, music has become the expressive art par excellence, and expression not just the paramount but the sole musical merit. "The principal, if not indeed the sole function of a perfect musical composition is the accurate expression of emotions and passions in all their varying and individual nuances." And again: "Expression is the soul of music; without it, music is just a pleasant toy; with it, music becomes an overwhelmingly powerful language which engulfs the heart."[9] Nor are we left in any doubt at all by Sulzer about whether instrumental music is included in this characterization; for, after remarking that "Every piece of music must have a definite character and evoke emotions of a special kind," he underscores the extension of "every" by adding: "This is so both of instrumental and vocal music."[10]

A side issue, perhaps, for us here, but nevertheless of considerable interest in other contexts, is Sulzer's conception of how the composer is to achieve the all-important aim of musical expression. "Having determined the character of his piece," Sulzer remarks, "he must put himself into the emotional state that he wishes others to experience." This seemingly impossible (and unnecessary) feat is to be achieved imaginatively: "His best course of action is to imagine some drama, happening or situation that will naturally induce the kind of state that he has in mind: and if his imagination is sufficiently fired by this, he should at once set to work, taking care not to introduce a musical passage (*Periode*) or figure (*Figur*) that is out of character with the piece."[11] This was not new advice to eighteenth-century performers, who were frequently advised in the Baroque, to "feel" the emotions of the pieces they were to play. But it may be somewhat a new thing to recommend it to composers. It is tempting to see this as the beginning of what was to become, in the late nineteenth and early twentieth centuries, the so-called expression theory of art. Susanne Langer, for one, has suggested that "the doctrine has come down to our day, and is widely accepted by musicians and philosophers alike," including, among the philosophers, Benedetto Croce, who is seen as a prime example of expression theory in its modern philosophical form.[12] This I think is a mistake. For what theorists like Sulzer and (before him) Mattheson were saying, I think, is not that music is an expression of the composer's emotions, and that that is why a composer must become sad in order to write sad music. (I cannot, after all, be correctly described as "expressing" an emotion I am not experiencing.)[13] Rather, "being sad" is recommended to composers by Sulzer as a preparation for writing sad music because in experiencing the emotion one can concentrate on its characteristics more easily and directly, and find the proper musical means of more accurately reflecting them.[14] It is clearly a self-conscious, craftsmanlike process that is being described here, not the "natural" spontaneity of "self-expression." And this is made all the more obvious by Sulzer's admonition to the composer that he take care "not to introduce a musical passage or figure that is out of character with the piece." Would such an admonition be appropriate or even make sense if what we were talking about was "expression"? If I am "expressing" my sadness, do I have to be cautioned not to grin?

Be all that as it may, this is not, as I have already said, particularly relevant to present concerns. What is relevant is Sulzer's description of the result of the composer's imaginative leap into the emotions: that is to say, *expressive music*. Sulzer writes:

Every emotion involves a sequence of images (*Vorstellungen*) somewhat akin to motion; the very phrase "motions of the affections" already indicates as much. There are emotions in which the images flow evenly like a gentle stream; there are others in which the sequence of images resembles a raging and turbulent flood, swollen with heavy rain, a flood that sweeps every obstruction before it. At times, the images within us resemble a wild sea that dashes violently against the shore, and then falls back, only to surge forward again with renewed force.

Music is ideally suited to the portrayal of all such movements. If the composer is sufficiently aware of them and if he is skilled enough to follow every movement in melody and harmony, these subjective changes will be aurally perceptible.[15]

It is not too fanciful, I think, to suggest that music, as Sulzer sees it, is a moving image of the emotive life, which is itself a moving play of mental imagery, very much in the manner of the association of ideas. In another place he calls the emotive parade that music is to reflect an "ebb and flow."[16] And, in yet another attempt to capture the way in which music embodies the emotive life in its expressive part, he says of the composer:

He must know whether the language he is to use is that of a man who is proud or humble, bold or timid, violent or gentle. He must know if the character is a supplicant or one in authority. Even if he comes upon his theme by accident, he should still examine it carefully if he is to sustain its character throughout the piece.[17]

This passage is really quite remarkable when one realizes that it comes right after Sulzer has made it unmistakably clear that he is talking about instrumental as well as vocal music. In other words, Sulzer is saying that even when the composer is writing for instruments alone, he is to think of the music as the utterance of a human being under the influence of some emotion or other. Instrumental music, for Sulzer, is a play of expressive sounds that reflects the subjective states and vocal expressions of human beings. And this helps us to understand the deeper significance of his suggestion that the composer "imagine some drama, happening or situation that will naturally induce the kind of [emotional] state that he has in mind . . ." to embody in tone, even where the music he is writing is textless, contextless, and "pure."

Sulzer was writing in 1771. Mozart was fifteen, which is to say, a full-fledged artist. Haydn had already brought sonata form to its early maturity. Sulzer, however, had nothing to say about them, or their kind of music. He still had as his musical models such figures of the musical Baroque as Graun, Hasse, and Handel.[18] But those who read him with more modern ears were bound to see his account of instrumental music as peculiarly suited to the new instrumental forms; and, indeed, the picture of the emotions with which he was working, far removed from Cartesianism and the *Affektenlehre* and much more closely akin to the association of ideas, was peculiarly unsuited to the composers he mentioned by name. Our next step must be to see how close the match between sonata form and the new theory of emotions is, given the historical license we now have, as well as the license of common musical sensibility, to see the instrumental music of this period as, among other things, a sequence of expressive musical qualities.

○ 4 ○ It is, of course, the commonest of commonplaces to describe sonata form as "dramatic." And if part of what that means is that it provides opportunity, within either a small or a large framework, for many different and perhaps contrasting expressive moods, rapidly giving place to one another, the description is certainly apt. I can venture no guess as to whether the new psychology of the late eighteenth century had a causal influence on the development of musical style in the Classical era. All I can do is point out and illustrate the (to me) obvious congruity between psychological theory and musical practice.

Let me cull from our examination, in the previous chapter, of associationist psychology some characteristic qualities imputed to the emotive life, on that view, and reflected, I shall argue, in sonata form. Three seem to me particularly relevant:

(a) The emotions, on the associationist view, tend often to blend into one another, the passage from one feeling state to another progressing by transition rather than quantum jump.

(b) But the association of ideas also leaves open the possibility of abrupt, violent change, with no apparent transition, preparation, or closure, just because associations are hostage to individual experience, and psychological connections so formed can join the most disparate emotions and ideas.

(c) Though in the train of emotive associations, emotions tend to move gradually into one another (a), the process itself is rapid and nervous: a lot gets packed into a small psychological space, because, unlike the Cartesian passions of the soul, the associationist emotion does not pursue an elaborate, preordained career but is always on its way to something else, even as it holds the stage.

If this, then, is the psychological reality that sonata form reflects, I think we can easily discern the musical analogues of the psychological facts. To start with, whether we see sonata form as a somewhat predictable sequence of melodic fragments, structural entities, key areas, all or none of the above, or any combination thereof, it is clear that we are confronted, most of the time, by a parade of expressive qualities that are part of a seamless musical fabric (at least when it is done well). And however musically bankrupt the notion of the "bridge passage" may have become to the musical analyst, it still helps to draw our attention, in the present context, to the fact that the course of emotive progression in sonata style is generally unbroken (with important exceptions soon to be discussed): that between what may seem to us to be central emotive "locations" in the expressive history of a movement there will usually be transitional phases that make a continuous passage from one to another: that make a seamless web.

Thus, in Example 19, chosen particularly for its concentration of expression (the full exposition is given here), one can distinctly distin-

EXAMPLE 19
Joseph Haydn, Symphony No. 49, "La Passione," first movement

Ex. 19 (*cont.*)

guish a first theme and mood in measures 1–10, a contrasting theme and mood in measures 22–30 (in the relative major), and a final, closing theme in measures 39–42, quite different still, both musically and in mood, from the previous two. But—and this is the important point— there is no true resting place, either musically or emotionally. For just as the three contrasting themes bleed into one another (or, perhaps, grow out of one another) in a continuous process, so the moods shade into one another through the bridge passages, and one cannot quite put one's finger on the exact place where (as I read the emotions) the profound melancholy of the first theme gives way to the rather more happy but somewhat yearning quality of the second, or the exact place where that brighter emotive tone gives way to the more subdued, halting quality of the closing theme, somewhere in mood between the first theme and the second. (The true emotional implications of the closing theme become manifest only in the recapitulation, where it is given in the tonic, F minor, and takes on a quite dejected mien—to appropriate a phrase from Tovey, "utterly broken with grief.")

In contrast to the instrumental da capo, then, sonata form presented a completely connected, continuous emotive "discourse," which quite obviously reflected the emotive reality of associationist psychology outlined in (a) above. This is, needless to say, neither an adverse judgment on the emotive verisimilitude of instrumental da capo, which reflected a different psychological reality, nor (even more unlikely) an adverse judgment on its musical validity, since, I dare say, neither the Brandenburg Concertos nor Handel's Opus 6 would be musically embarrassed in company with a symphony by Haydn or Mozart.

But if sonata form is a continuous emotive discourse, whereas the da capo form is, in effect, three separate emotive poses or set pieces, it nevertheless holds out the possibility, particularly when the movement is in the minor mode, of an abrupt change of mood without the customary bleeding of one emotion into another. And this same possibility is held out for the emotive life by the associationist psychology, not by the Cartesian (b).

The musical structure of sonata form particularly lends itself to a bridgeless transition from first to second key area when the exposition is in the minor mode because of the very close relation of minor to relative major, compared to the relation of tonic to dominant where the movement is in the major mode. The former is not really a change of key at all, and the ear can happily accept a more abrupt change in that case than in the change from tonic to dominant. (Of course, what the ear would accept one hundred years later, or now, has changed radically.)

From the point of view of emotive verisimilitude, this purely musical fact is serendipitous. For the abrupt, transitionless swing from major to minor is a perfect expressive analogue of the extreme emotional swing that the association of ideas makes a possible occurrence, particularly as the change of mode, even without any further change of musical character, is likely to be recognized as a change in emotive tone. It is no accident, therefore, that such movements, during a particular period of Haydn's life, earned the sobriquet "Sturm und Drang"; and although that may very well have been an historical misnomer, since Haydn probably never had a "period" of "Sturm und Drang," as a description of such music's expressive character it was psychologically accurate, and would be so at whatever date the movement was composed (Example 20).

This is not the only technique, in sonata style, for the abrupt emotional swing. There is a clearly recognizable "nervous," choppy kind of writing that achieves a similar effect without necessarily making a change in key

Example 20
Haydn, Symphony No. 49, second and fourth movements

or mode at all, but merely doing the business by sudden changes in thematic direction and pulse (Example 21).

That classical sonata form, overall, displays far more expressive variety than the instrumental da capo—again, no adverse judgment on the latter—is harder to illustrate but is, I think, obvious to anyone familiar with the music. In lieu of illustration, which would require the quotation of whole movements to accomplish convincingly, I can only present the claim to the experienced listener for consideration and, I hope, agreement. For it does seem to me abundantly clear, and beyond real dispute, that the most obvious phenomenal properties of the sonata-allegro movement are clear expressive analogues in music of that aspect of associationism outlined in (c) above: that is to say, the emotive life as a rapid and nervous process, evanescent and fleeting, busy and changeful. If instrumental music is seen the way Sulzer and others saw it in the late eighteenth century, as an emotive episode in a human conscious life, then it took associationism, or another theory like it in crucial respects, to make sonata form possible. For had the Cartesian psychology prevailed, the expressive "narrative" of a sonata movement would have seemed as impossible to Mozart and Haydn as the conscious life of the Underground Man. Of course I do not suggest that Haydn and Mozart read treatises on psychology. But they were not, after all, either imbeciles or intellectual hermits. They were abroad in the world, absorbed in its conceptual gossip; and it is probably this non-reflective conceptual osmosis, more than anything else, that gives most of us our firmest convictions about what is and what is not possible.

o 5 o   Opera is drama-made-music. How did the Mozartian finale achieve that transformation? The form of the dramatic ensemble, in Mozart's mature operatic works, was, as I have suggested, and as others have done before, the sonata-allegro. The form of the feelings that that musical structure was (among other things) meant to reflect was that of the association of ideas. And it was the happy congruity of that musical form with the nature of those feelings that, in part, gave Mozart's dramatic ensembles their "realism," their dramatic verisimilitude.

But an important qualification is in order here. I am not in the least suggesting that the Mozartian ensemble is *only* an emotive icon of the associationist psychology. My argument does not require such a restrictive premise, nor does the music warrant it. Obviously, many of Mozart's dramatic ensembles are, like arias, "frozen" moments of passionate expression. Others, however, are musical vehicles for dramatic action. This I do not deny. All I claim—and this I do not think can be denied—

Example 21

W. A. Mozart, Piano Sonata in B flat, K.281, first movement

is that even where the ensembles are dramatic in the fullest sense, they also are, in the fullest sense, expressive of the emotions of the characters who take part. Emotive expression is *always* an essential operative element in the Mozartian ensemble. And what made the kind of emotive expression we find there musically possible, and representationally successful, was the new turn that psychology took in the latter half of the eighteenth century. That is my argument.

It was, no doubt, the dramatic ensembles that Rosen had uppermost in his mind when he wrote:

> Mozart's achievement was revolutionary: for the first time on the operatic stage, the music could follow the dramatic movement while still arriving at a form that could justify itself, at least in its essentials, on purely musical grounds.
>
> Before Mozart (or before the development of the Italian comic opera for which Mozart was to find a definitive form), a musical drama had always been so arranged that the more formally organized music was reserved for the expression of feelings—generally one sentiment at a time—in an aria or duet, while the action was left to be conveyed in recitative. This meant that except in so far as the music had values of its own unrelated to the drama, it remained essentially an illustration and expression of the words; it could only be combined with the action in the most primitive way and in the least interesting fashion.[19]

Rosen's point, a valid one, is that Mozart found a way of "setting action to music" in the dramatic ensembles, whereas *opera seria* had, for the most part, rejected that possibility, relying rather, in the arias, upon the musical setting of emotive expression.[20] But in spite of Mozart's signal success in making action sing,[21] it would be a mistake to think that he did not rely very heavily indeed, in the dramatic ensembles as well as in the arias, on music as an expressive vehicle. For, in the end, action in the Mozart finale is carried forward in large part by the entrance (less frequently the exit) of characters; and when they arrive, they more often than not sing about how they feel: that is to say, emotive expression is still playing a prominent role. And Rosen's admission that, in Mozart's operas, the music is "still partially" an "expression of the [emotions of] the text"[22] does not go far enough to capture the full truth of the matter. The Mozart ensembles and ensemble-finales are, to be sure, action-made-music; but they remain, like the da capo aria of *opera seria*, expression-made-music in equal measure.

The most basic musical principles that animate the finale and larger dramatic ensembles are what might be called the *principle of aggregation*, or perhaps simply the *additive principle*; the *principle of permutations and combinations*; and the *principle of acceleration*. Lorenzo Da Ponte described them to a T but, oddly enough, failed to understand them as *musical* principles. He wrote:

> everybody sings; and every form of singing must be available—the *adagio*, the *allegro*, the *andante*, the intimate, the harmonious and then—noise, noise, noise; for the *finale* must always close in an uproar: which in musical jargon, is called the *chiusa* or *stretta*. . . . The *finale* must, through a dogma of the theatre, produce on the stage every singer of the cast, but here three hundred of them, and whether by ones, by twos, by threes or by sixes, tens or sixties; and they must have solos, duets, terzets, sextets, thirteenets, sixtyets; and if the plot of the drama does not permit, the poet must find a way to make it permit, in the face of reason, good sense, Aristotle, and all the powers of heaven or earth. . . .[23]

That Da Ponte thought the conventions governing the operatic finale, described so graphically in his *Memoirs*, "a dogma of the theatre"—by which he meant, one presumes the musical theatre—and not what they truly are, a dogma of pure instrumental music, is surprising, when one considers that he worked in close collaboration with Mozart, Salieri, Martini, and other notable composers of the time. The composers must have known better: and one can well imagine one of them—Mozart, I would have thought—replying to him one day, when confronted once too often with Da Ponte's condemnation of the finale as contrary to "reason" and "good sense," "My dear fellow, Aristotle be damned; opera is *music*, and these are the principles of *musical* reason and good sense."

Suppose I were writing a *sinfonia concertante* for violin, cello, oboe, bassoon, and orchestra. I would, of course, want to take advantage, on purely musical grounds, of all the possible combinations of sonorities: so I would be sure, in my composition, to give each instrument some solos, and to make as many possible mixes of instruments as I could: oboe with cello, violin with bassoon, violin with cello, oboe with violin and cello, and so on, as well as, of course, having them all play together. This is the principle of permutations and combinations at work in its familiar habitat; and it is the same principle that is at work in the finale, where, to Da Ponte's consternation, the singers "must have solos, duets, terzets, sextets, thirteenets, sixtyets. . . ." Indeed, no better description of the Mozartian dramatic ensemble can be given, from the musical point of view, than a *sinfonia concertante* for voices and orchestra.

The additive principle is an even more primitive and ubiquitous musical parameter. To take the most obvious cases, the fugue, canzona, ricercare, and various informal imitative forms start with one voice and end with them all. And it is a fairly well-recognized principle, at least in practice, that a composition usually ends with everyone playing. It may or may not start that way; but all forces come together at the close, to make a satisfying musical climax. When this principle is violated in any really obvious way, it is usually for some dramatic or programmatic effect, as in Haydn's "Farewell" Symphony (if the well-known story about it is really true), or the quiet ending of "Glory to God" in *Messiah*, where the shepherds are left, in the peace and quiet of the night, with only the first and second violins, after having received the rather noisy message from above, appropriately heralded by trumpets. Where there is no reason of "plot" for the violation of the convention, it is, of course, the violation of the convention itself that is the point, it being one of those cases in which musical expectation is tweaked. The additive principle is, needless to say, what eventuates in the finale, in "noise, noise, noise"; as Da Ponte correctly observes, "the *finale* must always close in an uproar. . . ." When an ensemble does not, as in the case of the quartet in *Idomeneo*, that is for dramatic purposes; and the violation of the convention underscores it. ("Alone I go to wander." [*Exit Idamante.*])

Speeding up the finale at the close—the stretto—is, again, whatever else it may be dramatically, a musical principle, reflected, for example, in the rule that the final movements of quartets, sonatas, symphonies, and other late-eighteenth-century instrumental compositions are generally faster than the first movements. Though Da Ponte did not, or pretended not to, understand the musical reasons behind this and the other principles of the finale that he poked fun at, he was a master at making texts that embodied them. It was partly through Da Ponte's talent and skill that drama was made music in Mozart's hands. In the much-discussed finale of the second act of *Figaro* and in the third-act sextet we have two rare opportunities of seeing how it was done: how drama was made ready for music. They are ideal cases, for our purposes, because we have here, as in none of Mozart's other mature operas, the play (a masterpiece in its own right) from which the libretto was made. *Die Entführung, Don Giovanni*, and *Così fan tutte* were each derived, in part, from pre-existent sources or well-established operatic plot themes and situations. *Figaro* alone was a direct and self-conscious transformation into operatic form of a pre-existent, fully formed dramatic work. So it provides as clear and unobstructed a view as we can ever hope to get into the workshop where the transformation of drama to music, for Mozart, began.

○ 6 ○   Da Ponte credits Mozart with having suggested that an opera might be fashioned from Beaumarchais' *Le Mariage de Figaro*;[24] and as there is little evidence of modesty, false or otherwise, in Da Ponte's character, I think we should believe him. For the rest of the process that wrested the book from the play the librettist takes full credit, although he does give us a lively impression of his interaction with the composer and of Mozart's active role in the proceedings that has the ring of truth (if not, perhaps, the whole truth). In any case, since it is clearly irrelevant to my argument whether the libretto was made by Da Ponte, Mozart, both, or neither, I shall speak of the librettist as Da Ponte *tout court* without fear of misunderstanding.

The end of Beaumarchais' second act almost wrote itself into finale form; for the additive principle was what the playwright was making use of, for comic purposes, from the entrance of the Count ("pincers in hand")—

Everything as I left it! Before you oblige me to break open the door, consider the consequences. Once again, will you open it?[25]

—to his exit, some twelve pages later (in Wood's translation), with everything apparently going his way again.

Da Ponte began the finale some lines after Almaviva's entrance speech, given in secco recitative (Example 22). The finale proper begins with Beaumarchais' line for the Count, "Come out, you little wretch!"[26] (Example 23). From then on until the exit of the Count, Beaumarchais' play and Da Ponte's libretto are in fairly close synchronization. Beaumarchais brings on his characters, and collects them, in just the way an *opera buffa* finale requires the business to be done; and Da Ponte had the wisdom simply to use Beaumarchais' text pretty much as he found it, merely pruning it here and there to make room for the music. So on march Beaumarchais' characters, the Count to join the Countess and Suzanne, Figaro ("I heard Your Lordship was unwell. . . . I came as soon as I could"[27]), Antonio ("They chuck all sorts of things down. They've just thrown a man out"[28]), Marceline, Bazile ("Don't give the authority, My Lord! Before you show him any favours you must do justice between

Example 22
Mozart, *Le nozze di Figaro*, Act II, Scene VIII

CONTE

Tut - to è   co - me il la-scia - i: vo - le - te   dun-que a-prir voi stes - sa,   o   deg - gio ...

EXAMPLE 23
Mozart, *Le nozze di Figaro*, Act II, Finale

us. He has obligations to me"[29]), et al. And so the stage is set for a full-scale *imbroglio*: all the "noise, noise, noise" that the composer might wish, provided by the librettist by more or less leaving the dramatist alone. (There is wisdom also in knowing when not to edit.)

It is only a page or two before Beaumarchais' second-act curtain that Da Ponte must intervene, and he does so with a sure hand. Beaumarchais wishes to end as he began, with just the Countess and Suzanne on stage. It makes a perfect symmetry: the quiet, intimate opening, the two women exchanging confidences; the gradual increase of characters, noise, and confusion; and then quiet again, with the Countess and Suzanne as before: "She kisses the Countess's hand and they go out."[30] From the literary and dramatic point of view, the second act of Beaumarchais' play has an elegant, entirely satisfying form. From the point of view of the operatic finale, however, the additive principle has been violated. Da Ponte set that to rights by ringing down *his* curtain with the noise and confusion at full tilt, all hands on deck.

Act III must clearly have posed a far greater problem for the poet. It is a trial scene, marvelously funny when staged, with all the necessary accouterments of the genre: an imbecile for a judge, a shyster for a lawyer, a fool for a client, and an unmannerly collection of back-talking, wise-cracking witnesses. As either a comic or a serious dramatic exercise, a trial is always a sure-fire success. If "When in doubt, have a trial scene" isn't an axiom of the theatre, it ought to be.

Musically, however, a trial is a trial—very nearly intractable. In the comic vein, of course, Gilbert and Sullivan succeeded in a small way; but their musical aspirations were, after all, hardly on a level with Mozart's, and the measure of their success is correspondingly less stringent. As a serious operatic undertaking, perhaps the trial scene in Britten's *Peter Grimes* comes closest to working out, although Britten indulged in more freedom from pure musical constraints than Mozart could have allowed himself and, as a result, did not achieve the pure musical interest that Mozart would have demanded of an operatic *scena*.

The reason for the musical intractability of a trial is not far to seek. For all of its natural, built-in drama, it is structurally amorphous. The participants come and go—with none of the dramatic build-up of the additive principle. The drama is an intellectual one—a drama of competing ideas and interests. It is not a drama of events nor, except secondarily, of emotions. As music, if it is not funny by design, it is, likely as not, going to be funny by accident.

Da Ponte solves the problem of the musical trial, in the third act of *Figaro*, in the most operatically traditional way: the very way in which it would have been solved in the *opera seria*, except that ensemble is substituted for aria. To begin with, the action and content of Beaumarchais' trial are drastically truncated. There are several cases decided in the third act of *La Mariage*, but Da Ponte cuts all of that away, leaving only the matter of Marcellina vs. Figaro. But more important, the legal business, including the "discovery"—that is, the revelation of Figaro's unsuspected parentage—is all accomplished in 38 measures of secco recitative. Where the concerted music picks up is just where the aria would commence in a Handel opera, to memorialize the pregnant emotive event: in this case, the surprise, awe, and wonder (not without tenderness as well) that the reuniting of child to parents might cause even under, shall we say, somewhat cynical circumstances. And this "moment" is sustained for 25 measures and a modulation to the dominant before anything really "happens" in the ensemble.

What is particularly ingenious about Mozart's and Da Ponte's solution is that we can have the "discovery" now in the ensemble as well, providing the ideal dramatic opportunity for a literal sonata recapitulation. For Susanna enters the scene at measure 26 of the Sextet, as yet ignorant of Figaro's true relationship to Marcellina and Bartolo. As she is finally brought into the secret too, we are musically ready for the recapitulation, and dramatically ready for renewed expressions of surprise, wonder, awe, and tenderness, the expressive materials of the exposition's "first theme."

Thus Da Ponte has given Mozart one of those rare occasions to embody not only the "spirit" of sonata form in a dramatic ensemble but something of the "letter" as well (if, that is, you believe sonata form to be anything more than "spirit"). But it is Mozart, the supreme craftsman, who seizes on the best possible way of pulling it off. For he had already started his recapitulation *before* Susanna knows the truth. Remember that the revelation comes to the others in secco recitative, and the exposition of the Sextet opens with the secret already out. Exact symmetry would require that Mozart start his recapitulation after Susanna's enlightenment; but that would have meant impeding the momentum of the piece. So instead the recapitulation begins with Marcellina's explanation to Susanna. "The words, of course, will no longer fit the opening melody, so it is the winds of the orchestra that play the melody . . . here, and Marcellina who decorates it."[31] Drama and sonata form are in perfect lock-step.

The sheer length of the second-act finale, 939 measures, is warning enough of its complexity. It has been the subject of musical analysis often enough to discourage me from adding my piece, especially as I come to it as a philosophical analyst and only secondarily as a musician. What I have to add that is new follows from the aesthetic argument I have been developing here. And I want to get to that as quickly as possible. All I want to do, as preliminary to that, is simply to reiterate for the second-act finale, as I have done for the third-act sextet, the widely accepted claim that, at least in general outline, it is in sonata form: not perhaps as sharply outlined as the sextet or other, more self-contained ensembles, but recognizable nonetheless. Certainly its dimensions tend to overpower formal constraints. But if one cannot, Beckmesser-like, recite the sonata litany over it, one can still feel, as Rosen would say, the same principle of resolution that characterizes the sonata spirit. I will leave it at that, and go on to make what contribution I can to our understanding of the relationship of the musical form of the ensembles to their "psychological" form. This will complete the circle that I have been trying to draw: the circle that will enclose within its perimeter Handel's *opera seria*, Mozart's *opera buffa*, the psychology of Descartes, and the psychology of associationism. Only then will I be able to reach, in the last chapter of this book, the conclusions that I wish to draw concerning the opera aesthetic.

o 7 o   The *buffa* ensemble is a more or less sectional affair; and its sections, like those of the *sinfonia concertante*—which, I have suggested, is the most closely analogous instrumental form—variously exploit the possible permutations and combinations of musical forces available.

In the larger ensembles, there is almost always a procession of characters traipsing on the stage for one reason of plot or another, and joining in: the additive principle at work. Thus the *buffa* ensemble, unlike the da capo aria, embodies dramatic action: things happen while the music proceeds. New people appear, the situation changes (which it may do anyway, even when everyone is present who is going to be, as in the first trio of *Figaro*). It is in this sense that in the ensembles Mozart and his age found a way for action to sing. But literally, after all, it is the singers that sing; and the characters that discourse and soliloquize. What do they discourse and soliloquize about?

To a large extent (I do not say wholly), *plus ça change, plus c'est la même chose.*

In the *opera seria*, as we have seen, the subject of the aria text is the emotion or feeling or attitude of the speaker (exceptions, of course, always allowed for). This subject is embodied in an expressive utterance, linguistically and musically, of that emotion or feeling or attitude. But in the operatic world, as in the real one, the expression of that emotion or feeling or attitude need not be direct; and it certainly need not use or mention any word naming the emotion or feeling or attitude expressed. I can express my anger by saying (or singing) "I am angry," but also, needless to say, by uttering half-a-hundred other propositions or exclamatory phrases that do not contain "anger," "angry," or any other word of the kind. (The one way of expressing an emotion, attitude, or feeling that is open to us but not to the inhabitants of opera is silence.)

This is so, to a high degree, I want to urge, in the world of Mozartian ensembles as well. That it is true of the arias needs, I take it, no argument at all. Let us, then, with this claim in mind, run through the emotive, propositional, and situational content of a Mozart ensemble: not the elephantine second-act finale of *Figaro*, but the more tractable third-act sextet.

Situation I. Discovery of Figaro's parentage by company present. Prevailing emotions expressed: affectionate tenderness changing to stunned surprise (measures 1–25) (Example 24).

Situation II. Entry of Susanna, money in hand, to pay Figaro's "damages." Prevailing emotions expressed: joy, by Susanna, at having discharged Figaro's debt to Marcellina and cleared the way for their marriage, leading to continued expressions of surprise, by Figaro et al., at the discovery of Figaro's parentage (measures 25–40) (Example 25).

Situation III. Susanna's misreading of parent-child affection as sexual passion. Prevailing emotions expressed: anger, jealousy, and outrage by

EXAMPLE 24
Mozart, *Figaro*, Act III, No. 18 (Sestetto)

Susanna, upon seeing Figaro and Marcellina embrace (measures 40–45) (Example 26).

Situation IV. General confusion. Prevailing emotions expressed: continued anger, outrage, and jealousy by Susanna; consternation by Count Almaviva and Don Curzio at the overthrow of their plans; wonder and awestruck admiration by Figaro, Marcellina, Bartolo, at Susanna's violent reaction to Figaro's presumed unfaithfulness (she boxes his ears) (measures 54–72) (Example 27).

Situation V. Discovery to Susanna of the true (parent-child) relationship of Figaro, Marcellina, and Bartolo. Prevailing emotions expressed: tender parental affection (again) by Marcellina, followed by wonder and awed surprise by Susanna and (again) by other parties present (measures 74–100) (Example 28).

Situation VI. All parties aware now of the true nature of the case. Prevailing emotions expressed: joy and satisfaction at the outcome by Figaro, Susanna, Bartolo, and Marcellina; anger and defiance at the outcome

EXAMPLE 25

Ex. 25 (*cont.*)

(simultaneously) by Curzio and Almaviva (measures 101–140) (Example 29).

To sum up, then, the "expressive content" of the sextet: we have, in the space of 140 measures, allegro moderato, common time, the following sequence of emotions: tenderness; surprise; joy; surprise; jealous anger; jealous anger, wonder, consternation (simultaneously); tenderness; surprise; joy, defiant anger (simultaneously)—all of this, of course, in the form of a sonata-allegro movement: Situations I–IV (Exposition); Situation V (Recapitulation); Situation VI (Coda).

The expressive range of this ensemble, as compared to that of any da capo aria, is enormous. If we take the average Handelian da capo aria to be 75 measures long (including the repeat), expressive of a sequence of three emotions, the third-act sextet of *Figaro*, in less than twice the musical length, sets forth, by my calculations, more than four times that many expressive attitudes or states. Now of course Mozart used six times the number of characters to do that; but the fact remains that between

Example 26

Handel's time and his the composer's beliefs about what sort of things emotions are must have changed radically for Mozart to have even conceived of the possibility of music changing its expressive character so many times, and so quickly, in so small a musical space. It will not do to reply that what made it possible was simply a musical form—the Classical first-movement sonata form—capable of doing that sort of thing. For the question would remain of why that form, with its expanded expressive range, developed in the first place. And if one believes, as I do, that music was thought of all along as, among other things, a sequence of expressive sounds, somehow reflecting at least a possible sequence of humanly experienceable emotive states, the answer forthcoming must sensibly be that changing beliefs about the emotive life—in particular, how rapidly and in what profusion human emotions flit across the psyche—made sonata form itself plausible as just that kind of expressive story.

What I am arguing, then, is that just as the da capo aria, a perfect musical form, perfectly represented the reality of Cartesian psychology, so the Mozartian ensemble, a perfect musical form, perfectly represented (among other things) a different psychological reality, that of the association of ideas and its progeny. It was just because Hartley's concept of

Example 27

EXAMPLE 28

Ex. 28 (cont.)

the human emotive life was one of fleeting, blending, proliferating subjective states that it would be represented by the sonata form, even in
such an expanded and sprawling version as *Figaro*'s second-act finale.
Whether one thinks of music as a sequence of emotive stimuli or, more
plausibly, as a sequence of expressive moments reflective of a possible
human experience, it is the new psychology of the eighteenth century
that makes possible the emotional canvas that a Mozart finale or a Classical "first movement" paints. If music is to stimulate in the listener the
emotions it is expressive of, the human psyche must be susceptible of
being stimulated in just that way, with just that profusion of emotions. If
Descartes is right, it cannot so respond; if Hartley is right, it can. And in
Mozart's day it was Hartleyan theories that prevailed. But even if, as I
believe, music is merely expressive of emotions rather than a stimulus to
them, its expressive face must, one would think be the face at least of
possible human experience, and not pure fantasy or the purely fortuitous, unintended result of formal musical thinking. Composers, after all,
contemplate and plan for the expressive qualities of their music, as well
as for the melodic, harmonic, contrapuntal, and structural ones, even
when writing for instruments alone with no text, title, or dramatic situation in hand. And it seems reasonable to believe that a composer would

think of imparting to his music only such sequences of expressive properties as would suggest themselves to him as humanly possible sequences. In other words, I think that, at least implicitly, music was thought of by composers, in its expressive aspect, as some kind of representation of experientially possible emotive arrays. (In the philosophers and musical theorists, after all, it was, as we have seen, an explicit belief as well; and the composers inhabited the same conceptual world.) So what was expressively conceivable for music could only be what was emotively conceivable for human beings. In Handel's time the acceptable psychological limits were set by Cartesianism; in Mozart's, by spinoffs of the association of ideas. The limits of Cartesianism are reflected musically, expressively, and dramatically by the da capo aria; the limits of associationism, musically, expressively, and dramatically by the sonata-ensemble. It was

EXAMPLE 29

Ex. 29 (*cont.*)

the perfect congruence of psychology with musical form that, at these two golden moments in the history of music, enabled the operatic aesthetic of drama-made-music to be realized more fully and completely than it ever had been before or ever was to be again.

○ 8 ○   In musical theatre, as well as in the novel, "realism" commands, I think, the tastes of most modern audiences. Because of that, the world that Mozart's three great ensemble-operas project is far more acceptable to us than the world of Handelian *opera seria*, for all of its musical perfection. For the world of Hartleyan psychology is closer to the way we think things are, at least in our "folk psychology," than is the world of the Cartesian *esprits animaux*; and Mozart's operas reflect that more "modern" psychology. Of the big three, *Così fan tutte* is surely the most psychologically unappealing in that regard. Much has been written in explanation, condemnation, and exculpation of that work because of it. Alas, that is to miss the whole point of where the perfection of an opera, of drama-made-music, lies. Indeed, if what I have argued so far is anywhere near the truth, *Così* is surely Mozart's most perfect purely operatic work and, by consequence, perhaps the most perfect purely operatic work in the repertoire—which is *not* to say the most perfect work of art in the musical theatre. That, in any case, is what I will try, in part, to show in the next chapter: the chapter that will conclude and, I hope, sum up and concentrate my musico-philosophical reflections on the opera aesthetic.

CHAPTER XI

Opera as music

∘ 1 ∘ Through an examination of the interaction between operatic practice and philosophical theory at three sensitive moments in music history, I have tried to extract a kind of "essence" of the opera that I have characterized as (quite self-consciously hyphenated) drama-made-music. The time has now come to put the finishing touches on this concept and raise some hard questions about it. To do that, however, a brief review of the foregoing historical and philosophical argument is necessary.

I began with a discussion of operatic origins. I suggested that the challenge which philosophy threw up to the first composers of opera, and which has continued to confront composers to this day, was to put human expression—particularly the expression of emotion and feeling—into musical form. The philosophical foundation of this challenge was, I argued, in the beginning, Platonic and Aristotelian. That is to say, it was the theory of *mimesis*, applied ruthlessly and thoroughly to music.

The theory was venerable and of great philosophical power. It was captivating, and as a philosophy of music it existed in splendid isolation. What philosophical justification there was for pure musical form—which was not to reach comparable stature until Kant's third *Critique*, or even respectability until the end of the seventeenth century—was yet to come. For these reasons, the theory of *mimesis* exerted an almost irresistible force on the first composers of opera. In itself it was highly satisfactory. That there was no philosophical threat to it from the direction of musical "purism" made it omnipotent. There were, of course, musical instinct, musical practice, and musical theory, and in the case of Monteverdi musical genius as well; and these are not to be underestimated as artistic forces. But opera was at the outset, and has continued to be, more intimately involved with and more responsive to philosophical speculation (broadly conceived) than any other musical form. Neither practice, theory, instinct, nor even genius could resist the force of *mimesis*. The result, on the positive side, was the *stile rappresentativo*: perhaps the most successful musical representation of passionate human utterance that we possess. On the negative, it was the failure of early opera, even in Monteverdi's hands, to achieve a truly successful musical form, for all of its unquestioned musical beauty. It is a failure that, I believe, is at least unconsciously felt by the majority of sensitive listeners, even in the presence of the most rigorous and conscientiously applied historical sympathy for an "alien" style.

If this is a correct diagnosis, the success of *opera seria* in its mature, optimal Handelian form becomes understandable, in part, as the fortuitous result of historical circumstances in both the musical and the philosophical worlds. For what philosophy could not give to Monteverdi in 1607 it would give to Handel in 1720: a fully worked-out philosophical aesthetics of musical representation and a fully worked-out psychology of the emotions for operatic music to represent, but, as an antidote to *mimesis*, at least the substantial beginnings of a "pure" musical aesthetics as well. This perfect mix of philosophical and psychological theory provided, I have argued, the conditions necessary (I do not say sufficient) for a completely successful solution to the problem of drama-made-music. That solution was the da capo aria: at once a perfect musical form and, in its form, a perfect musical representation of the emotive life as understood by its practitioners and audiences. When formal properties are enabled to coalesce, as they were to do in the da capo aria, with representational ones, successful drama-made-music is possible.

The formal and the representational again coalesced perfectly in the third of my music-historical moments: in the Mozartian dramatic ensemble. Again, philosophical and psychological theory made this possible (I will not say inevitable). Psychology had indeed changed from the closed, static universe of Descartes to the open, dynamic one of Hartley and his successors: a change ill suited to the da capo aria, and to the *opera seria* for which the da capo was the principal material substance. But musical forms had changed as well; and whether there was some subtle causal influence at work here no one, as far as I know, can say (or deny). What da capo form was to the Cartesian emotions, Classical sonata form was to the new associationist psychology of the Enlightenment: the perfect formal analogue in music to the human emotive life as understood at that time. And philosophical aesthetics provided the necessary impetus to both expressive representation and pure musical form; the latter, indeed, with far greater force than Baroque aesthetics could yet muster, with its still somewhat indecisive and unelaborated philosophical views on what was to become, in Kant's aesthetics, the basis for modern "formalism" in music.

Now, of course, no *opera seria* is composed entirely of da capo arias; *a fortiori*, no *opera buffa* is composed entirely of dramatic ensembles. Nor, indeed, is every da capo aria or dramatic ensemble an expressive representation or, perhaps, representational at all. So, clearly, this historical argument cannot tell us everything about the opera; that is not my claim.

But it is my claim that it tells us something very essential about it, and that this something is something like the expression of an ideal; or, to put it another way (to be explained more fully later on), the expression of one favored way to look at musical theatre that seems to embody more of what we mean by the term "opera" than what we mean by any other term customarily used to describe it.

There can be little reason to dissent from the assertion that the most pervasive theory of music in modern times—that is to say, from at least the end of the sixteenth century—where it is, broadly speaking, "philosophical" and not merely "technical," is the one (in, needless to say, numerous versions) that gives music an "emotional" content, as expressive representation, emotive stimulus, or both. There is no view more common than the view that music, whether vocal, programmatic, or purely instrumental, presents, if it presents anything "extramusical" at all, an expressive surface: a surface describable in emotive terms. It therefore must tell us something non-trivial about the concept of opera to discover that at two of the most notable points in its history, its central musical form—in *opera seria*, the da capo aria; in Mozartian *opera buffa*, the dramatic ensemble—was completely congruent with the "form" of the emotions, of the emotive life as it was interpreted to the composers by the leading "psychologists" of those times, Descartes and Hartley respectively. It tells us, I want to insist, two very important things. Most important, it tells us that a certain kind of artistic success—what I think of as lying closest to the ideal of successful *opera* (as opposed to music drama)—consists in the completest possible coalescence of musical form with musical representation: that is to say, operatic success is at its optimal level where what completely satisfies the "pure" musical faculty also completely satisfies as representation. Second, it tells us what should be a surprise to no one acquainted with the opera at any period in its history; that, at least for the most part, the most favored and most successful subject of musical representation in opera, the one that has, by and large, provided the best opportunity for musical form and musical representation to perfectly coalesce, is human emotion.

The Handelian *opera seria*, then, and the Mozartian *opera buffa* give us two examples of the operatic achievement I have been calling drama-made-music: specifically, emotive (or expressive) drama-made-music. I do not, I hasten to add, for a moment mean to suggest that emotive or expressive drama is the only kind of drama there is, or that drama-made-music can exist only as emotive (or expressive) drama-made-music. What I would claim is that the two operatic forms I have chosen as my exemplars are by no means anomalous in this regard. That the Handelian operatic aria and the Mozartian ensemble are emotive (or expressive) drama-made-music marks the rule, not the exception. But the important point for present purposes is not that they are any particular kind of drama-made-music—merely that they *are* drama-made-music. Therein lies one of their great successes as operatic forms; and if what makes something good of its kind also makes it *of* its kind, then we have learned, I suggest, that opera is indeed, in some essential respect, drama-made-music.

A whole bevy of questions must, I am quite well aware, be suggested by this conclusion—more questions, indeed, than I would be able to answer in this final chapter. Some of them are: What is the difference (marked out by the hyphens) between drama-made-music and the more familiar music drama? And if opera is, as I suggest, drama-made-music, is that the only thing it is? What of opera as drama? And what about the frequent claims that opera provides psychological or moral "insight"? What is the force of "is" in "opera is drama-made-music"? Must opera *always* be drama-made-music? Or is it merely an historical fact that it has been in the past but needn't be now or in the future? If I am claiming that opera is *essentially* drama-made-music, am I not unjustifiably placing *a priori* philosophical limits "from above" on what it is possible for an art-form to become—an effort doomed by the very open nature of the concept of art itself, and by the prerogative of artistic genius to make of an art-form anything that inspiration dictates? What, finally is the relation of my chapter title, "Opera as music," to my claim that opera is drama-made-music? Is opera drama, or music, or both? Am I denying the oft-repeated and sometimes deplored assertion that opera is a "mixed" genre, neither music nor drama but an admixture of the two? To some, but only some, of these pressing questions I want now to turn.

○ 2 ○   I want to begin by calling attention to the locution "*X* as *Y*" of which the title of this chapter is an instance. For it has more than merely literary or rhetorical significance. It does indeed have both of those: it is a convenient way to say what your subject is—opera and music in the present instance—and it also makes intended allusion to Joseph Kerman's much-admired book *Opera as Drama*, about which I shall have something more to say in a moment. But there is a deeper significance here than merely literary or rhetorical: call it philosophical if you wish; and I have meant to tap into it.

In a celebrated, much commented-upon, and influential passage in the *Philosophical Investigations*, Ludwig Wittgenstein made a great deal of the concept of "seeing as," in connection with an ambiguous drawing that could be "seen as" either a duck or a rabbit.[1] The notorious "duck-rabbit," as the figure came to be known in philosophical circles (it had originated as a psychological curiosity), has been reprinted so many times that it is unnecessary to do so yet again;[2] nor need the philosophical mare's nest of "aspect perceiving," which it is supposed to illustrate, concern us here. What I merely want to suggest is that locutions like "opera as drama," "opera as music," or what-you-will are relatives of the "seeing as" concept—perhaps even are short for "opera seen as drama," "opera seen as music"—and, as such, share in some of the non-controversial properties of this much-disputed concept that Wittgenstein made available to philosophers.

To speak of "opera as music" is to suggest some kind of choice; for what "X as Y" suggests is interpretation, and where there is interpretation there are alternatives. Where an object or text is interpretable, there are bound to be alternative interpretations; and even someone who thinks that some interpretations might be demonstrably false or bad or wrong is obliged to admit that, where a text or object is complex enough to be interpreted at all, there are bound to be some alternative interpretations *none* of which is demonstrably false or bad or wrong. In short, to describe X as Y is to suggest that X can be interpreted, which is to say, seen in more than one way, understood under more than one description. The title "Opera as music" is meant to suggest just that: that one way in which any opera may be seen is as music—specifically, as drama-made-music

Is there more to be said than just that: that *one* way to see opera is as drama-made-music? I said that the "X as Y" locution suggests choice. But what kind of choice would that be? Mere whim? Purely a matter of taste? The flip of a coin? I said that the "as" of "X as Y" suggests interpretation, and that in a text complex enough to be interpreted there are bound to be some alternative interpretations, none of which is wrong. If that is so, is there no way of rationally choosing one over the other? Or no way, at least, of rationally assessing the virtues and defects of each? And what would a downright "wrong" interpretation—a downright unacceptable way of seeing opera *as*—be like? To partially answer these disturbing questions, I am going to look now at two alternatives to opera as drama-made-music, namely, opera as drama and what I shall call opera as revelation. I want to suggest that opera as drama is a valid alternative to opera as drama-made-music, and to suggest, further, how the virtues of each might influence a rational choice between them. With regard to opera as revelation, I will argue that, at least in some of the characteristic forms it takes, it is an interpretational non-starter. Let me begin with opera as drama.

○ 3 ○   In his justly admired book *Opera as Drama*, Kerman expresses the thesis that "Opera is a type of drama whose integral existence is determined from point to point and in the whole by musical articulation."[3] And he contrasts this thesis with the two "most stultifying" views, as he calls them, "the one held by musicians, that opera is a low form of music, and the one apparently held by everybody else, that opera is a low form of drama."[4] I do not share the view that opera is either a low form of music *or* a low form of drama. I have tried to make out that it can be fruitfully seen as a musical form that has transmuted drama into music. But how does that view differ from Kerman's, that "opera is a type of drama whose integral existence is determined from point to point and in the whole by musical articulation?" I must begin here by being trite: it is a difference in emphasis, the difference between calling opera "musical drama" and calling it "dramatical music." But the cash value of this can only be seen, I think, on a case-by-case basis. Indeed, it is not by reading Kerman's introduction (from which I have quoted above) that we come to understand what his thesis is, but by reading what he says about individual operas and how he values them.

Consider, apropos of this, what Kerman has to say about *Così fan tutte*. It is ruthlessly consistent with the principle of dramatic integrity as he construes it, the same uncompromising attitude towards the operatic repertoire that has led one recent writer on opera to remark that "he reduced the canon of fully realized operatic masterpieces that adequately embodied the dramatic principle to less than a dozen . . ."[5]—*Figaro*, being the only work of Mozart's to survive the purge.

Kerman begins the indictment: "neither *Don Giovanni* nor *Così fan tutte* has the dramatic consistency and force of *Figaro* or the later *Magic Flute*." And he continues: "Even the most devoted Mozartian will have to admit that there is something unsatisfactory about *Così fan tutte*."[6]

Where is the dramatic flaw felt to lie? Well, on Kerman's view, as on almost anyone else's, in more than one place. But no one seems to feel very comfortable with the "psychology" of the thing. And that is the point on which I would like to dwell.

Kerman does not object to the psychology of the plot *per se*.

> Only a pedant will object to the compression of the action into a single day or to the fact that the girls do not recognize the Albanians. . . . It is even pompous to complain of the implied psychology, because the play is firmly posited on the view that emotion is essentially trivial—a legitimate comic exaggeration.[7]

What he does object to is what he sees as the interaction of that implied psychology with Mozart's music. The libretto itself Kerman thinks a perfect vehicle in its own right. "There is really no question that his libretto is technically first-rate, the intrique smooth and elegant, the construction masterly, the verse delightful." But its major psychological premise, of the shallowness of human emotion, clashes head-on with the "premise" of Mozart's music, which is the very opposite.

> Don Wolfgango, inevitably, took emotions seriously. Da Ponte should have known by this time that Mozart would pounce upon any feasible emotional matter, in however dry a book, and turn it to account.[8]

Thus, on Kerman's view, what we have from the point of view of opera as drama is a libretto with one psychology and music with another. "Mozart's music clarifies and damns Da Ponte's [emotive] cynicism, and so spoils his immaculate play."[9] It is not, of course, that *Così fan tutte* is a total disaster from the dramatic point of view. Both Mozart and Da Ponte were much too good for that. But where *Figaro* is a perfect work from the point of view of opera as drama, *Così* is a flawed one: the music pulls in one direction, toward the emotively deep and serious, while the book pulls in another, toward "the view that emotion is essentially trivial. . . ." Composer and librettist are on different emotional planes, and together they make a dramatically inconsistent whole.

Is this a mistaken interpretation of *Così fan tutte*? No: that is not what I am arguing. It is, on the contrary, right on the money, *from the opera-as-drama point of view*. Certainly one very rewarding way to take *Così fan tutte* is as a *dramma per musica*. It will pay off more handsomely under such a description than many other great operatic works. Mozart is Mozart, after all. But viewed in this way it must come off as a deeply flawed work, in the way Kerman has suggested and in other ways as well. Viewed in this way it will always leave one secretly wishing one were attending *Figaro* instead; for *Figaro* is the perfect instantiation of the ideal.

But let me suggest that there is another way of viewing *Così fan tutte*: as what I have tried to spell out in the present work under the concept of drama-made-music. What I want to argue is that under this description *Così fan tutte* emerges not as a flawed work but as Mozart's most perfect creation for the stage. This does not imply that my way of looking at the work is more correct or better than Kerman's: merely that it is different, and results in a different evaluation. It certainly does not imply that *Così* is a greater work of art when viewed under my description than when viewed under Kerman's. For an X might be more perfect Y than it is a Z, but because Zs are more valuable than Ys, being a flawed Z might still make it more valuable than being a perfect Y would do. (I will return to this in a moment.)

Wye Jamison Allanbrook concludes her valuable book on *Figaro* and *Don Giovanni* by describing *Così fan tutte*—the opera she *doesn't* talk about—as "an *opera seria* of an *opera buffa*."[10] As it is her closing sentence, there is no way of knowing what she might mean, so I can take the liberty of appropriating the phrase from her and saying what I would have meant by it if I had coined it myself. I wish I had; for I think that it is apt.

Da Ponte wrote, in *Così*, the perfect libretto. It is *the*, not *an, opera buffa* libretto; it is the ultimate distillate of them all. Its "characters" therefore are not Fiordiligi, Dorabella, Guglielmo, Ferrando; they are *the* soprano, *the* mezzo-soprano, *the* heroic tenor, etc. They are instruments in a *sinfonia concertante*, instruments with proper names. Indeed, so little did they matter as dramatic characters of the *Figaro* sort that Mozart apparently couldn't keep their names straight, although he wasn't in any confusion about their voices. In the autograph,

> Up to the finale of the first act, the first voice originally has Dorabella's name and the second voice Fiordiligi's. Later on the names are exchanged, probably merely for the sake of the names, since the well-known *individuality of the singers* . . . leaves no doubt which one was chosen as the first singer and which as the second.[11]

Imagine Mozart getting the names of Barbarina and Susanna mixed up! It is not just that they already existed in a famous play. But in art, if not in life, names are more than conventionalized tags for characters, like numbers on football players. They are part of their personal identities (for, after all, the character is, in a sense, just a name, since "he" or "she" has no existence beyond the world of the work in which he or she is called Barbarina or Susanna, Fiordiligi or Dorabella). Thus, like the characters of *opera seria*, the characters of *Così fan tutte* are as close to being character types as they can be without ceasing to be characters at all. They are stripped-down characters, characters in the raw, and that is why they leave more room for the purely musical parameters than do the characters of *Figaro* or *Don Giovanni*.

But the pure musicality of Da Ponte's libretto lies even more deeply, and more brilliantly, in the much-maligned plot itself, with all of its (from the opera-as-drama point of view) psychological improbability. I alluded in the previous chapter to a hypothetical *sinfonia concertante* for oboe, bassoon, violin, and cello when discussing Mozart's finales. Actually, as many of my readers will know, there is such a work by Joseph Haydn—one of his last orchestral pieces. The plot of *Così fan tutte* is, I want to suggest, a dramatic realization of just such an instrumental work. It is almost as if Mozart had said to Da Ponte: "Write me a play for oboe, bassoon, violin, and cello." The musical recipe of Haydn's work might well be stated as "Change your partners"; and that, in capsule, is the summary of Da Ponte's plot. Think of the oboe and bassoon as one natural pair, and the violin and cello as another. The musical ideal, of course, is for them both to contrast their sonorities, double-reed against string, and to mix them, oboe with cello and violin with bassoon. Haydn of course could mix and match these instruments as he wished, with no "external" constraints whatever on his musical fantasy—which had to answer only to his own musical taste and skill, and to the purely musical parameters of his age.

But consider, now, the two matched pairs, Figaro and Susanna, Count and Countess. The *sinfonia concertante* principle—what I called, earlier, the principle of permutations and combinations—dictates that the pairs should mix: we want to hear the Figaro-instrument sing not only with the Susanna-instrument but with the Countess-instrument as well, oboe with cello and violin with bassoon. Here, however, the composer's musical imagination is not unfettered. He must be provided a dramatic opportunity in the text to mix his sonorities; and of course there are some in *Figaro* as in any well-constructed opera libretto of the kind: the Count's flirtation with Susanna, in Act III, for example. It was just this, though, that Da Ponte was objecting to in his diatribe on finales in the *Memoirs*. For where, on the poet's view, the drama cannot reasonably provide such opportunities, he must write them in anyway, to satisfy musical demands, directly flouting, at times, what he takes to be sound dramatic principles. On the composer's side, sound musical principles, or at least the absolute freedom of his musical fantasy, must be compromised as well, if the story is to achieve some minimal credibility and, in the case of *Figaro*, bear some resemblance to a pre-existing story.

What Da Ponte achieved in the libretto of *Così fan tutte* was a plot line that simply *embodies* right from the start the *sinfonia concertante* principle—the principle of permutations and combinations. What better way, after all, to assure ample opportunity for everybody to sing a duet with everybody then invent a story in which everybody is in love with everybody (or at least pretends to be) at one point or another. By exchanging lovers, the four principal characters bestow upon the composer that complete freedom to "mix and match" sonorities that Haydn had in the *sinfonia concertante* for oboe, bassoon, violin, and cello but that Mozart never had had in opera heretofore. Indeed, if the *sinfonia concertante* has a "plot," it is, essentially, the plot of *Così fan tutte*. One can even imagine the familiar writer of program notes saying such banal things as: "But now, growing tired of the somewhat acerbic bassoon, the oboe becomes enamored, at measure 105, of the cello's warmer and more mellow sound, and they sing an impassioned duet based on the second subject . . . ," etc. What I am suggesting, then, is that the plot of *Così fan tutte* comes as close as any story line reasonably can to the "scenario" of an instrumental composition of the *sinfonia concertante* kind. From the point of view of opera as drama it cannot have the psychological or behavioral credibility of *The Marriage of Figaro*. If what happens in *Così fan tutte* is not "impossible," it is certainly "improbable" in the extreme. But from the point of view of this book—the point of view of opera as drama-made-music—it is the quintessentially musical libretto, and the opera that Mozart made of it his ultimate triumph. It gave his musical fantasy almost complete freedom, because Da Ponte's plot was a purely musical design— a purely musical "story." And Mozart could respond by letting it almost overflow with music. (As Kerman remarks, "it has been a long evening" of thirds and sixths.[12] And it seems to be a highly symbolic musical gesture that Mozart placed at the heart of *Così fan tutte* the purest of all purely musical forms, the canon, as if to set the seal of pure musicality on this, his most eminently musical work for the theatre.

o 4 o   Here, then, are two ways (of many, perhaps) to understand *Così fan tutte*; and I mean it, of course, to stand for all operatic works. We may understand it, or them, under the description (made current by Kerman) of "opera as drama"; or we can understand it, and them, as I have tried to suggest in this book, under the description of "drama-made-music." And I have insisted that both ways are right; both ways are rewarding, and as interpretations both are more or less consistent with the text (to the extent that we can speak of "the text" as something apart from its interpretations). On Kerman's interpretation, *Così* emerges as a deeply flawed though (I am sure Kerman would agree) estimable work. On my view it emerges as Mozart's most perfect opera—which may be to say *the* most perfect opera.

What does this tell us about *Così* as a work of art? What I want to emphasize is this: it by no means follows that *Così* emerges as a greater work of art under my description than under Kerman's. Or, to put it another way: under my description of opera as drama-made-music, *Così fan tutte* is a more perfect example of that kind than *The Marriage of Figaro*; but this in no way implies that, under my description, *Così* is a greater work of art. Indeed, I think the opposite: that although *Così* is the more perfect opera, which is to say, the greater drama-made-music, *Figaro* is the greater work. How can this be?

Quite simply: it can be because a work of the musical theatre may, in the long run, have more to offer as a work of art when seen as musical drama than when seen as drama-made-music, even though it emerges as more perfect under the latter description than under the former. *Così fan tutte*, I have argued, offers us the ultimate payoff under the description "drama-made-music": namely, artistic perfection. (The same might be said, in my opinion, for Handel's best operas.) Its ultimate artistic payoff, however, under the description "opera as drama" may very well be greater, even though under that description it is deeply flawed by psychological improbability and a certain obvious shallowness of character delineation. (Dorabella and Fiordiligi, Ferrando and Guglielmo, will never "live" for us with the vividness of Figaro, Cherubino et al.) When the eighteenth-century philosophers of art were busy with the distinction between the sublime and the beautiful, they frequently remarked that beautiful works are perfect, and sublime works flawed: the most pervasive illustration being the perfect beauty of Virgil as contrasted with the flawed sublimity of Homer. But Homer's sublimity, though flawed, was valued above Virgil's beauty, though perfect, because, overall, Homer's sublimity paid the higher aesthetic dividend. It is a similar logical point that I am making here.

Further, it may well be that the perfection of drama-made-music has, as a general rule, a lower overall artistic payoff than the perfection of opera as drama, because of the satisfactions that drama has to offer. If that were the case, it might explain why Handelian *opera seria*, for all of its perfection under the former description, fails to gain wide audience acceptance under the latter. (Another reason, of course, as I suggested in an earlier chapter, is the old-fashioned Cartesian psychology that it reflects.) In any event, the important conclusions to be underscored here are that "drama-made-music" and "opera as drama" are not mutually exclusive readings of musical theatre, but alternative, compatible ones; and that although the two readings may produce different evaluations of a given work, and certainly evaluations that are based, in part, on different criteria, these evaluations need not necessarily conflict with certain long-standing intuitions about individual works: for example, that *Così fan tutte*, which I view as Mozart's most perfect operatic work under the description "drama-made-music," is somehow a flawed and problematic one, inferior as a work of art to (say) *Figaro*, or Verdi's *Otello*.

A most important conclusion, however, that cannot be drawn from the compatibility of opera as drama and opera as drama-made-music is that all readings of opera are equally acceptable. I am a democrat in these matters, but not an anarchist. There are, it seems to me, readings of opera that must be rejected as irrational: as simply "off the wall." To these, under the head "opera as revelation," I want now to turn.

○ 5 ○ I want to begin with what might seem to be some rather pedantic carping at an author who, in general, is a model of care, restraint, and knowledgeability in his discussion of music. But my point here is that if even such innocent-sounding and familiar commonplaces about opera as those I am now going to cite are arguably false or unintelligible, we had better watch out when discussion passes from them to claims that on the very face of them must give pause to musical common sense and sensibility.

Winton Dean writes of Handel's dramatic works, "in the greatest of the operas and oratorios he tells us far more about human nature than we could ever guess from the libretto."[13] Such a statement easily passes us by in a book that is not at all prone to flights of fancy. We are used to encomiums like this, directed at great music; they are elicited, I suspect, by our bafflement about just what to say, since we don't really know what it is about great music that makes it great, and so grasp for metaphysical profundities in desperation. Aldous Huxley has a character in *Point Counterpoint* say that the slow movement of Beethoven's Opus 132 is a proof of the existence of God. We all, I think, accept that literary conceit for what it is and do not seriously think that we can find a demonstration of God's existence in that music, or any music. (It is disappointment enough to look for it in the works of philosophers.) How could music demonstrate the existence of God? And, more to the present purpose, how could Handel's music tell us more about human nature than his libretti? As bad as they may be as literary works (which is not to say they are bad libretti), they have the resources of language at their disposal. And no matter what the banalities about human nature they convey, they surpass the power of music to express propositions about human nature, banal or otherwise.

What Dean might have in mind here is illustrated in another place, where he says:

> The muddled and often ridiculous libretto of *Arminio* has a scene in which the hero, led in chains to the scaffold, contemplates what he calls "the proud theatre of death." As in Caesar's famous monologue in *Giulio Cesare*, Handel writes a superb accompanied recitative, full of chromatic inflections, that expresses with piercing intensity the brevity of life and the futility of mortal hopes.[14]

Well, if this is supposed to be an illustration of how Handel's music tells us about human nature, in this case revealing to us "the brevity of life and the futility of mortal hopes," I do not think it succeeds. Surely it is the *words* that say: life is short and hope is futile. Music cannot say that. What the music does is make that statement more intense; and it is an invalid step to go from there to the conclusions that the *music* says: life is short and hope is futile. Perhaps a clearer way of stating it is this. A character in *Arminio* expresses the proposition: life is short and hope is futile.

No doubt, had an actor spoken the poet's lines, he could never have expressed the proposition with the intensity and, therefore, the conviction that can be achieved by a singer singing them to Handel's music. Handel put in the intensity and the conviction that the poet could not, because Handel was an artistic genius and the poet was not. But the meaning, and hence the proposition, is in the words, not the music. Music cannot express such propositions; but it can emphasize or underscore them.

But perhaps, then, another kind of "revelatory" theory is open to us. If it is impossible for Handel's music to reveal to us truths about human life, might it not be possible for it to reveal truths about Handel? Indeed, doesn't it reveal something about what Handel *believed*, that he was aroused to such musical intensity by a text expressing the brevity of human life and the futility of mortal hope: namely, that *he* believed those things? As Dean says: "The heroic librettos are full of situations like this, and they constantly inspire music of this [high, intense] quality."[15] Doesn't the very consistency with which such sentiments elicited great music from Handel strongly suggest that Handel was in sympathy with such sentiments? Is that not a reasonable inference to be drawn from the music?

Dean certainly flirts with such a "revelatory" theory at one point; at least, such a theory can be teased out of what he says. Of Handel's "magic operas," he writes:

> The sorceress is of course a perennial operatic type. . . . The male victims [in Handel's magic operas] escape the snare and pair off happily, as the convention requires; but it is the fate of the sorceress—the spider, not the fly—that moves Handel. In each of these operas, he bestows his finest music on the creature who, despite the devilish use of her supernatural powers, cannot command the love of the mortal man she covets. . . . Handel's music transcends the librettos; the magic element, designed perhaps as an excuse for diversion and the titillation of the senses, becomes a vehicle for profound truths about human nature. In the process it tells us much about Handel's personality as an artist and a man.[16]

We have again the claim that Handel's operas reveal, as Dean puts it here, "profound truths about human nature." I can no more see it in the examples now adduced than in the ones adduced heretofore. What are these "profound truths"? That love cannot be won by foul means? That rejected lovers are unhappy, even if they are wicked? Or what? It is hard to accept that music can tell us these things. If it can, it is hard to know why we should care. It takes no genius to know these "profound truths."

And it surely must be something else in Handel's operas that interests us and makes them great, beyond the expression of these banalities, if indeed they are expressible at all in music or are expressed in Handel's.

There is, however, another claim being made in the above passage: that Handel's treatment of these defeated and rejected sorceresses tells us something about Handel himself: "tells us much about Handel's personality as an artist and as a man." I will leave aside the question of what aesthetic significance it might have for us if their music did indeed reveal things about composer's personalities and beliefs. (Obviously it does reveal *some* things—and some pretty trivial things, it should be added.) There have, indeed, been attempts to say what this aesthetic significance might be: that it puts us in contact with spiritually superior mentalities and states of consciousness, for example.[17] But all I am interested in here is the knowledge claim itself. What is the claim Dean is making about Handel's personality, what is its evidential base, and is that base sufficient to establish the claim?

The claim, very simply, seems to be that it was a part of Handel's personality to feel sympathy for rejected lovers, even villainous ones: "it is the fate of the sorceress—the spider, not the fly—that moves Handel." And the evidence for the claim is that "In each of these operas he bestows his finest music on the creature who, despite the devilish use of her supernatural powers, cannot command the love of the mortal man she covets."

Does the evidence prove sufficient to establish the claim? Hardly; for there is a necessary missing premise; and the premise seems false—at least, there is no convincing evidence of its truth. Dean's argument, with the missing premise supplied, must go something like this:

Composers usually compose their best music for the characters they are most in sympathy with.

The best music in Handel's magic operas is that for the women who have tried to win the love of a man through wicked and supernatural means and have failed of attaining that love.

Therefore, Handel is most in sympathy with the kind of woman "who, despite the devilish use of her supernatural powers, cannot command the love of the mortal man she covets."

I submit that we know far too little about the compositional process in music to claim that we have any evidence at all for the truth of the missing major premise, and that, at least on superficial reflection, which is about all we are in a position to give this matter, the premise seems patently false. To instance a case in point, in *Paradise Lost* most people find

Milton's portrayal of Satan far more engaging than his portrayal of God. His finest poetry is lavished on his villain. Should we conclude from this that Milton's sympathies were with the Prince of Darkness; that he was a Satanist and not a Christian? There is an alternative and far more plausible conclusion, of course, namely, that the character of Satan was poetically more interesting than that of God; that it gave more opportunities for literary treatment; that it excited Milton's poetic faculty more intensely because of its greater artistic potential. And is not the same hypothesis available for Handel? Is it not an equally plausible, perhaps more plausible, explanation of why Handel's music for his operatic sorceresses is some of his finest that their characters were more interesting than those of the rather bland heroes and heroines of *opera seria*; that they gave more opportunities for musical treatment; that they excited Handel's musical faculty more intensely because of their greater artistic potential?

When there are two (or more) competing and under-determined explanations for something and one is chosen without the other (or others) apparently being seriously considered, an underlying reason can frequently be nosed out, of which the chooser may not be fully aware at all. In the present case, it is not irrelevant to note that the explanation Dean puts forward is quite consistent with what philosophers call the "expression theory of art": the theory that art is, by nature, definitionally, the expression of emotion. It is a view so pervasive that one can reasonably assume everyone who writes about art believes it, unless the contrary is explicitly stated. And if one does accept this view, then it becomes quite easily understandable why one will choose, without considering others, the hypothesis that Handel's bestowing of his finest music on some given character type is an expression of his sympathy for that kind of character. It is only what the expression theory of art would imply, on the assumption that all art is an expression of human emotion and is understandable in terms of expression alone.

But the expression theory of art is a very questionable theory and has been under increasing criticism in recent years by philosophers. If it alone is the justification for choosing the hypothesis that Handel's personal sympathies are revealed by his music for sorceresses, rather than some other competing hypothesis, it is very weak justification indeed. In any case, any claim that operatic music reveals anything interesting about its composer should be greeted with a generous dollop of skepticism. If it is supposed to reveal things by expressing propositions, one can only respond with the gravest doubts about music's ability to express even the most trivial and simple ones, let alone any of notable content. And if it is supposed to reveal things by being a "symptom" of the composer's personality or psychological makeup, we must remind ourselves how little we really know in this regard, and how truly baffled we would be, for example, if we tried to figure out what kind of person Wagner was with only his music to guide us.

Now, if these minor forays into the theory of "opera as revelation," by a musicologist of usually sober and sound judgment, were the worst one had to fear from that quarter, it might be considered an unnecessary exercise in philosophical pedantry to refute them. Alas, there is far worse to come: claims about the revelatory powers of opera that are not merely minor lapses from musical and philosophical sobriety, but central, sustained, and serious claims, attributing to opera revelatory powers of a truly extraordinary kind. Some representative examples of this more elaborate version of "opera as revelation" must, I think, be confronted.

○ 6 ○   Let me strike the keynote of the kind of view I am now going to discuss with the following brief but, it seems to me, utterly astounding quotation from Irving Singer's book on "love" in the operas of Mozart and Beethoven. He writes:

> Guglielmo's music seems to say, we men are all as helpless as Cherubino. But what are we to do? We cannot live without women.[18]

This claim seems to me quite outlandish in its attribution, both in detail and in extent, of propositional content to music. And the phrase "seems to say," perhaps resorted to to soften the blow, hardly makes matters better. For it hardly is more believable that Guglielmo's music *seems* to say "we are all as helpless as Cherubino" and "We cannot live without women" or *seems* to ask the question "But what are we to do?" than that it *does* say them and *does* ask that question. I have to point to something in the music that might reasonably be taken to express these propositions, even to be able to be justified in making the weaker "seems" claim; one cannot sensibly say that anything "seems" to say anything. I can say that Swift's *A Modest Proposal* "seems" to say that we should eat babies but really says something else, because there are sentences in it that *can* plausibly (but mistakenly) be taken to express propositions to that effect. What can I point to in Guglielmo's music that any reasonable person might take (even mistakenly) to say "we are all as helpless as Cherubino. But what are we to do? We cannot live without women"? Singer is quite wise, I think, in never quoting a passage of music in his book. For if he did, if we had the notes before us, we would see, I think, as clearly as it is possible to see, that the music does not, cannot, say such things. Surely this is the "revelation" theory run amok.

Now there are passages in Singer's book that are consistent with being not about the music, that is, about the operas he is talking about, but about their libretti. And as the kinds of claims he makes, particularly about characters, are not inappropriate claims to make about literary works, which libretti certainly are, I have no quarrel with them as a matter of logic: that is to say, they are claims which may not be true but which at least could be true; it is within the power of literary works to say the kinds of things, do the kinds of things, attributed to them. This is so of the general run of opera criticism and analysis, both the older and the more recent, of which the following, from the work of the Mozart scholar Hermann Abert, is a good example.

> The 19th century tried to make Elvira's previous history more respectable, but in vain; she is simply, as the libretto says, "abbandonata da Don Giovanni," and so in the same position as many others. At the same time she is a passionate woman whose love for Don Giovanni is not merely a passing episode but the decisive experience of her life. She is of all the women in the opera the one who in her whole being is closest to Don Giovanni. His love has kindled in her a spark of the same consuming passion that burns in him. But whereas he, being the man, is constantly lured by a sensuous desire for new adventures, she can find fulfilment of her longing only in him. Her aim is therefore not to be revenged but to win back Don Giovanni's love; this is always apparent even in her fiercest outbursts of hatred. And even when she has to recognize the hopelessness of her quest she strives to save her beloved from the fatal consequences of his actions. Therefore she returns at the end neither as a pious "sister" to win his soul for Heaven nor, like Gretchen, to bring about his "salvation," a thought far from Mozart's mind; she simply wants to save the man she loves from annihilation.[19]

What is said up until the last sentence, where Mozart's name is invoked, is entirely consistent with being a discussion of what we can glean about the character of Donna Elvira from Da Ponte's words. And words are certainly capable of delineating characters in the complex way suggested here, where music, I would insist, is not. With that I have no quarrel. The question is, are Da Ponte's words capable of it? And I think the answer must be "no." If they were, Da Ponte would be a far more significant literary figure than we know him to be: not a minor artist but a playwright of the first rank. This is a clear case of "over-interpretation."

This reflection leads to recognition of what seems to me to be a pervasive operatic illusion: what might be called the "illusion of psychological depth." Were we to possess (say) only Da Ponte's libretto for *Don Gio-*

vanni, it seems to me utterly impossible that anyone would ever have been tempted to see the kind of complexity of character in Donna Elvira that Hermann Abert does, or, to take perhaps the most extreme case in the literature, the well-nigh cosmic depth of character that Kierkegaard sees in Don Giovanni. The strange paradox here is that words *can* impart such significance, but Da Ponte's can't; whereas music *can't*, even when, as in the case of Mozart, it is music of genius. The depth is an illusion, brought about by the fact that the music is surpassingly beautiful and makes these otherwise dead characters live, *just as if* they were products of literary genius and lived—like Dostoyevsky's characters, for example—because of the depth and complexity that literary language can impart. We look for the same complexity and depth in Don Giovanni and Donna Elvira, Otello and Desdemona, because that is what we know accounts for the living quality of great characters in literary fiction; for these great operatic characters do indeed have that kind of life. But it is not in the words, and cannot be in the music; it is, I suggest, in the fantasy of the critic. No doubt, the beauty of the music makes these characters lives, I do not pretend to know how—it is a brute aesthetic fact. However, their "depth" and "complexity" are illusion merely: the product of musical beauty, not psychological insight, which can only be expressed in the requisite way, by discursive language.

I do not mean to suggest, by the way, that music is completely powerless to "characterize"; it does, in perfectly familiar and understandable ways, as where Mozart depicts the simplicity of Papageno with "simple" tunes, and the nobility of Zarastro with noble hymn-like ones. But when it comes to Dostoyevskyan depth and complexity, composers have the genius but not the means, their poets the means but not the genius.

What, however, about the few cases where an operatic libretto is a work of the first literary rank in its own right? *Wozzeck*, for example, or *Pelléas at Mélisande*, or Hugo von Hoffmannsthal's collaborations with Richard Strauss? Here the literary texts will doubtless support claims of character complexity and depth. But the problem in this regard, I would suggest, is that there is liable to be a confusion of the literary with the operatic text: what might be called the "fallacy of misplaced psychological depth."

Certainly, Alban Berg's text for *Wozzeck*, although it is a condensation of the play, possesses enough of Büchner's words to retain much of the psychological depth and complexity that make the original seem so prophetically insightful from the psychoanalytic point of view. Is that a property of Berg's book, or of his opera? Although this distinction is terribly hard to make in practice, it does exist in logic, and must not be lost sight of in making critical statements about operatic works. I want to argue that the kind of depth and complexity that are possessed by Büchner's character Woyzeck, and, by consequence, by the character Wozzeck in Berg's musically unadorned libretto, do not belong to that character in Berg's opera. Here is why.

Imagine that a native speaker and reader of German is attending a performance of Büchner's *Woyzeck*. The "object" he will be aware of throughout the performance will, of course, be a function, in part, of his intelligence, education, experience, and concentration on that particular occasion. But if he possesses the background requisite for appreciation of the play, and if he concentrates sufficiently on what he is seeing and hearing, he will find enacted before him a play in which the main character, Woyzeck, emerges as a person of great depth and complexity. But imagine, now, that he is attending a performance of Alban Berg's *Wozzeck*. How might he become aware of that complex and deep personality, Wozzeck, that he has become familiar with from attending Büchner's play? He had better concentrate very hard indeed on what words are being enunciated by the man who sings the part; and good luck to him— for we all know, from our own experiences of opera, that it is well-nigh impossible to understand in any great detail, even in our native language, the words that opera singers sing. What he will hear, no matter how hard he concentrates, will be only a part of the text, and that through a glass darkly, obscured by the music. Indeed, to hear the text in a way that will reveal the depth and complexity of Büchner's Woyzeck, he will have to treat Berg's score as so much background noise, to be filtered out as much as possible. In the end, the "object" that is perceived will be neither Büchner's text nor Berg's opera, but a completely garbled version of both.

Undaunted, our stubborn friend decides to solve this problem by reading the libretto very, very carefully before he next attends a performance of Berg's *Wozzeck*; indeed, just to make sure, he commits it to memory. All to no avail: for when he attends a performance again, he will still face the choice of dividing his attention, in some reasonable way, between the music and words, as is necessary and proper in the experience of *opera*, or concentrating on the words, with the music, now become a perceptual nuisance, pushed as far into the background as possible. If he chooses the former course, he will perceive the "object" *Wozzeck*, by Alban Berg. But the character Wozzeck, in that work, will not have the depth and complexity of the character in Georg Büchner's play (as condensed by Berg). There will not be the proper relation of words to consciousness in our subject's field for *that* character to emerge; the depth and complexity of Büchner's Woyzeck, dependent as they are on the propositional content of a very sophisticated literary language, will be sacrificed in the process of giving Berg's music the concentration it requires. In other words, when a drama becomes drama-made-music, or for that matter just musical drama, if its characters have great psychological depth and complexity to begin with, as they do in Berg's libretto for *Wozzeck*, those must be lost. Nor will it help for our listener to choose the second alternative, concentrate on the words, and obliterate the music as best he can. For he will then not be hearing Berg's opera *Wozzeck* at all, but either a travesty of it or a travesty of Büchner's play, depending on how you want to look at it. Neither alternative is worth serious consideration. Whatever the character of Wozzeck might be in either of these two "objects," it is not the character we are talking about. Our conclusion must be that where the libretto of an opera will sustain an analysis "in depth" of its characters (which will be seldom), it is a fallacy to think of that as an analysis "in depth" of the characters in the opera which the setting of the libretto produces; for that is a different work, a different "object" altogether, and to confuse the two is to commit what I have been calling the "fallacy of misplaced depth."

○ 7 ○   Just as there are extremes to which the revelation theory of opera has been carried where the revelation is supposed to be of truths about "life," "the world," "human nature," "psychology," and so forth, there are extremes to which it has been taken where there is something about the composer that is supposed to be being revealed. Again, the example I will adduce is from Singer. He writes:

> In the operas written with Da Ponte Mozart sounds like a man who does not really believe in love between the sexes—at least not love as a unique and lasting oneness in which each participant unselfishly devotes himself to the welfare of the other. In *Don Giovanni* only Ottavio and Donna Anna could possibly qualify as true lovers in this sense, and their union is benighted by a supervening struggle between life and death—Don Giovanni vs. the Commendatore—that makes their relationship seem rather uninteresting. In *Figaro* the Countess, Susanna, and even Figaro may be loving persons; but the opera is intriguing, and forever depends upon the phenomenon of intrigue, because we can never be certain that anyone in it really loves anyone else. In *Così* the philosophical demonstration tends to indicate that love is not a human possibility at all, unless we reinterpret it as an easygoing arrangement that enables men and women to live together without expecting too much from one another. In these three Italian operas there is no such thing as complete, harmonious, innocent (but also passionate) love. On the contrary, the drama is always generated by diffi-

culties internal to each couple such that we can never know whether they are truly in love. Even after the happy endings of *Così* and *Figaro*, and despite the benign promise of their multiple marriages, we cannot be sure that human beings are capable of authentic oneness of this sort.[20]

What are we to say to the assertion that "In the operas written with Da Ponte Mozart sounds like a man who does not really believe in love between the sexes—at least not love as unique and lasting oneness in which each participant unselfishly devotes himself to the welfare of the other"? Can Mozart's operas really tell us that about Mozart; tell us that Mozart is a man who didn't believe in love? (The question gains added emphasis in the face of Mozart's letters, which clearly contradict the claim.) Can operas really tell us things like that about their composers?

Does the *music* tell us that about Mozart? Singer says that "In the operas written with Da Ponte Mozart *sounds like* a man who does not really believe in love between the sexes . . ."; and that sounds as if he is talking about music. (He says not "seems like a man" but "sounds like a man.") But in the rest of the passage, where evidence is adduced for that claim, it is not music that is talked about at all, but rather relationships between male and female lovers in the plots. In effect, then, Singer is talking about the libretti, about the words. And that is not very surprising. For how could music tell us any such things about Mozart?

But how can the libretti tell us that either? The libretti are by Lorenzo Da Ponte. If they tell us anything, they tell us about *his* views on "love between the sexes." Brigid Brophy had a ready answer for this. Mozart's librettists may have written these texts; but Mozart chose to set them rather than others; so they surely must have expressed *his* views as well. "It was by a very scrutinising selection over a very wide field, followed by his personal re-working of the material obtained by careful selection, that Mozart adopted into his own psychology characters and situations which had been in the first place Varesco's, Stephanie's, Beaumarchais', da Ponte's."[21] And so, for example, "We need not hesitate to accept *Don Giovanni* as Mozart's own unconscious autobiography, although the story was an old one and the actual libretto by da Ponte."[22] In support of this contention, the evidence of his letters is invoked: "The letters shew him at the utmost pains to secure the best available librettists and then at the utmost pains to work the raw material they supplied into a shape acceptable—adoptable—to himself."[23]

Now, that libretti can tell us interesting things about the composers who chose and set them may sometimes be true but is an *ignoratio elenchi* in the present argument, since we are concerned here with what the *operas* tell us; and for reasons very much like those already adduced in the preceding section, operas cannot tell us the kinds of things Singer thinks they can about composers. I shall get to those reasons in a moment. But before I do, even though it is something of an irrelevancy, I would like to say just a little bit about what Mozart's libretti can, or rather cannot, tell us, for Brophy's reference to Mozart's letters seems to me to be something of a scare tactic that should be faced down. What do the letters really tell us?

To be brief, they tell us that Mozart, all of his adult life, longed for *scritture*, i.e., contracts to write operas; for he would not, could not write an opera without one. (He couldn't afford to.) They tell us that when he did have the *scritura*, his choice of libretti was hardly, as Brophy suggests, "a very scrutinising selection over a very wide field," but was, on the contrary, very much of a Hobson's choice. (Does she really believe that, after "a very scrutinising selection over a very wide field," Mozart would have "chosen" libretti by the likes of the Abbé Varesco, Stephanie the younger, or Emanuel Schikaneder?) He was a hostage to the whims of princes, censors, singers, *Schauspieldirektors*, and the intrigues of his rivals. He "chose" what came along, or the moment was lost. But he certainly took every opportunity he could of messing about with the book, in order to suit it to his music: this is made abundantly clear throughout his correspondence, and particularly in that concerning *Idomeneo* and *Die Entführung aus dem Serail*. About this Brophy is quite correct, except—and this is of the essence—that there is absolutely no evidence at all of his messing about in the ways Brophy suggests and Singer requires. On the contrary, the evidence of the letters suggests that what Mozart was engaged in had nothing to do with tinkering for the sake of getting libretti to "express" his views on love, sex, passion, sensuality, or anything else that might have to do with his "world view," if he had any (which I doubt). To suggest it is to read his letters through nineteenth-century eyes, and through a sensibility formed by the expression theory of art. Mozart's tampering with his libretti had a very different purpose from that; his letters show this quite explicitly, and in detail.

What the correspondence shows us is the working musician in the theatre, principally concerned with having opportunities for writing the right music in the right places, on grounds that have little to do with "expression." The discussion with librettists, as reported by Mozart, and Mozart's discussion of the libretti themselves reveal, first and foremost, the craftsmanlike concerns of the practicing composer. He wants his musical climax here or there, he needs an opportunity in a text for a particular kind of movement, an aria or an ensemble, in a particular place, and so on. He talks about the needs of his singers, the particular strengths and weaknesses of their voices, their ranges. He talks of adding pieces, moving them there to here. He even writes music and then asks for a text. In all of this there is not the slightest hint (fortunately, I am tempted to add) of "philosophy," not the slightest allusion to all those higher goals of "art" that besprinkle the writings of nineteenth-century composers. Well, but surely he spoke about the "psychological motivations" of his operatic characters? Indeed he did, and the discussion is about on the level of profundity reached when you and your wife discuss why you don't like her brother Albert. That Mozart paid close attention to the texts he was setting, that he tried, when possible, to work with his poets, that he had very definite ideas about what a good opera libretto was and what a good setting of it was—all this his letters amply document. But when we turn to the details, as Brophy insists we do, what we find is that all of these concerns are expressed in the terms not of the theoretician but of the craftsman. They give absolutely no evidence of Mozart's "higher purposes." I think Mozart knew more about what opera can do than anyone else I can think of. What *I* think he thought might very well be the motto for this book: *What music can't do, opera can't do.*

But, as I have said, all of this is a red herring. For the question is not what a libretto might tell us about a composer, but what an opera might; and to confuse the two is to commit, in a slightly different form, what I called the "fallacy of misplaced psychological depth."

If I said that the novels of Jane Austen reveal truths about their author, I might mean (at least) two different things: that *qua* novels, *qua* art works, they reveal, as part of our aesthetic experience of them, truths about their author, and that this is part of their overall value *qua* works of art; or simply that scrutinized in a certain way, through the lens of social history, or psychoanalysis, or whatever, they give clues, evidence, symptoms of their author's personality traits, beliefs, prejudices, or unconscious motivations. Let us for convenience call the first "aesthetic revelation" and the second "symptomatic revelation."

When we say that a composer's operas reveal something about him or her, the same ambiguity enters in. We might mean "symptomatic revelation" or we might mean "aesthetic revelation." But the kinds of things Singer thinks Mozart's operas reveal about him can, because of the propositional content required, be revealed only by close scrutiny of the libretti (assuming, of course, that he has not over-interpreted the libretti—which, as a matter of fact, I think he has done). This, needless to say, cannot be an aesthetic encounter with the opera and is not "aesthetic revelation" *qua* opera. It may be "aesthetic revelation" *qua* libretto, i.e. *qua* literary work, in which case it will tell us something about the poet; or it may be thought of as scrutinizing a part of the opera in a

particular way, from a particular viewpoint, in which case it will be
"symptomatic revelation." But what is of interest, in the aesthetics of
opera, can only be what opera can reveal about the composer *qua* opera;
and to scrutinize the libretto does not yield that kind of revelation
because it is not an aesthetic encounter with *the opera*. Nor can we get
around this by going to a performance and there fixating on the words.
For we will then be in the very same position as our unfortunate spectator
of *Wozzeck*, trying to experience the depth and complexity of Büchner's
character. If he is successful in extracting the propositional content of
the words, in order to gain insight into the beliefs of the composer about
life, love, and the rest, it will only be a result of "successfully" masking
the music; and whatever you want to say he is thus experiencing, it is not
opera.

If the notion that part of the aesthetic character of opera is revelation—either of truths about the world, or of truths about the composer—
is to have any validity at all, it will have to stay close to what music, even
when married to a text and a story, is able to convey in the way of propositional content; and that is so minimal as to be worthless in explaining
anything that might be important to the value and nature of opera as an
art-form. If we must value operas for their revelatory powers, we must
rank them very low indeed. I cannot see how, valued that way, they could
merit any serious attention at all. (Perhaps that was Johnson's point.) And
making exalted, extravagant claims for the revelatory powers simply
leads to nonsense. The music will not support the claims; and *What music
can't do, opera can't do.*

o 8 o   I have discussed, now, three ways of looking at opera: as
drama, as revelation, and—the theme of this book—as what I have called
drama-made-music. Of opera as revelation I will say no more, for it is
not, on my view, a viable interpretive stance. Of opera as drama, a stance
which is both viable and valuable, I will say no more because so much has
been said about it by those more qualified than myself. And of drama-
made-music I will say little more, because I have already said just about
all I have to say. In fact, I will make an end with what, to me at least,
seems a baffling mystery: Why should opera as drama-made-music exist
at all? What possible appeal can such a point of view have?

If I asked this question of opera as drama, I think there would be a
ready answer available. There is, indeed, a very deep question as to why
we have *drama* at all, a question as old as Plato and Aristotle. But if you
take that as a given, the reason we have opera as drama, or poetry as
drama, is that music and poetry, each in distinctively different ways and

in some ways that are the same, enhance dramatic representation at places where prose cannot; so we want these other dramatic genres to satisfy the full range of dramatic enjoyments (if that is not too pallid a term) that we are capable of. The ways in which music can do this, in opera as drama, in incidental music, oratorio, passion, melodrama, *dramma per musica* have been written of widely, and sometimes wisely and well, from Galilei to Kerman; and I need say no more about them here. If there is not general agreement on all of them (and of course there is not), there is a kind of consensus, overall, that music does enhance drama, and that we have *some* understanding of how.

But why drama-made-music? Why drama transmuted, as it were, into pure musical form? What would be its *raison d'être*? Opera as drama is understandable: it is a form of dramatic representation with values that are defined by the drama but are, some of them at least, unique to it and not shared by drama in its other forms. If, however, there is a way of understanding opera such that it is a genre not of drama but of music, with drama as part of its material substance, as it were, *its* values must be defined in musical terms; and given the recalcitrance of the dramatic material to musical transformation, it surely must always come off second to "just plain music": "a low form of music" (to appropriate Kerman's phrase).[24] Why should I want to hear this imperfect music, made from unmusical stuff, when I can hear pure music, in its unadulterated and perfect form? What does opera as drama-made-music have that music as music doesn't have, have better, and have more fully? That is the mystery.

Well, I don't really know the answer. But I can offer two conjectures which, although not entirely satisfactory to me, may at least advance inquiry in something like the right direction.

My first conjecture starts from an analogy. Some of Picasso's most intriguing "sculptures" (the art books call them "assemblages") are constructed out of clearly recognizable pieces of "junk." The most famous, perhaps, and the most strikingly simple, is the 1943 *Head of a Bull* consisting only of a bicycle saddle and handlebars (Musée Pìcasso, Paris). Now, if I were to naively ask why Picasso should choose to make representational sculptures out of such recalcitrant materials when he could have made much better likenesses with clay or bronze, the answer would, of course, be, in part, that Picasso was not aiming at "realistic" representation (whatever you take that to be) at all; and that is doubtless true. A more complete answer would be that Picasso was aiming at as "realistic" a representation as possible, in these assemblages, given the restraints he had placed himself under, given the artistic problem he had posed to himself of making representations out of recognizable pieces of "reality."

Part of the pleasure we take in these sculptures is appreciating the freedom in constraint that the great artist achieves. However, there is this to them also. Picasso has, essentially, set *us* a problem as well: the task of picking out and identifying the things out of which the sculpture is made, which itself makes these objects intriguing, and then watching the junk fade back into the representation again, thus sustaining further interest.

But cannot the very same argument be made for opera as drama-made-music? To be sure, I might make "better" music, satisfying the pure musical parameters more fully, by simply setting myself the task of composing a string quartet, rather than setting myself the one, so beset with vagaries, of making pure music out of a libretto by Zeno or Metastasio. Yet would not making such an argument be an exact analogue to, and just as naive as, the one that questions the purpose of making representations out of junk when clay or bronze would do "better"? Is not the answer to it analogous as well? The composer of drama-made-music tries to realize the pure musical parameters as fully as he can, given the artistic constraints under which he has placed himself, of making music out of drama; and recognizing that must be part of the aesthetic delight we take in the result. At the same time, the composer has set us, his audience, the task of seeing (hearing) the drama in the music, seeing (hearing) how it fades back into the musical texture. What the junk is to Picasso's sculptures, the drama is to the composer's opera—a preformed part that we delight in recognizing and in seeing transformed into something else: representation in the former case, musical form—da capo aria, sonata-ensemble, minuet-chorus, or whatever—in the latter. Junk-assemblages are not better than marble statues, or worse: some are better than some marble statues, some worse. Operas viewed as drama-made-music are not better or worse than string quartets: some are better than some string quartets, some worse. That is not the point. The point is that Picasso's junk-sculptures are both the same as and different from representational marble statues. They are the same, of course, in that they afford the viewer the pleasures of representational art. They are different—and this is their justification—in that they afford other pleasures that marble statues cannot: the pleasures of playing hide-and-seek with pieces of "reality." And, likewise, opera as drama-made-music is both the same as and different from symphonies, string quartets, trio sonatas. It is the same, of course, in that it affords the pleasures and satisfactions of pure musical form. It is different—and this is *its* justification—in that it affords a pleasure and satisfaction that "pure" music cannot: the pleasure and satisfaction of recognizing the non-musical part in the musical whole, as one recognizes the part of "reality"—the saddle or handlebars—in the Picasso assemblage.

○ 9 ○ This, then, is my first and highly conjectural answer to the question Why drama-made-music? It has a strength and a weakness. The strength is that it connects the phenomenon in question with another, more readily understandable one in a related area, and this gives us some confidence that we are dealing not with something strange and singular but, perhaps, with a common, or at least not uncommon, artistic or aesthetic experience. Reduction to the familiar is, after all, the core of explanation.

The weakness is that the explanation really doesn't tell us why there is this relation between music and *drama*. Granted, dramatic texts can serve as "material" for music, as junk can serve as material for representational sculpture, and provide an analogous aesthetic experience with analogous aesthetic satisfactions. But lots of other things could too. I might set a telephone book to music, with the same aesthetic goals in view. Indeed, it would provide an even greater musical challenge with perhaps, as a result, even a greater potential for aesthetic payoff. How much more difficult, after all, to make music out of telephone numbers than out of drama; for the latter at least sometimes has "musical" form whereas the former have little form at all, and what little they do have is mind-deadeningly repetitive. Yet the relation of music to *drama* seems so unshakable, so perennial, so ancient, so "right," that there must be some reason why this particular material is so often resorted to in music. And that reason our first explanation does not address at all.

This leads me to my second conjecture, which takes its departure from an observation of Rosen's quoted in the preceding chapter. It may be recalled that Rosen speaks of "the same need of resolution" both in sonata form and in drama.[25] Now, it seems to me one might fairly generalize from this statement about a specific musical form, or group of forms, to the syntactical structure of music itself from the late sixteenth century, if not before, to at least the advent of "modernism" in the twentieth century, and in much of twentieth-century music to the present moment. This music is, quintessentially, the art of generating and resolving tension or, if you prefer the dramatic term (which just about tips my hand), *conflict*. I certainly do not want to suggest that this is a characteristic of all musics—certainly not all non-Western musics, and perhaps not even all Western musics. But it is, one is tempted to say, the central syntactic concept that motivates not only the sonata-allegro, but all music in the major/minor key system and, perhaps, all tonal music.

What the exact nature of this central syntactic feature is is not, of course, agreed upon by theorists and aestheticians. Some think of it as psychological: as a disposition of music to arouse tension, and to resolve it, in the auditor. I think this is Meyer's view in his first and perhaps most influential book, *Emotion and Meaning in Music*. But there are other ways of construing it: as a "phenomenological" property of music, that we perceive in it but do not "feel" as tension and release in ourselves; or (if this does not amount to the same thing) as a "quasi-grammatical" property of the music that we perceive in the way we might perceive the "unresolved" quality of an incomplete sentence and the "resolution" of a complete one, which I take to be something like Meyer's later view. (There may, indeed, be more possibilities than just these.) However, amidst such disagreements there is general agreement, one would think, about the centrality, no matter how construed, of tension and release in the music of the West; and the centrality of that property, not its thorough analysis, is all I need (or can) establish for the present.

Further, it should be remarked that the resolution of tension or conflict in music is more complete, and in that sense more satisfying, than it can ever be in spoken drama. That is because music, unlike natural languages, is "a syntax without a semantics." In the spoken drama, conflict involves people and ideas; it is frequently moral conflict. In what we take to be its deepest, most profound form, tragedy, the conflicts are often the most difficult ones of all: indeed, those for which no solution seems possible, or for which every proffered solution is unsatisfying in some elemental way. And the intellectual problems posed, centering, it is fair to say, upon the problem of evil (or, as it has recently and unmemorably been put, the problem of why bad things happen to good people), admit of no answer at all: at least, no answer that has not perennially been rejected in the ongoing philosophical dialogue. It is small wonder, then, that tragic drama and drama in general, when they raise conflicts and pose problems worthy of their finer moments, cannot ever give completely satisfying resolutions and answers. For they are the perennial conflicts and problems that have characterized Western philosophy as an enterprise, where (as C. L. Stevenson once characterized the doctoral examinations at a great American university) the same questions get asked; it's just the answers that change.

Of course, I am not suggesting that "intellectual" resolution of conflict is always or necessarily the only kind spoken drama offers. I take it that Shakespeare does not offer us a "theoretical" resolution (like the one Aeschylus gives of the moral problem of the *Oresteia*) of the terrible conflict in *King Lear* but, instead, only the "consolation" of supremely beautiful poetry. And there is always, needless to say, the possibility of the dramatist saying (theoretically) "no" to any resolution or answer at all, as a recognition that none is possible, thus purposely leaving tension undischarged. The point I want to make, however, is that most drama, as we understand that concept in the West, generates conflict, of an intellectual,

emotional, moral, or personal kind, and endeavors to resolve it concep-
tually, or poetically, or "aesthetically," or in all those ways at once.
Because spoken drama is linguistic and language has a semantics as well
as a syntax, spoken drama must be "about" something; its conflict must
have genuine linguistic reference to something beyond it. And that something is genuine conflicts in the world of human affairs. The world of
human affairs, practical, personal, moral, intellectual, emotional, is a
world that continues to puzzle us and that we continue to question. There
can be no entirely satisfactory and satisfying resolution there, nor in the
dramatic works that represent it to us.

Music, on the other hand, being a syntax without a semantics, has no
references to this messy world of human conflict (although I do not deny
that we feel some "reverberations" of the "real world" there). It sets up
pure, autonomous, exclusively "syntactical" conflict or tension, and provides a resolution in pure, autonomous, exclusively "syntactical" terms.
Like a game of chess, where the resolution is perfectly defined in checkmate and is therefore completely satisfying within the world of chess,
music is, so far as tension is concerned, a closed system within which perfect resolution is possible, with no strings left untied. Where that is not
accomplished, it is seen either as a musical defect or as an intentional
departure, for aesthetic effect, from the paradigm. I do not, of course,
suggest that the "rules" of the "game" are as clearly defined in music as
in chess, or that there is not a range of possible resolutions of musical
conflict, making musical resolution, unlike "checkmate," a concept of
degree. (One cannot, after all, be more or less checkmated, whereas a
resolution in music can be more or less satisfactory *qua* resolution: more
or less a "resolution," in other words.) An individual musical work,
within some genre and within some given stylistic system, sets up its own
musical—which is to say, syntactical—conflicts and tensions and, along
with them, the implicit possibilities—the "rules," if you will—of their resolution. These "rules" and "possibilities" are not unique to a work: they
are the "rules" and "possibilities" impressed, in part, from without, from
the system or genre that makes a work to be in one historical or typolog-
ical style or another. They are unique to the extent that the work is original; and if there were no originality in a work at all, it would, necessarily,
be identical with some other work and, hence, not "a work" in its own
right. But, further, I am not suggesting that the possibilities, the rules for
resolution of tension, are such—like the rules and possibilities of some
formal systems—that only one single resolution is necessary and inevitable in a given work. Had Beethoven ended his Ninth Symphony with
the purely instrumental movement he is supposed to have been contem-
plating at one point, and had he done a truly Beethoven-like job of it, we

would be none the wiser: there *was* more than one way to musically resolve the work, as "inevitable" as the resolution we do in fact have may seem, and that, *pari passu*, goes for individual movements and parts of individual movements as well. Musical "inevitability" is, to some extent, Monday-morning quarterbacking.

To sum up, then: musical works, being closed systems with no semantics, no reference, can resolve the conflicts they raise in a complete and completely satisfying way. Spoken (or read) drama cannot, because its conflicts are representations of our own; and they, alas, are irreconcilable when they are deep, and dramatically beneath notice when they are shallow. Of course, dramatic worlds are fictional worlds, and because of that, being to a certain extent self-contained themselves, with their own rules of resolution, they are more able to dissipate conflict and tension than the world of the human condition—from which we derive the concept of poetic justice. Nevertheless, a fictional world, no matter how remote, must make contact with the real one, else how could we understand the fictional world at all? A god may come down on wires, or a prince resolve in a single speech the politics of Denmark. But we know that these are tokens for a world where no such clean and clear resolutions are possible; and so, even though defined by the rules of fictional worlds in which they occur, they are never ultimately resolutions for us, with no further questions to ask or doubts to experience.

Having observed the essential nature of both drama and music to be the generation and resolution of conflict or tension, and having observed, as well, the essential differences between them in these regards, we are now in a position to consider a second conjectural answer to the question: Why opera as drama-made-music? Our answer is in two parts, corresponding to the two questions: Why drama-made-music rather than something-else-made-music? and Why opera as drama-made-music rather than merely opera as drama? Or, in other words, What does opera as drama-made-music have to offer that drama, or opera as drama, or just plain music does not?

The first part of our answer is obvious and simple. The reason drama is such an available material for transmutation into music is that both drama and music have as their deepest and most pervasive aesthetic feature the generation and resolution of conflict, the building and releasing of tension. It is a marriage made in heaven and, no doubt, already consummated in Greece. Yes: other non-musical materials can be, and have been, made into music. But drama becomes music more readily because, at the core, the "semantics" of drama and the "syntax" of music embody the same principle. And the relation, by the way, is reflexive. Talk about music so easily falls into the dramatic mode for the very same reason that drama so often falls into the musical. The temptation to see purely musical conflict and resolution as "drama" is merely the reverse of the centuries-old urge to transmute drama into pure musical form.

The second part of the answer comes as an implication of the argument that music can provide perfect resolutions to its constituent conflicts whereas drama cannot. The question is: Granted we have "pure" music, spoken drama, and opera as drama, why should we have another thing altogether that I have characterized as drama-made-music? Why should that be a valuable point of view from which to experience musical theatre? What particular aesthetic satisfaction can it provide that opera as drama cannot provide in the opera house, and instrumental music cannot provide out of it? The answer is that opera as drama, being a species of drama (as Kerman quite rightly concludes), can only give the imperfect resolution of which drama is capable, whereas when an opera can rewardingly be viewed as drama-made-music it can approach very closely to that *complete* syntactical resolution that only music can give. Pure instrumental music can give the resolution but it cannot give the drama. Opera as drama is musically intensified drama, but with only the unstable resolution that spoken drama can give; pure instrumental music is the resolution without the drama, syntax without semantics; and drama-made-music is drama pushed almost to the vanishing point but, in the process, so thoroughly transmuted into musical form that it can give almost that complete resolution of pure musical syntax.

∘ 10 ∘   These, then, are my (highly conjectural) answers to the question Why opera as drama-made-music? They do not satisfy even me; and I see no reason therefore that they should satisfy my reader, who would be less likely than I to view them with charity or indulgence. They need, certainly, to be developed further. They open up whole new areas of inquiry, raise new questions, and perhaps should have come at another book's beginning rather than at this book's end. In the event, it may be, for all I know, that there are no satisfying answers to the question Why opera as drama-made-music? In which case, we may have to conclude, in the spirit of Dr. Johnson, that drama-made-music is an irrational entertainment. But those who cultivate only such entertainments as are "rational" will surely miss more of what is good in life than rationality would countenance, leaving us with the paradoxical conclusion that no defense at all seems to be about as good a defense as we will ever really need.

Chapter I *Ecstasy and prophecy*

1. Quoted in Hugo Leichtentritt, "The Reform of Trent and its Effect on Music," *The Musical Quarterly*, 30 (1944), p. 319; and also in Gustave Reese, *Music in the Renaissance* (New York: Norton, 1954), p. 448.
2. *The New English Bible* (Oxford University Press and Cambridge University Press, 1961), p. 296.
3. Aristotle, *Poetics* (1447a), trans. W. Hamilton Fyfe (Cambridge, Mass.: Harvard University Press, The Loeb Classical Library, 1953), p. 5.
4. Ibid. (1449b), p. 23.
5. Quoted in Reese, *Music in the Renaissance*, p. 449; italics mine.
6. Heinrich Glarean, *Dodecachordon*, in *Source Readings in Music History*, ed. Oliver Strunk (New York: Norton, 1950), pp. 226–227.
7. Reese, *Music in the Renaissance*, p. 449.
8. Leichtentritt, "The Reform of Trent," p. 320.
9. Reese, *Music in the Renaissance*, p. 480.

Chapter II *The art of invention: opera as invented art*

1. Erwin Panofsky, "Style and Medium in the Motion Pictures," *Film: An Anthology*, ed. Daniel Talbot (Berkeley: University of California Press, 1959), p. 15.
2. Nino Pirrotta, "Studies in the Music of Renaissance Theatre," Part I of Nino Pirrotta and Elena Povoledo, *Music and Theatre from Poliziano to Monteverdi*, trans. Karen Eales (Cambridge: Cambridge University Press, 1982), p. 6. And see, also, Romain Rolland, "The Beginnings of Opera," *Some Musicians of Former Days*, trans. Mary Blaiklock (New York: Henry Holt, 1915).
3. Pirrotta, *Music and Theatre*, p. 28.
4. Ibid., p. 36.
5. Ibid.
6. Ibid., p. 236
7. Ibid., p. 201.
8. Ibid., p. 202.
9. Ibid., p. 237.
10. Ibid., p. ix.
11. Ibid., p. 201.
12. Panofsky, "Style and Medium in the Motion Pictures," p. 15.

Chapter III   *Enter Philosophy (in Classical attire)*

1. See Claude V. Palisca, "Girolamo Mei: Mentor to the Florentine Camerata," *The Musical Quarterly*, 40 (1954).
2. Plato, *Republic*, trans. John Llewelyn Davies and David James Vaughan (London: Macmillan, 1950), p. 93.
3. Ibid. (393), pp. 85–86.
4. Ibid. (395), p. 88.
5. Palisca, "Girolamo Mei," p. 7.
6. Aristotle, *Poetics* (1447a), pp. 5–7.
7. Ibid. (1447b), p. 9.
8. Aristotle, *Poetics* (1339b–1340a), trans. S. H. Butcher, in *Aristotle on Poetry and Music*, ed. Milton C. Nahm (Indianapolis: Bobbs-Merrill, Library of Liberal Arts, 1956), p. 45.
9. Thomas Twining, *Two Dissertations on Poetical and Musical Imitation*, appended to his translation of Aristotle's *Treatise on Poetry* (London, 1789), pp. 47–48.
10. Aristotle, *Politics*, ibid.
11. Ibid.
12. *Poetics* (1449), p. 23.
13. Quoted in Palisca, "Girolamo Mei," p. 10.
14. Ibid.
15. Ibid., p. 11.
16. Ibid.
17. Ibid., p. 16.
18. Vincenzo Galilei, *Dialogo della musica antica e della moderna*, in Strunk, *Source Readings in Music History*, p. 315.
19. Ibid., pp. 316–317.
20. For further reflections on the relation of representation to expression, in Galilei and others, see Peter Kivy, *Sound and Semblance: Reflections on Musical Representation* (Princeton: Princeton University Press, 1984), Chapter VII.
21. Strunk, *Source Readings in Music History*, p. 317.
22. Ibid., pp. 319 and 318.
23. Jacopo Peri, Foreword to *Euridice*, in Strunk, *Source Readings in Music History*, p. 374.
24. Giulio Caccini, Foreword to *Le nuove musiche*, in Strunk, *Source Readings in Music History*, p. 378.
25. Ibid., p. 380.
26. Ibid., p. 381.
27. Ibid., pp. 379 and 378.
28. Galilei, *Dialogo*, ibid., p. 307.
29. Palisca, "Girolamo Mei," p. 10.
30. Peter Kivy, *The Corded Shell: Reflections on Musical Expression* (Princeton: Princeton University Press, 1980), pp. 21–23, 28–38, 42–43, 112–113, et passim.

Chapter IV *The musical parameters*

1. Strunk, *Source Readings in Music History*, pp. 313–314.
2. On this see Kivy, *Sound and Semblance.*
3. Aristotle, *Poetics* (1450b–1451a), p. 31.
4. Brian Baxter, "Conventions and Art," *The British Journal of Aesthetics*, 23 (1983), p. 331.
5. See, for example, Leonard Meyer's *Emotion and Meaning in Music* (Chicago: University of Chicago Press, 1956), and his attempt to deal with this problem in "On Rehearing Music," *Journal of the American Musicological Society*, 14 (1961).
6. Immanuel Kant, *Critique of Aesthetic Judgement*, trans. James Creed Meredith (Oxford: Clarendon Press, 1911), pp. 188–190.
7. Eduard Hanslick, *The Beautiful in Music*, trans. Gustav Cohen (New York: Liberal Arts Press, 1957), p. 48.
8. *Letters of Mozart and His Family*, trans. Emily Anderson (London: Macmillan, 1938), vol. III, p. 1144.
9. Ibid., vol. III, p. 1145.
10. Joseph Kerman, *Opera as Drama* (New York: Vintage Books, 1956), p. 26. I am not forgetting, nor do I think was Kerman, the famous dispute between Monteverdi and Giovanni Maria Artusi over points of music theory and practice having to do with the *seconda practica*. But as they are not directed specifically at the "problem of opera," they do not, as I see it, constitute a counterexample for Kerman, or a source for me.

Chapter V *Enter Orpheus (Philosophy attending)*

1. Robert Donington, "Monteverdi's First Opera," *The Monteverdi Reader*, ed. Denis Arnold and Nigel Fortune (New York: Norton, 1968), p. 270.
2. Leo Schrade, *Monteverdi: Creator of Modern Music* (New York: Norton, 1950), p. 227.
3. Ibid., p. 231.
4. Donington, "Monteverdi's First Opera," p. 261.
5. I reproduce the example essentially as it appears in Donington's essay, ibid., p. 262.
6. Ibid., p. 271.
7. You may also, in a more sophisticated version of this game, *add* to a melodic line to whip it into shape, "filling in" the "implied" notes that the composer has left out. For many examples of this, see Rudolph Reti, *The Thematic Process in Music* (London: Faber and Faber, 1961), where some truly surprising alterations take place in the interests of "thematic unity."
8. Donington, "Monteverdi's First Opera," pp. 260–261.
9. I follow here the edition of Howard Mayer Brown (Madison: A-R Editions, 1981).
10. Editor's Preface to ibid., p. xi.

11. Donington, "Monteverdi's First Opera," pp. 270–271.

12. Frank Sibley, "Aesthetic Concepts," *The Philosophical Review*, 68 (1959).

13. Donington, "Monteverdi's First Opera," p. 260.

14. On this, see Peter Kivy, *Speaking of Art* (The Hague: Martinus Nijhoff, 1973), pp. 5–21.

15. Donington, "Monteverdi's First Opera," p. 271.

16. Schrade, *Monteverdi*, p. 227.

17. Gottfried Wilhelm von Leibniz, *Discourse on Metaphysics*, ed. Peter G. Lucas and Leslie Grint (Manchester: Manchester University Press, 1953), pp. 9–10 (Section VI); italics mine.

18. Brown (ed.), *Euridice*, editor's Preface, p. ix.

19. Schrade, *Monteverdi*, p. 226.

20. Donington, "Monteverdi's First Opera," p. 263.

21. Domenico de' Paoli, " 'Orfeo' and 'Pelléas,' " *Music and Letters*, 20 (1939), p. 394.

22. Ibid., pp. 396–397.

23. Ibid., p. 389.

24. Ibid.

25. Ibid., p. 383.

26. That it is not is amply demonstrated, unless one just begs the question, by various works of Varèse and other contemporary composers, as well as by the music of Bali and other non-Western musics.

27. Paoli, " 'Orfeo' and 'Pelléas,' " p. 390. Paoli's "continuous melody" must be what Wagnerian argot calls "endless melody."

28. Giovanni Guareschi, *The Little World of Don Camillo*, trans. Una Vincenzo Troubridge (New York: Pocket Books, 1954), p. 5.

Chapter VI   *Philosophy and Psychology (in early modern dress)*

1. Hegel, *Aesthetics*, trans. T. M. Knox (Oxford: Clarendon Press, 1975), vol. I, p. 28.

2. Ibid.

3. Ibid.

4. *Eckermann's Conversations with Goethe*, trans. R. O. Moon (London: Morgan, Laird, n.d.), p. 351 (Monday, 14 February 1831).

5. René Descartes, *The Passions of the Soul*, in *Essential Works of Descartes*, trans. Lowell Bair (New York: Bantam Matrix Books, 1966), p. 109 (Part I, Article 3).

6. Ibid. (Part I, Article 4).

7. Ibid., p. 117 (Part I, Article 17).

8. Ibid., p. 140 (Part II, Article 68).

9. Ibid., p. 181 (Part III, Article 149).

10. Ibid., p. 141 (Part II, Article 69).

11. Ibid., p. 111 (Part I, Article 7).

12. Ibid., pp. 121–122 (Part I, Article 27).

13. Ibid., pp. 152–153 (Part II, Article 91).

14. Ibid., p. 189 (Part III, Article 165).
15. Ibid., p. 188 (Part III, Article 162).
16. Ibid. (Article 163).
17. Ibid., p. 201 (Part III, Article 193).
18. Ibid. (Article 194).
19. René Descartes, *Compendium of Music*, trans. Walter Robert, ed. Charles Kent (American Institute of Musicology, 1961), p. 11.
20. Ibid., p. 27.
21. Ibid., p. 51.
22. Ibid., pp. 14–15.
23. *The Passions of the Soul*, p. 113 (Part I, Article 11).
24. *Compendium of Music*, p. 15.
25. Francis Hutcheson, *Inquiry Concerning Beauty, Order, Harmony, Design*, ed. Peter Kivy (The Hague: Martinus Nijhoff, 1973), p. 81 (Section VI, Article xii). I follow the reading of the first edition (1725) throughout.
26. For my previously expressed and elaborated views in this regard, see: Peter Kivy, "What Mattheson said," *The Music Review*, 32 (1973); *The Corded Shell*, Chapter IV; "Mattheson as Philosopher of Art," *The Musical Quarterly*, 70 (1984).
27. For a good biography of Mattheson and a rather perfunctory survey of his theoretical writings, see Beekman C. Cannon, *Johann Mattheson: Spectator in Music* (New Haven: Yale University Press, 1947).
28. Daniel Webb, *Observations on the Correspondence Between Poetry and Music* (London, 1769), pp. 1–2.
29. *De oratore*.
30. Webb, *Observations*, pp. 4–6.
31. Ibid., pp. 6 8.
32. Ibid., pp. 10–11.
33. On this, see Kivy, *The Corded Shell*, Chapter X.
34. Webb, *Observations*, pp. 11–12.
35. Johann Mattheson, *Der vollkommene Capellmeister*, trans. Ernest C. Harriss (Ann Arbor: UMI Research Press, 1981), p. 104, (Part I, Chapter iii, Article 51).
36. Ibid. (Article 55).
37. In my early article "What Mattheson said," I tried to show how they were derived directly from Descartes' *Passions of the Soul*. I think now that that was a mistake.
38. Mattheson, *Der vollkommene Capellmeister*, pp. 104–105 (Part I, Chapter iii, Articles 56–61).
39. Ibid., pp. 106–111 (Articles 64–89), *passim*.
40. Ibid., p. 104 (Article 54).
41. "Mattheson as Philosopher of Art."
42. Descartes, *Compendium of Music*, pp. 11–13.
43. Gottfried Wilhelm Leibniz, "On Wisdom," *Philosophical Papers and Letters*,

trans. and ed. Leroy E. Loemker (Chicago: University of Chicago Press, 1956), vol. II, p. 698.

44. Leibniz, "Principles of Nature and Grace," *Philosophical Papers and Letters*, vol. II, p. 1042.

45. See, for example, Jerome Stolnitz, "On the Origins of 'Aesthetic Disinterestedness,'" *Journal of Aesthetics and Art Criticism*, 20 (1961).

46. On this, see Paul O. Kristeller, "The Modern System of the Arts (II)," *Journal of the History of Ideas*, 13 (1952).

47. Hutcheson, *Inquiry*, p. 34 (Section I, Article ix).

48. Ibid., p. 40 (Section II, Article iii).

49. Ibid., p. 39 (Section I, Article xvi). I am moving very quickly here over dangerous ground. For a more leisurely and thorough look at the territory, see Peter Kivy, *The Seventh Sense: A Study of Francis Hutcheson's Aesthetics and Its Influence in Eighteenth-Century Britain* (New York: Burt Franklin, 1976), Chapters II–VI.

50. Hutcheson, *Inquiry*, p. 39 (Section I, Article xvi).

51. Ibid., p. 54 (Section IV, Article i).

52. Ibid., p. 46 (Section II, Article xiii).

53. Ibid., p. 53 (Section VI, Article xii).

54. Charles Avison, *An Essay on Musical Expression*, 3rd ed. (London, 1775), p. 4.

55. Ibid. Italics mine.

56. [Jean-Baptiste] Abbé Du Bos, *Critical Reflections on Poetry, Painting and Music*, trans. Thomas Nugent (London, 1748), vol. I, p. 1.

57. Ibid., vol. I, p. 5.

58. Ibid., vol. I, pp. 22–23.

59. Ibid., vol. I, p. 24.

60. Ibid., vol. I, p. 364.

61. Ibid., vol. I, pp. 360–361.

62. Ibid., vol. I, pp. 363–365.

63. Ibid., vol. I, p. 362.

64. Actually, something like Du Bos' account has been suggested by Kendall Walton, in his "Fearing Fictions," *Journal of Philosophy*, 75 (1978), where he speaks of emotions raised by art as "make believe." And for another recent "solution" to the problem, see Jerrold Levinson, "Music and Negative Emotion," *Pacific Philosophical Quarterly*, 63 (1982).

Chapter VII   *The irrational entertainment as rational solution*

1. Robert S. Freeman, *Opera Without Drama: Currents of Change in Italian Opera, 1675–1725* (Ann Arbor: UMI Research Press, 1981), p. 1.

2. Edward J. Dent, *Opera* (Harmondsworth, Penguin Books, 1949), p. 40.

3. Charles Burney, *A General History of Music*, ed. Frank Mercer (New York: Dover Publications, 1957), vol. II, p. 676.

4. Andrew Porter, "Completest Concerts," *The New Yorker*, March 12, 1984, p. 121.

5. This is not to be taken, by the way, as a plea on Burney's part for opera in

English. As he remarks (quite correctly in my view): "What do we understand when English is singing on our Stage without a book?" (*History*, vol. II, p. 676n).

6. Freeman, *Opera Without Drama*, p. 255.

7. *Lives of the English Poets*, ed. G. B. Hill (New York: Octagon Books, 1967), vol. II, p. 106. I am grateful to John Middendorf for tracking this quotation down for me.

8. This is Burney's phrase (*History*, vol. II, p. 677); but it is the view he attacks, not the one he endorses.

9. I would rather hear an opera by Caldara or Fux, as written, than the Halle "versions" of Handel's.

10. *History*, vol. II, p. 675.

11. Tuesday, 6 March 1711: in Strunk, *Source Readings in Music History*, pp. 511–512.

12. Anonymous, *Reflections upon Theatrical Expressions in Tragedy* (1755), in Newman Flower, *George Frideric Handel: His Personality and His Times* (New York: Charles Scribner's Sons, 1948), p. 241.

13. Winton Dean, *Handel and the Opera Seria* (Berkeley and Los Angeles: University of California Press, 1968), pp. 7–8.

14. Ibid., p. 8.

15. Ibid., p. 213.

16. Strunk, *Source Readings in Music History*, p. 530.

17. *Saggio sopra l'opera in musica*, in Strunk, *Source Readings in Music History*, p. 665.

18. Christoph Willibald Gluck, Dedication to *Alceste*, in Strunk, *Source Readings in Music History*, p. 674.

19. Strunk, *Source Readings in Music History*, p. 665.

20. For my detailed views on what the parameters and capabilities of musical story-telling are, see *Sound and Semblance*, Chapter IX.

21. Strunk, *Source Readings in Music History*, p. 588.

22. Ibid.

23. With the possible exception of *Xerxes*, where Handel comes close to writing a genuine comic opera.

24. Monroe C. Beardsley, "The Relevance of Reasons in Art Criticism," *The Aesthetic Point of View: Selected Essays*, ed. Michael J. Wreen and Donald M. Callen (Ithaca and London: Cornell University Press, 1982), especially pp. 346ff.

25. [John] Brown, *A Dissertation on the Rise, Union, and Power, the Progressions, Separations, and Corruptions of Poetry and Music* (London, 1763), p. 232.

26. Jean-Jacques Rousseau, *A Dictionary of Music*, trans. William Waring (London, n.d.), p. 295 (in the article "Opera").

27. Isaiah Berlin, "Winston Churchill in 1940," *Personal Impressions*, ed. Henry Hardy (Harmondsworth: Penguin Books, 1980), p. 5.

28. See note 5 above.

29. The English translation is by Nigel Fortune, as provided in the libretto that accompanies the Westminster recording of the opera.

30. Meyer, *Emotion and Meaning in Music*, p. 161.
31. Ibid., p. 171.
32. Dean, *Handel and the Opera Seria*, p. 152.
33. The English translation is by Aaron Hill, as provided in the libretto that accompanies the Columbia Masterworks recording of the opera. (Hill was the co-author, with Giacomo Rossi, of the original Italian libretto.)
34. Dean, *Handel and the Opera Seria*, p. 9.
35. From the anonymous English translation provided in the libretto that accompanies the London (Editions de l'Oiseau-Lyre) recording of the opera.
36. See note 33 above.
37. Strunk, *Source Readings in Music History*, p. 669.
38. Ibid., p. 674.
39. *The Collected Correspondence and Papers of Christoph Willibald Gluck*, ed. Hedwig and E. H. Mueller von Asow (New York: St. Martin's Press, 1962), p. 106.
40. Ibid., p. 117.
41. Ibid., pp. 107–108.

Chapter VIII   *Listening with the ear of theory*

1. Dean, *Handel and the Opera Seria*, p. 24.
2. Ibid., p. 6.
3. See, for example, Stuart Hampshire, "Logic and Appreciation," *Aesthetics and Language*, ed. William Elton (Oxford: Oxford University Press, 1954).
4. Dean, *Handel and the Opera Seria*, p. 20.
5. On this see Arthur C. Danto, *The Transfiguration of the Commonplace: A Philosophy of Art* (Cambridge, Mass.: Harvard University Press, 1981).
6. I take the idea of "world projection" from Nicholas Wolterstorff's *Works and Worlds of Art* (Oxford: Clarendon Press, 1980).

Chapter IX   *Expanding universe*

1. Thomas Hobbes, *Leviathan* (New York: E. P. Dutton, 1950), pp. 16–17 (I, iii).
2. Ibid.
3. John Locke, *An Essay Concerning Human Understanding*, ed. A. C. Fraser (New York: Dover Publications, 1959), vol. I, pp. 530–531 (II, xxxiii, 7).
4. David Hartley, *Observations on Man, His Frame, His Duty, and His Expectations*, 6th ed. (London, 1834), p. iii.
5. John Gay, *Concerning the Fundamental Principles of Virtue or Morality*, in *British Moralists*, ed. L. A. Selby-Bigge (Indianapolis and New York: Bobbs-Merrill, 1964), vol. II, p. 270; italics mine.
6. Ibid., p. 284.
7. Ibid., pp. 284–285.
8. Ibid., p. 281.
9. Sir Isaac Newton, *Opticks* (New York: Dover Publications, 1952), pp. 353–354.
10. Hartley, *Observations on Man*, p. 8.
11. Ibid., p. 4.

12. Ibid., p. 41.
13. Ibid., p. 1.
14. Ibid., p. 36.
15. Ibid., pp. 38–39.
16. Ibid., p. 44.
17. Ibid., p. 231.
18. Ibid.
19. Ibid.
20. Ibid., p. 264.
21. Ibid., p. 232.
22. Ibid., p. 300.
23. Ibid., p. 235.
24. For a complete account of Hutcheson's position in this regard, see Kivy, *The Seventh Sense*, pp. 75–85.
25. Hutcheson, *Inquiry Concerning Beauty*, p. 80 (VI, xi).
26. Hartley, *Observations on Man*, p. 267.
27. Ibid.
28. Ibid., p. 270.
29. I am not saying that there were no musical masterpieces; only that music was simply not seen that way at the time.
30. Avison, *Essay on Musical Expression*, pp. 3–4.
31. Ibid., pp. 4–7.
32. Ibid., p. 71.
33. Alexander Gerard, *An Essay on Taste*, 3rd ed. (Edinburgh, 1780), p. 61.
34. For a full account of Alison, see Kivy, *The Seventh Sense*, pp. 188–202.
35. Archibald Alison, *Essays on the Nature and Principles of Taste* (Cambridge, Mass., 1812), p. 105.
36. Ibid., p. 144.
37. Ibid., p. 146.
38. Ibid., p. 162.
39. Ibid., p. 144.
40. Ibid., p. 147.
41. Ibid.
42. Ibid., p. 148.
43. Ibid., pp. 162–163.
44. Ibid., p. 124.
45. On this, see Alan Tormey, *The Concept of Expression: A Study in Philosophical Psychology and Aesthetics* (Princeton: Princeton University Press, 1971).
46. Alison, *Essays*, p. 157.
47. Ibid., p. 158.

Chapter X *Form, feeling, finale*

1. Charles Rosen, *The Classical Style: Haydn, Mozart, Beethoven* (New York: Norton, 1972), p. 303.
2. Ibid., p. 296.

3. Siegmund Levarie, *"Le Nozze di Figaro": A Critical Analysis* (New York: Da Capo Press, 1977), p. 57.

4. Rosen, *The Classical Style*, p. 304.

5. Ibid., pp. 295–296.

6. Johann Nicolaus Forkel, *Ueber die Theorie der Musik, insofern sie Liebhabern und Kennern der Kunst notwendig und nützlich ist*, in *Music and Aesthetics in the Eighteenth and Early-Nineteenth Centuries*, ed. Peter le Huray and James Day (Cambridge: Cambridge University Press, 1981), p. 176. The complete thought is this: "If music is a language of the passions and emotions, if not a single person's emotions coincide with those of another, would it not then follow that, in default of suitable precepts and rules deduced from nature and from experience, art would have to be left to the caprice and wilfulness of each individual?"

7. Johann Georg Sulzer, *Allgemeine Theorie der schönen Künste, in einzelnen, nach alphabetischer Ordnung der Künstwörter aufeinanderfolgenden Artikeln abgehandelt*, in le Huray and Day, *Music and Aesthetics*, p. 123.

8. Ibid., p. 124; italics mine.

9. Ibid.

10. Ibid., p. 126.

11. Ibid., pp. 126–127.

12. Susanne K. Langer, *Philosophy in a New Key: A Study in the Symbolism of Reason, Rite, and Art* (New York: Mentor Books, 1959), p. 183.

13. On this see, Tormey, *The Concept of Expression*, Chapter II, and, especially, p. 43.

14. For a similar argument with regard to Mattheson, see Kivy, "Mattheson as Philosopher of Art."

15. Le Huray and Day, *Music and Aesthetics*, pp. 125–126.

16. Ibid., p. 127.

17. Ibid., p. 126. Cf. Jerrold Levinson, "Truth in Music," *Journal of Aesthetics and Art Criticism*, 40 (1981).

18. Le Huray and Day, *Music and Aesthetics*, pp. 125 and 130.

19. Rosen, *The Classical Style*, p. 173.

20. Ibid., p. 177.

21. Wieland is quoted by Rosen as saying that "Action cannot be sung" (ibid.).

22. Ibid., pp. 172–173.

23. *The Memoirs of Lorenzo Da Ponte*, trans. Elisabeth Abbott (Philadelphia and London: Lippincott, 1929), p. 133.

24. Ibid., pp. 149–150.

25. Pierre-Augustin Caron de Beaumarchais, *"The Barber of Seville" and "The Marriage of Figaro,"* trans. John Wood (Harmondsworth: Penguin Books, 1964), p. 142.

26. Ibid., p. 143.

27. Ibid., p. 148.

28. Ibid., p. 149.

29. Ibid., p. 152.

30. Ibid., p. 156.
31. Rosen, *The Classical Style*, p. 294.

Chapter XI *Opera as music*

1. Ludwig Wittgenstein, *Philosophical Investigations*, trans. G.E.M. Anscombe (New York: Macmillan, 1953), pp. 203ff.
2. I am guilty of having done it once myself, in *Speaking of Art*, where what I have to say about the matter can be seen in Chapter V.
3. Kerman, *Opera as Drama*, p. 13.
4. Ibid., p. 21.
5. Herbert Lindenberger, *Opera: The Extravagant Art* (Ithaca and London: Cornell University Press, 1984), p. 57.
6. Kerman, *Opera as Drama*, p. 109.
7. Ibid., p. 112.
8. Ibid., pp. 111 and 113.
9. Ibid., p. 115.
10. Wye Jamison Allanbrook, *Rhythmic Gesture in Mozart: "Le Nozze Di Figaro" and "Don Giovanni"* (Chicago and London: University of Chicago Press, 1983), p. 328.
11. The 1883 edition of the *Revisionsbericht* of the *Gesamtausgabe*, quoted in Alan Tyson, "Notes on the Composition of Mozart's *Così fan tutte*," *Journal of the American Musicological Society*, 37 (1984), p. 364; my italics.
12. Kerman, *Opera as Drama*, p. 116.
13. Dean, *Handel and the Opera Seria*, p. 122.
14. Ibid., p. 61.
15. Ibid.
16. Ibid., p. 82.
17. See, for such a defense, J.W.N. Sullivan, *Beethoven: His Spiritual Development* (New York: Vintage Books, 1960).
18. Irving Singer, *Mozart and Beethoven: The Concept of Love in Their Operas* (Baltimore and London: The Johns Hopkins University Press, 1977), p. 89.
19. Hermann Abert, *Mozart's "Don Giovanni,"* trans. Peter Gellhorn (London: Eulenburg Books, 1981), pp. 69–70.
20. Singer, *Mozart and Beethoven*, pp. 103–104.
21. Brigid Brophy, *Mozart the Dramatist* (New York: Harcourt, Brace and World, 1964), p. 31.
22. Ibid., p. 29.
23. Ibid.
24. See note 4 above.
25. See Chapter IX, note 5 above.

Abert, Hermann. *Mozart's "Don Giovanni."* Translated by Peter Gellhorn. London: Eulenburg Books, 1981.

Alison, Archibald. *Essays on the Nature and Principles of Taste.* Cambridge, Mass., 1812.

Allanbrook, Wye Jamison. *Rhythmic Gesture in Mozart: "Le Nozze Di Figaro" and "Don Giovanni."* Chicago and London: University of Chicago Press, 1983.

Aristotle. *Poetics.* Translated by W. Hamilton Fyfe. Cambridge, Mass.: Harvard University Press, The Loeb Classical Library, 1953.

Avison, Charles. *Essays on Musical Expression.* 3rd ed. London, 1775.

Baxter, Brian. "Conventions and Art." *The British Journal of Aesthetics*, 23 (1983).

Beardsley, Monroe. "The Relevance of Reasons in Art Criticism." *The Aesthetic Point of View: Selected Essays.* Edited by Michael J. Wreen and Donald M. Callen. Ithaca and London: Cornell University Press, 1982.

Beaumarchais, Pierre-Augustin Caron de. *"The Barber of Seville" and "The Marriage of Figaro."* Translated by John Wood. Harmondsworth: Penguin Books, 1964.

Berlin, Isaiah. *Personal Impressions.* Edited by Henry Hardy. Harmondsworth: Penguin Books, 1980.

Brophy, Brigid. *Mozart the Dramatist.* New York: Harcourt, Brace and World, 1964.

Brown, [John]. *A Dissertation on the Rise, Union, and Power, the Progressions, Separations, and Corruptions of Poetry and Music.* London, 1763.

Burney, Charles. *A General History of Music.* Edited by Frank Mercer. 2 vols. New York: Dover Publications, 1957.

Cannon, Beekman C. *Johann Mattheson: Spectator in Music.* New Haven: Yale University Press, 1947.

Da Ponte, Lorenzo. *The Memoirs of Lorenzo Da Ponte.* Translated by Elizabeth Abbott. Philadelphia and London: Lippincott, 1929.

Danto, Arthur C. *The Transfiguration of the Commonplace: A Philosophy of Art.* Cambridge, Mass.: Harvard University Press, 1981.

Dean, Winton. *Handel and the Opera Seria.* Berkeley and Los Angeles: University of California Press, 1968.

Dent, Edward J. *Opera.* Harmondsworth: Penguin Books, 1949.

Descartes, René. *Compendium of Music.* Translated by Walter Robert, edited by Charles Kent. American Institute of Musicology, 1961.

———. *The Passions of the Soul.* Translated by Lowell Bair. *Essential Works of Descartes.* New York: Bantam Matrix Books, 1966.

Donington, Robert. "Monteverdi's First Opera." *The Monteverdi Reader.* Edited by Denis Arnold and Nigel Fortune. New York: Norton, 1968.

Du Bos, [Jean-Baptiste]. *Critical Reflections on Poetry, Painting and Music.* Translated by Thomas Nugent. 3 vols. London, 1748.

Flower, Newman. *George Frideric Handel: His Personality and His Times*. New York: Charles Scribner's Sons, 1948.

Freeman, Robert S. *Opera Without Drama: Currents of Change in Italian Opera, 1675– 1725*. Ann Arbor: UMI Research Press, 1981.

Gay, John. *Concerning the Fundamental Principles of Virtue or Morality. British Moralists*. Edited by L. A. Selby-Bigge. 2 vols. Indianapolis and New York: Bobbs-Merrill, 1964.

Gerard, Alexander. *An Essay on Taste*. 3rd ed. London, 1780.

Gluck, Christoph Willibald. *The Collected Correspondence and Papers of Christoph Willibald Gluck*. Edited by Hedwig and E. H. Mueller von Asow. New York: St. Martin's Press, 1962.

Goethe, J. W. von. *Eckermann's Conversations with Goethe*. Translated by R. O. Moon. London: Morgan, Laird, n.d.

Guareschi, Giovanni. *The Little World of Don Camillo*. Translated by Una Vincenzo. New York: Pocket Books, 1954.

Hampshire, Stuart. "Logic and Appreciation." *Aesthetics and Language*. Edited by William Elton. Oxford: Oxford University Press, 1954.

Hanslick, Eduard. *The Beautiful in Music*. Translated by Gustav Cohen. New York: Liberal Arts Press, 1957.

Hartley, David. *Observations on Man, His Frame, His Duty, and His Expectations*. 6th ed. London, 1834.

Hegel, G.W.F. *Aesthetics*. Translated by T.M. Knox. 2 vols. Oxford: Clarendon Press, 1975.

Hobbes, Thomas. *Leviathan*. New York: E. P. Dutton, 1950.

Hutcheson, Francis. *Inquiry Concerning Beauty, Order, Harmony, Design*. Edited by Peter Kivy. The Hague: Martinus Nijhoff, 1973.

Johnson, Samuel. *Lives of the English Poets*. Edited by G. B. Hill. 3 vols. New York: Octagon Books, 1967.

Kant, Immanuel. *Critique of Aesthetic Judgement*. Translated by James Creed Meredith. Oxford: Clarendon Press, 1911.

Kerman, Joseph. *Opera as Drama*. New York: Vintage Books, 1956.

Kivy, Peter. *The Corded Shell: Reflections on Musical Expression*. Princeton: Princeton University Press, 1980.

———. "Mattheson as Philosopher of Art." *The Musical Quarterly*, 70 (1984).

———. *The Seventh Sense: A Study of Francis Hutcheson's Aesthetics and Its Influence in Eighteenth-Century Britain*. New York: Burt Franklin, 1976.

———. *Sound and Semblance: Reflections on Musical Representation*. Princeton: Princeton University Press, 1984.

———. *Speaking of Art*. The Hague: Martinus Nijhoff, 1973.

———. "What Mattheson said." *The Music Review*, 32 (1973).

Kristeller, Paul O. "The Modern System of the Arts (II)." *Journal of the History of Ideas*, 13 (1952).

Langer, Susanne K. *Philosophy in a New Key: A Study in the Symbolism of Reason, Rite, and Art*. New York: Mentor Books, 1959.

le Huray, Peter, and James Day, eds. *Music and Aesthetics in the Eighteenth and Early-Nineteenth Centuries*. Cambridge: Cambridge University Press, 1981.

Leibniz, Gottfried Wilhelm von. *Discourse on Metaphysics*. Edited by Peter G. Lucas and Leslie Grint. Manchester: Manchester University Press, 1953.

———. *Philosophical Papers and Letters*. Translated by Leroy E. Loemker. 2 vols. Chicago: University of Chicago Press, 1956.

Leichtentritt, Hugo. "The Reform of Trent and its Effect on Music." *The Musical Quarterly*, 30 (1944).

Levarie, Siegmund. *"Le Nozze di Figaro": A Critical Analysis*. New York: Da Capo Press, 1977.

Levinson, Jerrold, "Music and Negative Emotion." *Pacific Philosophical Quarterly*, 63 (1982).

———. "Truth in Music." *Journal of Aesthetics and Art Criticism*, 40 (1981).

Lindenberger, Herbert. *Opera: The Extravagant Art*. Ithaca and London: Cornell University Press, 1984.

Locke, John. *An Essay Concerning Human Understanding*. Edited by A. C. Fraser. 2 vols. New York: Dover Publications, 1959.

Mattheson, Johann. *Der vollkommene Capellmeister*. Translated by Ernest C. Harriss. Ann Arbor: UMI Research Press, 1981.

Meyer, Leonard. *Emotion and Meaning in Music*. Chicago: University of Chicago Press, 1956.

———. "On Rehearing Music." *Journal of the American Musicological Society*, 14 (1961).

Mozart, W. A. *Letters of Mozart and His Family*. Translated by Emily Anderson. 3 vols. London: Macmillan, 1938.

Nahm, Milton C., ed. *Aristotle on Poetry and Music*. Indianapolis: Bobbs-Merrill, Library of Liberal Arts, 1956.

Newton, Isaac. *Opticks*. New York: Dover Publications, 1952.

Palisca, Claude V. "Girolamo Mei: Mentor to the Florentine Camerata." *The Musical Quarterly*, 40 (1954).

Panofsky, Erwin. "Style and Medium in the Motion Pictures." *Film: An Anthology*. Edited by Daniel Talbot. Berkeley: University of California Press, 1959.

Paoli, Domenico de'. " 'Orfeo' and 'Pelléas.' " *Music and Letters*, 20 (1939).

Paul. Corinthians I. *The New English Bible*. Oxford University Press and Cambridge University Press, 1961.

Peri, Jacopo. *Euridice*, ed. Howard Mayer Brown. Madison: A-R Editions, 1981.

Pirrotta, Nino, and Povoledo, Elena. *Music and Theatre from Poliziano to Monteverdi*. Translated by Karen Eales. Cambridge: Cambridge University Press, 1982.

Plato. *Republic*. Translated by John Llewelyn Davies and David James Vaughan. London: Macmillan, 1950.

Porter, Andrew. "Completest Concerts." *The New Yorker*, March 12, 1984.

Reese, Gustave. *Music in the Renaissance*. New York: Norton, 1954.

Reti, Rudolph. *The Thematic Process in Music*. London: Faber and Faber, 1961.

Robinson, Paul. *Opera and Ideas from Mozart to Strauss*. New York: Harper and Row, 1985.

Rolland, Romain. *Some Musicians of Former Days*. Translated by Mary Blaiklock. New York: Henry Holt, 1915.

Rosen, Charles. *The Classical Style: Haydn, Mozart, Beethoven*. New York: Norton, 1972.

Rousseau, Jean-Jacques. *A Dictionary of Music*. Translated by William Waring. London, n.d.

Schrade, Leo. *Monteverdi: Creator of Modern Music*. New York: Norton, 1950.

Sibley, Frank. "Aesthetic Concepts." *Philosophical Review*, 68 (1959).

Singer, Irving. *Mozart and Beethoven: The Concept of Love in Their Operas*. Baltimore and London: The Johns Hopkins University Press, 1977.

Stolnitz, Jerome. "On the Origins of 'Aesthetic Disinterestedness.' " *Journal of Aesthetics and Art Criticism*, 20 (1961).

Strunk, Oliver, ed. *Source Readings in Music History*. New York: Norton, 1950.

Sullivan, J.W.N. *Beethoven: His Spiritual Development*. New York: Vintage Books, 1960.

Tormey, Alan. *The Concept of Expression: A Study in Philosophical Psychology and Aesthetics*. Princeton: Princeton University Press, 1971.

Twining, Thomas. *Two Dissertations on Poetical and Musical Imitation*. Appended to *Aristotle's Treatise on Poetry*. Translated by Thomas Twining. London, 1789.

Tyson, Alan. "Notes on the Composition of *Così fan tutte*." *Journal of the American Musicological Society*, 37 (1984).

Walton, Kendall. "Fearing Fictions." *Journal of Philosophy*, 75 (1978).

Webb, Daniel. *Observations on the Correspondence Between Poetry and Music*. London, 1769.

Wittgenstein, Ludwig. *Philosophical Investigations*. Translated by G.E.M. Anscombe. New York: Macmillan, 1953.

Wolterstorff, Nicholas. *Works and Worlds of Art*. Oxford: Clarendon Press, 1980.

INDEX